WHEN SKEPTICS ASK

"Dr. Geisler has put us all in his debt. He has set out the tough questions for Christianity and given credible answers. The serious Christian would do well to study what he has to say."

Paul Feinberg

WHEN SKEPTICS ASK

Norman L. Geisler
and
Ronald M. Brooks

BakerBooks
a division of Baker Publishing Group
Grand Rapids, Michigan

Published by Baker Books
a division of Baker Publishing Group
P.O. Box 6287, Grand Rapids, MI 49516-6287
www.bakerbooks.com

New paperback edition published 2008
ISBN 978-0-8010-7164-5

Previously published by Victor Books, a division of Scripture Press

Printed in the United States of America

The Library of Congress has catologed the original edition as follows:
Geisler, Norman L.
 When skeptics ask / Norman L. Geisler and Ronald M. Brooks
  p. cm.
 Includes bibliographical references.
 ISBN 10: 0-08010-1141-8
 ISBN 978-0-08010-1141-2
 1. Apologetics—20th century—Miscellanea. I. Brooks, Ronald M. (Ronald Matthew), 1957–. II. Title.
BT1102.G436 1990
239—dc20   89-29002

Art on page 49 © 1989 M. C. Escher Heirs/Cordon Art-Baarn-Holland. Used by permission.

Art on pages 121-22 taken from W. D. Edwards, W. J. Gabel, and F. E. Hosmer, "On the Physical Death of Christ," *Journal of the American Medical Association* 255 (21 March 1986): 1454-63. Used by permission of Mayo Foundation.

Chart on page 155 taken from Norman L. Geisler and William E. Nix, *General Introduction to the Bible* (Chicago: Moody Press, 1981), 169. Used by permission.

Chart on page 227 taken from Norman L. Geisler and J. Kerby Anderson, *Origin Science: A Proposal for the Creation-Evolution Controversy* (Grand Rapids: Baker, 1987), 149. Used by permission.

Charts on pages 236 and 238 taken from Norman L. Geisler, *The Re-Incarnation Sensation* (Wheaton, Ill.: Tyndale House Publishers, 1986). Used by permission. All rights reserved.

Unless otherwise noted, all Scripture is taken from the New American Standard Bible®, Copyright © 1960, 1962, 1963, 1968, 1971, 1972, 1973, 1975, 1977, 1995 by The Lockman Foundation. Used by permission.

Scripture markd NIV is taken from the HOLY BIBLE, NEW INTERNATIONAL VERSION®. NIV®. Copyright © 1973, 1978, 1984 by International Bible Society. Used by permission of Zondervan. All rights reserved

Scripture marked KJV is taken from the King James Version of the Bible.

CONTENTS

*This book is dedicated
to all who would seek
a reason for the hope
that is in them.*

1

THE NEED TO ANSWER EVERY MAN

"You know, all this stuff about arguments for God's existence and evidence for the Resurrection is interesting, and I know there is a place for it, but I've never needed it," the pastor said as he looked in the rearview mirror to change lanes. The young man seated next to him remained silent for a moment, slightly shocked by this statement. The pastor continued, "The people I share the Gospel with just don't ask those questions. They aren't interested in whether truth is objective, or what ancient historians said about Jesus and the Resurrection, or solutions to the problem of evil. Most people just aren't the kind that are philosophical about what they believe."

Finally the young man blurted out, "REALLY? That's the only kind of questions I ever get!" He had come from a family that was Christian in name only and raised in a part of the country where religion was typically ridiculed. When he finally became a Christian in college, he had to work out a lot of difficult questions about his faith, and the unbelievers he had contact with had been thoroughly trained skeptics and agnostics. Through his whole life he had been keenly aware of the fact that the world is opposed to Christianity on intellectual grounds. Whenever he shared Christ with someone, he or she would inevitably raise some of the objections that he himself had once voiced. It seemed inconceivable, from his experience, that a pastor could minister without ever confronting the same kind of opposition.

These two men were engaged in two different ministries. Both are valid and both are necessary. The pastor's ministry focused on evangelism, but the other man was used by God in a separate and distinct ministry of pre-evangelism. Rather than first trying to lead people to Christ, he removed the obstacles to faith. Rather than just preaching the Word, he spent more time using reason to explain why objections are groundless. Instead of asking immediately for a spiritual commitment, he sought intellectual agreement on the issues that must be understood before the Gospel can be accepted. For example, if someone does not believe that God exists and that He can perform miracles, then it makes no sense to him to say that God raised Jesus from the dead, because that is a miracle—a big one! Not all people have questions of this kind, but when they do, they need answers before they can believe. Before we can share the Gospel, we sometimes have to smooth the road, remove the obstacles, and answer the questions that are keeping that person from accepting the Lord. The following chart clarifies the difference between evangelism and pre-evangelism.

EVANGELISM	PRE-EVANGELISM
Done by all Christians	Done by any Christian when needed
Anytime/anyplace	Only if an objection is raised
Content is Gospel	Content is all of Christian doctrine
Based on revelation	Based on reason
States Gospel	Clarify Christian teaching
Goal is faith	Goal is understanding

So evangelism and pre-evangelism are different ministries. We know that the Bible tells us all to do evangelism, but what about pre-evangelism? Is that only for a few geniuses and specially gifted people, or should we all be involved? Do we really need to answer every man? There are three simple reasons why we need to be involved in pre-evangelism.

UNBELIEVERS HAVE GOOD QUESTIONS

The objections that unbelievers raise are usually not trivial. They often cut deep into the heart of the Christian faith and challenge its very foundations. If miracles are not possible, then why should we believe Christ was God? If God can't control evil, is He really worthy of worship? Face it: if these objections can't be answered, then we may as well believe in fairy tales. These are reasonable questions which deserve reasonable answers.

WE HAVE GOOD ANSWERS

Most skeptics have only heard the questions and believed that there were no answers. But we have some great answers to their questions. Christianity is true. That means that reality will always be on our side, and we just need to find the appropriate evidence to answer whatever question is asked. Fortunately, Christian thinkers have been answering these questions ever since Paul's time, and we can draw on their knowledge to help us find the answers we want.

GOD COMMANDS US TO GIVE THEM THE ANSWERS

This is the most important reason of all. God told us to do it. In 1 Peter 3:15 we read, "But in your hearts set apart Christ as Lord. Always be prepared to give an answer to everyone who asks you to give the reason for the hope that you have" (NIV). This verse says several important things. First, it says that we should be ready. We may never run across someone who asks the tough questions about our faith, but we should still be ready just in case. But being ready is not just a matter of having the right information available; it is also an attitude of readiness and eagerness to share with others the truth of what we believe. Second, we are to give a reason to those who ask the questions. It is not expected that everyone needs pre-evangelism, but when people do need it, we must be able and willing to give them an answer. Finally, giving these answers links doing pre-evangelism with making Christ Lord in our hearts. If He is really Lord, then we should be obedient to Him by "destroying speculations and every lofty thing raised up against the knowledge of God, and . . . taking every thought captive to the obedience of Christ" (2 Cor. 10:5). In other words, we should be confronting issues in our own minds and in the expressed thoughts of others that are preventing them from knowing God. That is what pre-evangelism is all about.

But this is not the only command to do pre-evangelism. There is also Jude 3, "Beloved, while I was making every effort to write you about our common salvation, I felt the necessity to write to you appealing that you contend earnestly for the faith which was once for all delivered to the saints." The people Jude was writing to had been assaulted by false teachers, and he needed to encourage them to protect the faith as it had been revealed through Christ. Jude makes a significant statement in verse 22 about our attitude as we do this when he says, "Have mercy on some, who are doubting." There is also Titus 1:9, which makes a knowledge of Christian evidences a requirement for church leadership. An elder in the church should be "holding fast the faithful word which is in accordance with the teaching, that he may be able both to exhort in sound doctrine and to refute those who contradict." Paul also gives us an indication of our attitude in this work in 2 Timothy 2:24-25. "And the Lord's bondservant must not be quarrelsome, but be kind to all, able to teach, patient when wronged, with gentleness correcting those who are in opposition, if perhaps God may grant them repentance leading to the knowledge of the truth." Anyone attempting to answer the questions of unbelievers will surely be wronged and be tempted to lose patience, but our ultimate goal is that they might come to a knowledge of the truth that Jesus has died for their sins. With so important a task at hand, we must not neglect obedience to this command.

BUT WHAT ABOUT. . .?

No doubt some of you have already thought of some reasons why we don't need to be involved in pre-evangelism. Some even seem to be "biblical" reasons. There is no way that we can answer all those objections, but there are a few common ones that we should take a little time to address.

"THE BIBLE SAYS,
'DO NOT ANSWER A FOOL ACCORDING TO HIS FOLLY.'"
We agree with Proverbs 26:4. We also agree with verse 5 which says, "Answer a fool as his folly deserves, lest he be wise in his own eyes." Either the Book of Proverbs was put together by a madman, or the lesson of the passage is that we have to be careful in how and when we choose to confront false ideas. Don't just argue with someone who will not listen to reason, or you will be just as foolish as he. But if you are able to show a person the error of his thinking in a way that he can understand, perhaps he will seek God's wisdom rather than relying on his own.

"LOGIC IS NOT VALID.
IT CAN'T TELL US ANYTHING ABOUT GOD."
Look at this carefully. It says that logic doesn't apply to these issues. But the statement is logical about these issues. It is logical because it claims to be true while its opposite is false. That claim, called the law of noncontradiction, is the basis of all logic.

In order to say that logic doesn't apply to God, you have to apply logic to God in that very statement. So logic is inescapable. You can't deny logic with your words unless you affirm it with the very same words. It is undeniable. When a truth cannot be denied, it must be true. So this objection is false. Logic can tell us some things about God. For instance, since God is truth, He cannot lie (Heb. 6:18). Logic is a valid tool for discovering truth and can be used effectively with non-Christians who don't believe that the Bible is a revelation from God.

"IF PRE-EVANGELISM IS BIBLICAL,
THEN WHY DON'T WE SEE IT DONE IN THE BIBLE?"
That's a good question. It may be that we aren't looking for it, or we don't recognize it when we see it. Moses did pre-evangelism. The first chapter of Genesis clearly confronts the mythical accounts of creation known in his day. Elijah did it. The whole scene at Mount Carmel with the prophets of Baal is designed to show the superiority of Yahweh. Jesus did it. His meeting with the woman at the well is a good example of confronting social, religious, and moral barriers to faith.

Paul did it a lot. On at least four occasions (Acts 14:8-18; 17:16-34; 24:5-21; 26:1-29), we see Paul making his case for the faith to unbelievers from different religious backgrounds. In addition to this are the commands that we have already discussed and the many times the New Testament authors confront false teachings in their writings. There are many examples of pre-evangelism throughout the Scriptures as God has reached out to the world with the message of His love.

Unbelievers have good questions. Christianity has good answers. And God has told us to give them the answers they are looking for. Not everyone has deep philosophical questions, and God never guarantees our success. Success is His business. But He has told us to be ready. That is what this book is all about.

2

QUESTIONS ABOUT GOD

The existence of a personal, moral God is fundamental to all that Christians believe. If there is no moral God, there is no moral being against whom we have sinned; therefore, salvation is not needed. Furthermore, if there is no God, there could be no acts of God (miracles), and the stories of Jesus can only be understood as fiction or myth. So the first question that must be addressed in pre-evangelism is, "Does God exist?" The second question is very closely related to the first: "If God exists, what kind of God is He?" Both of these questions will be answered in this chapter, and in chapter 3 we will look at questions about other gods.

DOES GOD EXIST?

ARGUMENTS FOR THE EXISTENCE OF GOD

There have traditionally been four basic arguments used to prove God's existence. They are called the cosmological, teleological, axiological, and ontological arguments. But since these are technical terms, let's just call them the arguments from Creation (*cosmos* means creation), design (*telos* means purpose), moral law (*axios* means judgment), and being (*ontos* means being).

Argument from Creation
The basic idea of this argument is that, since there is a universe, it must have been caused by something beyond itself. It is based

History of the Argument from Creation
Paul said that all men know about God "for God has made it evident to them. For since the Creation of the world His invisible attributes, His eternal power and divine nature, have been clearly seen, being understood through what has been made" (Rom. 1:19-20). Plato is the first thinker known to have developed an argument based on causation. Aristotle followed. Muslim philosophers al-farabi and Avicenna also used this type of reasoning, as did the Jewish thinker Moses Maimonides. In Christian thought, Augustine, Aquinas, Anselm, Descartes, Leibniz, and others to the present day have found it valuable, making it the most widely noted argument for God's existence.

on the law of causality, which says that every limited thing is caused by something other than itself. There are two different forms of this argument, so we will show them to you separately. The first form says that the universe needed a cause at its beginning; the second form argues that it needs a cause right now to continue existing.

The universe was caused at the beginning
This argument says that the universe is limited in that it had a beginning and that its beginning was caused by something beyond the universe. It can be stated this way:

1. The universe had a beginning.
2. Anything that has a beginning must have been caused by something else.
3. Therefore, the universe was caused by something else, and this cause was God.

In order to avoid this conclusion, some people say that the universe is eternal; it never had a beginning–it just always existed. Carl Sagan said, "The cosmos is all that is, or ever was, or ever will be."[1] But we have two ways to answer this objection. First, the scientific evidence strongly supports the idea that the universe had a beginning The view usually held by those who claim that the universe is eternal, called the steady state theory, leads some to believe that the universe is constantly producing hydrogen atoms from nothing.[2] It would be simpler to believe that God created the universe from nothing. Also, the consensus of scientists studying the origin of the universe is that it came into being in a sudden and cataclysmic way. This is called the Big Bang theory. The main evidence for the universe having a beginning is the second law of thermodynamics, which says the universe is running out of usable energy. But if it is running down, then it could not be eternal. What is winding down must have been wound up. Other evidence for the Big Bang is that we can still find the radiation from it and see the movement that it caused (see chap. 10 for details). Robert Jastrow, founder-director of NASA's Goddard Institute of Space Studies, has said, "A sound explanation may exist for the explosive birth of our Universe; but if it does, science cannot find out what the explanation is. The scientist's pursuit of the past ends in the moment of creation."[3]

But beyond the scientific evidence that shows the universe began, there is a philosophical reason to believe that the world had a starting point. This argument shows that time cannot go back into the past forever. You see it is impossible to pass through an infinite series of moments. You might be able to imagine passing through an infinite number of dimensionless points on a line by moving your finger from one end to the other, but time is not dimensionless or imaginary. It is real and each moment that passes uses up real time that we can't go back to. It is more like moving your finger across an endless number of books in a library. You would never get to the last book. Even if you thought you had found the last book, there could always be one more added, then another and another. . . . You can never finish an infinite series of real things. If the past is infinite (which is another way of saying, "If the universe had always existed without a beginning"), then we could never have passed through time to get to today. If the past is an infinite series of moments, and right now is where that series stops, then we would have passed through an infinite series and that is impossible. If the world never had a beginning, then we could not have reached today. But we have reached today: so time must have begun at a particular point in the past, and today has come at a definite time since then. Therefore, the world is a finite event after all and it needs a cause for its beginning.

Two Kinds of Infinite Series

There are two kinds of infinite series, one is abstract and the other is concrete. An abstract infinite series is a mathematical infinite. For example, as any mathematician knows, there are an infinite number of points on a line between point A and point B, no matter how short (or long) the line may be. Let's say the points are two bookends about three feet apart. Now, as we all know, while there are an infinite number of abstract mathematical points between the two bookends, nevertheless, we cannot get an infinite number of actual books between them, no matter how thin the pages are! Nor does it matter how many feet of distance we place between the bookends; we still cannot get an infinite number of books there. So while abstract, mathematical infinite series are possible, actual, concrete infinite series are not.

Now that we have seen that the universe needs a cause of its *beginning*, let's move on to the second form of the argument. This argument shows that the universe needs a cause of its existence *right now*.

The universe needs a cause for its continuing existence

Something is keeping us in existence right now so we don't just disappear. Something has not only caused the world to come into being (Gen. 1:1), but is also continuing and conserving its existence in the present (Col. 1:17). The world needs both an originating cause and a conserving cause. In a sense, this question is the most basic question that can be asked, "Why is there something rather than nothing?" It can be put this way:

1. *Finite, changing things exist.* For example, me. I would have to exist to deny that I exist; so either way, I must really exist.
2. *Every finite changing thing must be caused by something else* If it is limited and it changes, then it cannot be something that exists independently. If it existed independently, or necessarily, then it would have always existed without any kind of change.
3. *There cannot be an infinite regress of these causes.* In other words, you can't go on explaining how this finite thing

causes this finite thing, which causes this other finite thing, and on and on, because that really just puts off the explanation indefinitely. It doesn't explain anything. Besides, if we are talking about why finite things are existing right now, then no matter how many finite causes you line up, eventually you will have one that would be both causing its own existence and be an effect of that cause at the same moment. That is nonsense. So no infinite regress can explain why I am existing right now.

4. *Therefore, there must be a first uncaused cause of every finite, changing thing that exists.*

This argument shows why there must be a present, conserving cause of the world, but it doesn't tell us very much about what kind of God exists. How do we know that this is really the God of the Bible?

TWO ASPECTS OF CREATION

Originating Cause

Continuing Cause

In the beginning, God created the heavens and the earth. Gen. 1:1

Time

Time

All things have been created by Him and for Him. And He is before all things and in Him all things hold together. Col. 1:16-17

Argument from design

This argument, like others that we will mention briefly, reason from some specific aspect of creation to a Creator who put it there. It argues from design to an intelligent Designer.

1. All designs imply a designer.
2. There is great design in the universe.
3. Therefore, there must be a Great Designer of the universe.

The first premise we know from experience. Anytime we see a complex design, we know by previous experience that it came from the mind of a designer. Watches imply watchmakers; buildings imply architects; paintings imply artists; and coded messages imply an intelligent sender. It is always our expectation because we see it happening over and over. This is another way of stating the principle of causality.

Also, the greater the design, the greater the designer. Beavers make log dams, but they have never constructed anything like Hoover Dam. Likewise, a thousand monkeys sitting at typewriters would never write *Hamlet*. But Shakespeare did it on the first try. The more complex the design, the greater the intelligence required to produce it.

We ought to mention here that there is a difference between

History of the Argument from Design

"For Thou didst form my inward parts; Thou didst weave me in my mother's womb. I will give thanks to Thee, for I am fearfully and wonderfully made. Wonderful are Thy works, and my soul knows it very well" (Ps. 139:13-14). Responding to the birth of the Enlightenment and the scientific method, William Paley (1743–1805) insisted that if someone found a watch in an empty field, he would rightly conclude that there had been a watchmaker because of the obvious design. The same must be said of the design found in nature. The skeptic David Hume even stated the argument in his *Dialogues Concerning Natural Religion,* as have several others. However, there have been at least as many objectors to it as there have been proponents of it. The classic exponent was William Paley, and the most noted opponent was David Hume.

simple patterns and complex design. Snowflakes or quartz crystals have simple patterns repeated over and over, but have completely natural causes. On the other hand, we don't find sentences written in stone unless some intelligent being wrote them. That doesn't happen naturally. The difference is that snowflakes and crystals have a simple repeated pattern. But language communicates complex information, not just the same thing over and over. Complex information occurs when the natural elements are given boundary conditions. So when a rockhound sees small round rocks in a stream, it doesn't surprise him because natural erosion rounds them that way. But when he finds an arrowhead he realizes that some intelligent being has deliberately altered the natural form of the rock. He sees complexity here that cannot be explained by natural forces. Now the design that we are talking about in this argument is complex design, not simple patterns; the more complex that design is, the greater the intelligence required to produce it.

That's where the next premise comes in. The design we see in the universe is complex. The universe is a very intricate system of forces that work together for the mutual benefit of the whole. Life is a very complex development. A single DNA molecule, the building block of all life, carries the same amount of information as one volume of an encyclopedia. No one seeing an encyclopedia lying in the forest would hesitate to think that it had an intelligent cause; so when we find a living creature composed of millions of DNA-based cells, we ought to assume that it likewise has an intelligent cause. Even clearer is the fact that some of these living creatures are intelligent themselves Even Carl Sagan admits:

> The information content of the human brain expressed in bits is probably comparable to the total number of connections among neurons—about a hundred trillion, 10^{14} bits. If written out in English, say, that information would fill some twenty million volumes, as many as in the world's largest libraries. The equivalent of twenty million books is inside the heads of every one of us. The brain is a very big place in a very small space.   The neurochemistry of the brain is astonishingly busy, the circuitry of a machine more wonderful than any devised by humans.[4]

Some have objected to this argument on the basis of chance. They claim that when the dice are rolled any combination could happen. However, this is not very convincing for several reasons. First, the design argument is not really an argument from chance but from design, which we know from repeated observation to have an intelligent cause. Second, science is based on repeated observation, not on chance. So this objection to the design argument is not scientific. Finally, even if it were a chance (probability) argument, the chances are a lot higher that there is a designer. One scientist figured the odds for a one-cell animal to emerge by pure chance at 1 in 10^{40000}. The odds for an infinitely more complex human being to emerge by chance are too high to calculate! The only reasonable conclusion is that there is a great Designer behind the design in the world.

Argument from moral law
Similar arguments, based on the moral order of the universe rather than the physical order, can be offered. These argue that the cause of the universe must be moral, in addition to being powerful and intelligent.

1. All men are conscious of an objective moral law.
2. Moral laws imply a moral Lawgiver.
3. Therefore, there must be a supreme moral Lawgiver.

History of the Moral Argument
This argument did not gain prominence until the early nineteenth century after the writings of Immanuel Kant. Kant insisted that there was no way to have absolute knowledge about God and he rejected all of the traditional arguments for God's existence. He did, however, approve of the moral approach, not as a proof for God's existence, but as a way to show that God is a necessary postulate for moral living. In other words, we can't know that God exists, but we must act like He exists to make sense of morality. Later thinkers have refined the argument to show that there is a rational basis for God's existence to be found in morality. There have also been attempted disproofs of God's existence on moral grounds based on ideas coming from Pierre Bayle and Albert Camus.

In a sense, this argument also follows the principle of causality But moral laws are different from the natural laws that we have dealt with before. Moral laws don't *describe what is; they prescribe what ought to be*. They are not simply a description of the way men behave, and are not known by observing what men do. If they were, our idea of morality would surely be different. Instead, they tell us what men ought to do, whether they are doing it or not. Thus, any moral "ought" comes from beyond the natural universe. You can't explain it by anything that happens in the universe and it can't be reduced to the things men do in the universe. It transcends the natural order and requires a transcendent cause.

Now some might say that this moral law is not really objective; it is nothing but a subjective judgment that comes from social conventions. However, this view fails to account for the fact that all men hold the same things to be wrong (like murder, rape, theft, and lying). Also, their criticism sounds very much like a subjective judgment, because they are saying that our value judgments are wrong. Now if there is no objective moral law, then there can be no right or wrong value judgments. If our views of morality are subjective, then so are theirs. But if they claim to be making an objective statement about moral law, then they are

---

Same, Different, or Similar?
How much like God are we? How much can an effect tell us about its cause? Some have said that the effect must be exactly the same a its cause. Qualities such as existence or goodness in the effect are the same as those qualities in its cause. If that is true, then we should all be pantheists, because we are all God, eternal and divine. In reaction, some have said that we are entirely different from God—there is no similarity between what He is and what we are. But that would mean that we have no positive knowledge about God. We could only say that Goa is "not this" and "not that," but we could never say what He is. The middle road is to say that we are similar to God—the same, but in a different way. Existence, goodness, love, all mean the same thing for both us and for God. We have them in a limited way, and He is unlimited. So we can say what God is, but in some things, we must also say that He is not limited as we are—"eternal," "unchanging," "nonspatial," etc.

implying that there is a moral law in the very act of trying to deny it. They are caught both ways. Even their "nothing but" statement requires "more than" knowledge which shows that they secretly hold to some absolute standard which is beyond subjective judgments. Finally, we find that even those who say that there is no moral order *expect* to be treated with fairness, courtesy, and dignity. If one of them raised this objection and we replied with, "Oh, shut up. Who cares what you think?" we might find that he does believe there are some moral "oughts." Everyone expects others to follow some moral codes, even those who try to deny them. But moral law is an undeniable fact.

Argument from being

A fourth argument attempts to prove that God must exist by definition. It says that once we get an idea of what God is, that idea necessarily involves existence. There are several forms of this argument, but let's just talk about the idea of God as a perfect Being.

1. Whatever perfection can be attributed to the most perfect Being possible (conceivable) *must* be attributed to it (otherwise it would not be the most perfect being possible).
2. Necessary existence is a perfection which can be attributed to the most perfect Being.

History of the Argument from Being

When God revealed His name to Moses, He said, "I AM THAT I AM," making it clear that existence is His chief attribute (Ex. 3:14, KJV). The eleventh-century monk Anselm of Canterbury used this idea to formulate a proof for God's existence from the very idea of God, without having to look at the evidence in Creation. Anselm referred to it as a "proof from prayer" because he thought of it while meditating on the idea of a perfect Being; hence, the name of the treatise where it is found is the *Monologion,* meaning a one-way prayer. In another of his writings, the *Proslogion,* he dialogues with God about nature and develops an argument from Creation also. In modern philosophy, the argument from being is found in the writings of Descartes, Spinoza, Leibniz, and Hartshorne.

3. Therefore, necessary existence must be attributed to the most perfect Being.

To answer the first question, necessary existence means that something exists and cannot not exist. When we say this of God, it means that it is impossible for Him not to exist. This is the most perfect kind of existence because it can't go away.

Now this argument succeeds in showing that our idea of God must include necessary existence; but it fails to show that God actually exists. It shows that we must *think* of God as existing necessarily; but it does not prove that He must necessarily *exist*. This is an equivocation that has confused many people, so don't feel stupid for having trouble with it. The problem is that it only talks about the way we think of God, not whether or not He really exists. It might be restated this way:

1. If God exists, we conceive of Him as a necessary Being.
2. By definition, a necessary Being must exist and cannot not exist.
3. Therefore, if God exists, then He must exist and cannot not exist.

It is like saying: *if* there are triangles, then they must have three sides. Of course, there may not be any triangles. You see, the argument never really gets past that initial "if." It never gets around to proving the big question that it claims to answer. The only way to make it prove that God exists is to smuggle in the

---

All Roads Lead to a Cause
We have seen that all of the traditional arguments ultimately rest on the idea of causality. The argument from being needs the confirmation that something exists in which perfection and being is found. The argument from design implies that the design was caused. Likewise, morality, justice, and truth as principals of an argument all assume that there is some cause for these things. This leads us back to the argument from Creation as the basic argument which proves God's existence, for as one student said, it is the "causemological" argument.

argument from Creation. It can be useful, though, because it shows that, if there is a God, He exists in a necessary way. That makes this idea of God different from some other ways to conceive of Him, as we will see later.

Now for the $64,000 Question: If all these arguments have some validity but rely on the principle of causality, what is the best way to prove that God exists? If you answer, "The argument from Creation," you are on the right track. But what if we can combine all of these arguments into a cohesive whole that proves what kind of being God is as well as His existence? That is what we will do in the following pages.

WHAT KIND OF GOD EXISTS?

If we want to show that God exists and that He is the God of the Bible, then we need to show that all of the things in the arguments mentioned are true. Each one contributes something to our knowledge of God and, taken together, they form a picture that can only fit the one true God.

GOD IS POWERFUL

The argument from Creation proves not only that God exists, but that He has power. Only a God with incredible power could create and sustain the whole universe. His energy would have to be greater than all the energy that was ever available in the whole Creation, for He not only caused all things, He holds them together and keeps them in existence and still sustains His own existence. That is more power than we can imagine.

GOD IS INTELLIGENT

Even Carl Sagan admits that the design of the universe is far beyond anything that man could devise. The argument from design shows us that whatever caused the universe not only had great power, but also great intelligence. God knows things—things that we cannot understand. This opens the possibility for God to know all sorts of other things, but more on that later. For now it is enough to say that God at least knows everything there is to know about the way we think, because He designed our brains.

GOD IS MORAL

The existence of a moral law in the mind of a moral Lawgiver shows us that God is a moral Being. He is neither beyond morality (like some kings think they are) nor beneath morality (like a rock). He is by nature moral. This means that part of what He knows is the difference between right and wrong. But we can take this one step further: He is not only moral; He is good. We know that part of what He created was people, and persons are good, in and of themselves. The fact that persons always expect to be treated better than things shows that. Even someone denying that people have value at least expects you to value his opinion as a person. But whatever creates good things must be good itself (a cause can't give what it hasn't got). So God is not only moral, He is good.

GOD IS NECESSARY

The argument from the idea of a necessary being may not prove that God exists, but it sure does tell us a lot about God once we know that He does exist (by the argument from Creation). We said already that necessary existence means that He cannot not exist—so He had no beginning and no end. But it also means that He cannot "come to be" in any other way. He must be *as He is* necessarily. He can't become something new. That removes all change from His being—He is unchanging. And without change, time is not possible, because time is just a way to measure change—so He is eternal (e = no, *tern* = time; no-time). In fact, since a necessary being cannot not be, He can have no limits. A limitation means "to not be" in some sense, and that is impossible—so He is infinite. Also, He can't be limited to categories like

---

Change can only be essential, like changing from a dog to a horse, or accidental, like changing from a brunette to a blond. Essential changes change what a thing is; accidental ones only change little details. God can't change His essence because that would mean not existing (remember: His essence is to exist). He can't change any details because everything He's got is wrapped up in His existence. Therefore, God is changeless.

ere and there," because unlimited being must be in all places at all times—therefore, He is omnipresent. All of these are attributes that follow just from knowing that He is necessary.

But His necessity also tells us something about His other attributes. Because of His necessity, He can only have whatever He has in a necessary way. That means, as we have seen, without beginning, without change, and without limitation. So while the argument from Creation tells us that He has power, the argument from the idea of a perfect being shows that it is perfect, unlimited power. The argument from design tells us that He is intelligent, but His necessity informs us that His knowledge is uncreated, unchanging, and infinite. The moral order suggests that He is good, but the perfection of His being means that He must be all good in a perfect and unlimited way. Anything that God is He must be in accordance with His nature; so His power, knowledge, and goodness are as perfect as His being.

GOD IS UNIQUE

We have said that God is all-powerful, all-knowing, all-good, infinite, uncreated, unchanging, eternal, and omnipresent. But how many beings like that can there be? He is a class of one by definition. If there were two unlimited beings, how could you tell them apart? They have no limits to define where one stops and the other begins—but neither one can "stop" or "begin" anyway. There can only be one infinite Being and no other.

GOD IS LORD OVER CREATION

The argument from Creation does more than prove that God exists; it also proves that He is the Creator. There is no way to distinguish two infinite creatures, but God is distinct from the finite world that He has made. The whole point of the argument from Creation is that the universe cannot explain its own existence—that it is not God. The same point can be made if we consider an individual. I exist: but I have no way to account for my existence in myself. It is painfully clear that my being is not necessary—I could cease to exist at any moment and the world would go right on without me. Only by recognizing an infinite Being, a necessary cause for my being—One who gives me being—can I make sense of my existence. And as the all-powerful, all-knowing Creator, He has control over the creation. Not only does God exist, but His creation also exists distinct from Him.

GOD IS YAHWEH

Is this the God of the Bible? At the burning bush, God told Moses His name and said, "I AM WHO I AM" (Ex. 3:14). This signifies that the central characteristic of the God of the Bible is existence. His very nature is existence. Popeye can say, "I am what I am." But only God can say, "I AM WHO I AM." He is the "I AM." The Bible also calls God eternal (Col. 1:17; Heb. 1:2), unchanging (Mal. 3:6; Heb. 6:18), infinite (1 Kings 8:27; Isa. 66:1), all-good (Ps. 86:5; Luke 18:19), and all-powerful (Heb. 1:3; Matt. 19:26). Since these beings are the same in all these respects, and there can't be two infinite beings, then this God that the arguments point us to is the God of the Bible.

SOME OBJECTIONS

IF EVERYTHING NEEDS A CAUSE, THEN WHAT CAUSED GOD?

This question comes up a lot. The problem is that people don't listen well to what we have to say. We didn't say that everything needs a cause; we said everything *that has a beginning* needs a cause. Only finite, contingent things need a cause. God didn't have a beginning; He is infinite and He is necessary. God is the uncaused cause of all finite things. If God needed a cause, we would begin an infinite regress of causes that would never answer the question. As it is, we can't ask, "Who caused God?" because God is the first cause. You can't go back any farther than a first.

IF GOD CREATED ALL THINGS, THEN HOW DID HE CREATE HIMSELF?

Again, only finite, contingent beings need causes. Necessary beings don't. We never said that God is a self-caused Being. That would be impossible. However, we can turn this objection into an argument for God. There are only three possible kinds of being:

self-caused, caused by another, and uncaused. Which are we? Self-caused is impossible with respect to existence; we can't bring ourselves into existence. Uncaused would mean that we are necessary, eternal, infinite beings, which we are not; so we must be caused by another. If we are caused by another, what kind of being is He? Again, self-caused is impossible; if He were caused by another, that leads to an infinite regress; so He must be uncaused.

NO STATEMENTS ABOUT EXISTENCE ARE NECESSARY

Some critics have attempted an ontological disproof of God by saying that we just can't talk about God in terms of necessary truths. However, the statement itself appears to be a necessary statement about God saying that such statements can't be made. Now either it is a necessarily true statement or it is not. If it is, then the act of asserting it proves it to be false, for it says that such statements are impossible. If it is not necessarily true, then some necessary statements are possible and the objection vanishes. Let's just be fair: if they can make negative statements about existence (God does not exist), then why can't we make positive ones?

THE MORAL LAW IS EITHER
BEYOND GOD OR ARBITRARY

Bertrand Russell asked where God derived the moral law. He said that either it is beyond God and He is subject to it (and hence, not the ultimate good), or it is an arbitrary selection of codes that originated in God's will. So either God is not ultimate or He is arbitrary; in either case He is not fit to be worshiped. Russell fails to exhaust the possibilities, however, and we can sidestep the horns of his dilemma. Our contention is that the moral law is rooted in God's good and loving nature. This is not an ultimate beyond God, but within Him. And it is impossible for God to will something that is not in accordance with His nature. God is good and cannot will evil arbitrarily. So there is no dilemma.

CAN GOD MAKE A MOUNTAIN SO BIG
THAT HE CAN'T MOVE IT?

This is another meaningless question. It asks, "Is there something that is more than infinite?" It is logically impossible for anything to be more than infinite, because infinite has no end. The same applies to questions like, "Can God make a square circle?" It is just like asking, "What is the smell of blue?" It is a category mistake—colors don't smell and circles can't be square. These are logical impossibilities. They contradict themselves when we try to think about them. God's omnipotence does not mean that He can do what is impossible, only that He has the power to do anything that is actually possible, even if it is impossible for us. Any mountain that God makes, He can control, put where He wants, and disintegrate if He likes. You can't ask for more power than that.

IF GOD HAS NO LIMITS, THEN HE MUST BE BOTH GOOD AND EVIL, EXISTENCE AND NONEXISTENCE, STRONG AND WEAK

When we say that God is unlimited, we mean that He is unlimited in His perfections. Now evil is not a perfection; it is an imperfection. The same is true of nonexistence, weakness, ignorance, finitude, temporality, and any other characteristic that implies limitation or imperfection. We might say that God is "limited" in that He can't enter into limitations, like time, space, weakness, evil—at least not as God. He is only "limited" by His unlimited perfection.

IF GOD IS A NECESSARY BEING, THEN THE WORLD IS TOO

This assumes that a necessary being must do all that it does necessarily, but our definition was only that He must be all that He is. All that is in God's nature is necessary, but anything that He does extends beyond His nature and is done by His free will. One cannot even say that it was necessary for Him to create. His love may have given Him the *desire* to create, but it did not *demand* that He do so. He must be as He is, but He can do what He pleases as long as it doesn't contradict His nature.

IF GOD IS ETERNAL, WHEN DID HE CREATE THE WORLD?

This asks a confused question. Being in time, we can imagine a moment before the beginning of time, yet there really was no

such moment. God did not create the world *in* time; He is respon
sible for the creation *of* time. There was no time "before" time.
There was only eternity. The word "when" assumes that there was
a time before time. This is like asking, "Where was the man when
he jumped off the bridge?" On the bridge? That was before he
jumped. In the air? That was after. In this question, "when" assumes a definite point for a process action. Jumping is the process
of going from the bridge to the air. In the question about Creation, it tries to put God into time rather than starting it. We can
speak of a creation *of time*, but not *in time*.

IF GOD KNOWS EVERYTHING,
AND HIS KNOWLEDGE CAN'T CHANGE,
THEN EVERYTHING IS PREDETERMINED AND
THERE IS NO FREE WILL

Knowing what men *will* do with their freedom is not the same as
ordaining what they **must** do against their free choice. God's
knowledge is not necessarily incompatible with free will. There is
no problem in saying that God created men with free will so that
they could return His love, even though He knows that some will
not make that decision. God is responsible for the fact of freedom,
but men are responsible for the acts of freedom. In His knowledge, God might even persuade men to make certain decisions,
but there is no reason to suppose that He coerces any decision so
as to destroy freedom. He works persuasively, but not coercively.

GOD IS NOTHING BUT A PSYCHOLOGICAL CRUTCH,
A WISH, A PROJECTION OF WHAT WE HOPE IS TRUE

This kind of argument makes a serious error. How can men know
that God is "nothing but" a projection, unless they have "more
than" knowledge? To be sure that man's consciousness is the limit
of reality and that there is nothing beyond it, one must go beyond
the limits of man's consciousness. But if one can go beyond, then
there weren't limits. This objection says that nothing exists outside
our minds, but a person must go outside the boundaries of his
own mind to say that. If the objection were true, it must be false.
It defeats itself.

It was a long hard climb, but we have a solid argument that *the*

God, not just *a* God, exists. At this point we are tempted to fold our hands and sit back as if there were no other questions that could possibly be asked. However, we have only established that this God exists; we have not shown that anything that the Bible says He did or said is true. That's what the rest of the book is about. Also, we have not done anything to distinguish this concept of God from any other concept of God. This task will be taken up in the next chapter.

NOTES

1. Carl Sagan, *Cosmos* (New York: Random House, 1980), p. 4.

2. Robert Jastrow, *God and the Astronomers* (New York· Warner Books, 1978), p. 99

3. Ibid., p. 105.

4. Sagan, op. cit., p. 278.

3

QUESTIONS ABOUT OTHER GODS

There are many different "gods" competing for the hearts and minds of people today. The way we think about what God is like and His relationship to the world determines a lot about the way we see other things in our everyday lives. For example, people with different beliefs about God might approach the problems of world hunger or civil rights in different ways. A person who believes that everything is part of God, as Eastern pantheists do, will consider anything painful or evil to be unreal; so he might conduct seminars on meditation to make the victims realize that their problems are only illusions. A person who thinks of God as developing along with the progress of the world is very likely to be involved in famine relief programs and Amnesty International in a firm belief that he is helping to make God better. One who has faith in the God of the Bible would show compassion to those in need and provide food, clothes, and shelter.

These persons have different ways of looking at the problem and different motivations for solving it because of their diverse views of God. How one understands God determines so much about the way he sees the world. We call these different concepts worldviews. There are six worldviews that oppose Christianity which we want to discuss:

1. Atheism—the view that there is no God
2. Deism—the view that God exists, but doesn't perform miracles
3. Pantheism—the view that all is God

4. Panentheism—the view that God is developing along with the world
5. Finite Godism—the view that God exists but is limited and/or imperfect
6. Polytheism—the view that there are many gods.

For each of these we will discuss its view of God, the world, evil, miracles, and values or ethics. This chart organizes the various worldviews according to the logically possible options concerning God. Each level of the chart asks one of the four basic questions about God: How many gods are there? Are they finite or infinite?

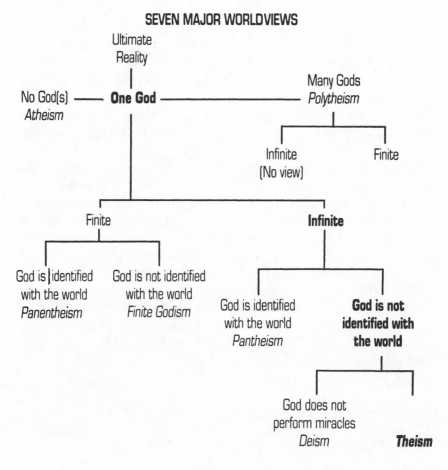

SEVEN MAJOR WORLDVIEWS

Are they identified with the world or not? Are miracles possible? Each worldview is found in *italics* and the road leading to the Christian conclusion is in **bold** type.

ATHEISM—WHAT IF THERE IS NO GOD?

Though a recent poll indicates that only about 5 percent of Americans do not believe in God, the influence of atheistic thinkers in our time is certainly widespread. Most college students have studied the writings or the thoughts of existentialist Jean-Paul Sartre, communist Karl Marx, capitalist Ayn Rand, or psychologists Sigmund Freud and B.F. Skinner. In the 1960s, the following passage from Friedrich Nietzsche became a motto for the "God is dead" movement:

"Where is God gone?" he called out. "I mean to tell you! *We have killed him*—you and I! We are all his murderers! . . . Do we not hear the noise of the grave diggers who are burying God? . . . God is dead! God remains dead!"[1]

Religion Without God?
In 1961, the Supreme Court ruled that there are some atheistic religions and cited among them Hinayana Buddhism, Taoism, and secular humanism. Here are some of the beliefs of secular humanism:
1. "Religious humanists regard the universe as self-existing and not created."
2. "Humanism believes that man is a part of the universe and that he has emerged as the result of a continuous process."
3. "We can discover no divine purpose or providence for the human species. . . . No deity will save us; we must save ourselves."
4. "We affirm that moral values derive their source from human experience. Ethics are autonomous and situational, needing no theological or ideological sanction."
5. "Moral education for children and adults is an important way of developing awareness and sexual maturity."
6. "To enhance freedom and dignity the individual must experience a full range of civil liberties in all societies. This includes . . . an individual's right to die with dignity, euthanasia, and the right to suicide." [All quotes from *Humanist Manifestos I and II,* ed. by Paul Kurtz (Buffalo: Prometheus Books, 1973).]

Not all atheists are quite as militant, however. Karl Marx echoed the sentiments of many modern atheists when he wrote, "Nowadays, in our evolutionary conception of the universe, there is absolutely no room for either a creator or a ruler."[2]

While a *skeptic* doubts that God exists, and an *agnostic* says that he doesn't know if God is out there, the *atheist* claims to know that there is no God. There is only the world and the natural forces that operate it.

WHAT DO ATHEISTS BELIEVE ABOUT GOD?

There are different kinds of atheism. Some believe that God once existed, but died in the body of Jesus Christ. Others say that it is impossible to talk about God because we can't know anything about Him, so He may as well not exist. Still others say that there is no longer any need for the God-myth that once flourished among men. But the classic view holds that there never was and never will be a God either in the world or beyond it. Those who hold this view object that the arguments used to prove God's existence are faulty. God is simply a creation of human imagination.

WHAT DO ATHEISTS BELIEVE ABOUT THE WORLD?

Many believe the world is uncreated and eternal. Others say it came into existence "out of nothing and by nothing." It is self-sustaining and self-perpetuating. They argue that if everything needs a cause, then one can ask, "What caused the first cause?" So they claim that there must have been a series of causes that reaches back into the past forever. Some simply say that the universe is not caused; it is just there.

WHAT DO ATHEISTS BELIEVE ABOUT EVIL?

While atheists deny God's existence, they affirm the reality of evil. They think the existence of evil is one of the primary evidences that there is no God. One atheist philosopher even wonders what could possibly make a Christian admit that his beliefs are false if he still believes in the existence of God while evil is present in the world. Some also argue that it is absurd to believe in God since God made all things, and evil is a thing, so God must have made evil.

WHAT DO ATHEISTS BELIEVE ABOUT VALUES?

If there is no God, and man is merely a collection of chemicals, then there is no reason to believe that anything has eternal value. Atheists believe that morals are relative and situational. There may be some enduring ethical principles, but these were created by man, not revealed by God. Goodness is defined as whatever works to achieve the desired results.

Atheist philosophers have asked some questions which challenge us to think about our faith. However, the objections that are raised about God's existence have already been addressed in our arguments in chapter 2. Briefly stated, an infinite series of causes is impossible and unnecessary, because Christians never said that *everything* needs a cause—only *events* or things that change need causes. Asking, "What caused the first cause?" is like asking, "What does a square triangle look like?" or, "What is the smell of blue?" It is a meaningless question. Triangles can't have four sides; colors don't smell; and first causes don't have causes because they are first. (See chap. 4 to answer questions about evil.)

DEISM—WHAT IF GOD MADE THE WORLD AND THEN LEFT IT ALONE?

Deists hold a view of God very much like the Christian view, except they don't think God performs miracles—ever. They agree that God made the world, but He just lets it run on natural principles. He oversees human history, but He doesn't intervene. They might compare God to a watchmaker who made the watch, wound it up, and then left it alone to run down.

Springing out of the eighteenth-century enlightenment, deists put reason above revelation (which is a miracle). Some famous deists include Thomas Hobbes, Thomas Paine, and Benjamin Franklin. Thomas Jefferson used his deistic views to cut all of the miracles from the Bible. His Gospel of John ends in chapter 19 with the words, "Now, in the place where He was crucified, there was a garden; and in the garden a new sepulcher, wherein was never a man yet laid. There they laid Jesus, and rolled a great stone to the door of the sepulcher, and departed."[3] Everything after that (John 20–21) is about the Resurrection.

Thomas Paine (1737–1809) was one of the most militant deists, as he showed in *The Age of Reason* (1794–95). He maintained that the Enlightenment had ended the need for a revealed religion and the age of science had come, saying, "THE WORD OF GOD IS THE CREATION WE BEHOLD." The universe "reveals to man all that is necessary for man to know of God." He especially despised Christianity, fearing that it would threaten a republican government.

"Of all the systems of religion that were ever invented, there is none more derogatory to the Almighty, more unedifying to man, more repugnant to reason, or more contradictory in itself, than this thing called Christianity. Too absurd for belief, too impossible to convince, and too inconsistent for practice, it renders the heart torpid, or produces only atheists and fanatics. As an engine of power, it serves the purpose of despotism; and as a means of wealth, the avarice of priests; but so far as respects the good of man in general, it leads to nothing here or hereafter." [All quotes from *The Complete Works of Thomas Paine,* ed. by Calvin Blanchard (Chicago: Belford, Clark & Co., 1885).]

WHAT DO DEISTS BELIEVE ABOUT GOD?

Deists believe almost everything that a theist does about God, except that they don't believe in miracles. They believe He is beyond the world, personal, all-good, all-loving, all-powerful, and all-knowing. They even pray to Him. However, they believe that God never specially intervenes in the world to help mankind. Since this also means that Jesus was not God (that would be a miracle), there is no reason for them to believe that God is a Trinity. The idea of three Persons in one nature (the Trinity) is to them just bad math. Because judgment would be an intervention of God in human affairs, some deists are universalists, claiming that no one will be judged.

WHAT DO DEISTS BELIEVE ABOUT THE WORLD?

Like theists, deists think the world was created by God and that we can know something about God by looking at the world. In fact, they say that the world is God's only revelation. He has given us reason so that we might understand Him through the things He has made.

WHAT DO DEISTS BELIEVE ABOUT EVIL?

Deists agree that man's actions are the source of evil. Most deists recognize an evil principle at work within man. Some blame evil on the abuse or neglect of using reason to rule one's life. For most deists, then, man will face either reward or judgment in the afterlife.

WHAT DO DEISTS BELIEVE ABOUT VALUES?

They hold that all moral laws are grounded in nature; however, since reason is the only means of knowing moral laws, there is disagreement as to what laws are binding and how universal they are. Some recognize the human desire for happiness as the single moral principle which guides all actions. All specific moral laws would then be applied differently in different circumstances as reason dictates.

HOW SHOULD WE RESPOND TO DEISM?

Deism is inconsistent on its most basic premise. Deists believe in the biggest miracle of all (Creation) but reject what they consider to be all the little miracles. If God was good enough and powerful enough to create the world, isn't it reasonable to assume that He could and would take care of it too? If He can make something out of nothing, then He can certainly make something out of something; as for example, Jesus made wine out of water. Unlike the seventeenth-century Enlightenment thinkers, scientists today do not consider natural laws to be universal or absolute. They *describe* what we see in nature, but they do not *dictate* what ought to be.

PANTHEISM—WHAT IF THE WORLD IS GOD?

Eastern religions have long been the seat of pantheistic thought, but this philosophy is now coming to the West through the New Age movement in the form of yoga, meditation, macrobiotic diets, and channeling. The central focus of pantheism is that all is God and God is all. In addition to Hinduism, Taoism, and some forms of Buddhism, pantheism is also the view of Western religions such as Christian Science, Unity, Scientology, and Theosophy. Even

Pantheism: Hollywood Style

"I want to introduce some Zen here," says Irvin Kershner, director of *The Empire Strikes Back,* who refers to Yoda as "a Zen master." George Lucas confessed, "I was trying to say in a very simple way . . . that there is a God and there is both a good side and a bad side. You have a choice between them, but the world works better if you're on the good side." The *Star Wars* films intentionally teach a religious message that God is a Force. We know it by feeling, matter is nothing, we can use the Force to rid ourselves of anger, fear, and aggression, and we can have immortality by being absorbed by it (as Obe Wan Kenobe was). "People can croak, 'Entertainment! Entertainment!' until they're blue in the face. The fact remains that films like *Star Wars* have become jerry-built substitutes for the great myths and rituals of belief, hope, and redemption that used to shape cultures before mass secular society took over." [Quotes from *Rolling Stone* (July 24, 1980, p. 37), *Time* (May 25, 1983, p. 68), and *Newsweek* (January 1, 1979, p. 50).]

some early Greek philosophers were pantheistic, as were later European thinkers like G.W.F. Hegel and Benedict de Spinoza. This worldview has recently been popularized in the *Star Wars* films.

WHAT DO PANTHEISTS BELIEVE ABOUT GOD?

God, to a pantheist, is the absolute being that unites all things. Some say that God is simply above multiplicity, others that He manifests Himself in many forms, and still others that He is a force which permeates all things. However, they agree that He is an it, not a person. Also, it is so completely different from anything we know that we cannot know anything about it. So reason is of no benefit in understanding ultimate reality. One Hindu Scripture says,

Him [Brahman] the eye does not see, nor the tongue express, nor the mind grasp. Him we neither know nor are able to teach. Different is he from the known, and . . . from the unknown.

He truly knows Brahman who knows him as beyond knowledge; he who thinks he knows, knows not. The ignorant think that Brahman is known, but the wise know him to be beyond knowledge.[4]

The condition for coming to know anything about God (or the Tao) is to realize that truth is found in contradictions (in Taoism, this is called the Tao). So one must meditate to empty the mind of reason and then contemplate such questions as, "What is the sound of one hand clapping?" These questions, which have no answer except the question itself, are designed to open the mind to the realization that atman (the world, multiplicity, evil, illusion) is Brahman (God, unity, good, reality). Hence, God is all and all is God. Man exists to realize that he too is God.

Though not known by reason, the essence of God is that He is mind. Hence, there can be no material existence, because mind is all. (What is mind? No matter. What is matter? Never mind.) As D.T. Suzuki put it, "This Nature [i.e., man's spiritual nature] is the Mind, and the Mind is the Buddha, and the Buddha is the Way, and the Way is Zen."[5] Likewise, the third-century A.D. philosopher Plotinus said that the first emanation from the Absolute One was *Nous* (Greek for mind), wherein God thinks about Himself and all multiplicity flows from there.

WHAT DO PANTHEISTS BELIEVE ABOUT THE WORLD?

The world was not created by God, but eternally emanates from Him. Theists say that God created from nothing (*ex nihilo*), but pantheists say that God brings forth the world from Himself (*ex Deo*). Of course, some pantheists (such as most Hindus and Mary Baker Eddy) say that the world does not really exist at all. It is illusion (maya). In order to overcome the illusion of matter, pain, and evil, we must learn to believe that all is God, including ourselves, and the illusion will have no grip on us.

Because God is not beyond the world but in it, there can be no miracles in the sense of *supernatural* events. There can be *supernormal* events, though, such as levitation, prophecy through channeling, healings, and ability to resist pain (like walking on hot coals). These things are not done by any power outside the universe, however. They are accomplished by people realizing their divine potential and using the divine power all around them.

WHAT DO PANTHEISTS BELIEVE ABOUT EVIL?

"Here also is found . . . the cardinal point in Christian Science,

No Difference?

The late Francis Schaeffer tells of this experience with a pantheist: "One day I was talking to a group of people in the digs of a young South African in Cambridge. Among others, there was present a young Indian who was of Sikh background but a Hindu by. religion. He started to speak strongly against Christianity, but did not understand the problems of his own beliefs. So I said, 'Am I not correct in saying that on the basis of your system, cruelty and noncruelty are ultimately equal, that there is no intrinsic difference between them?' He agreed . . . the student in whose room we met, who clearly understood the implications of what the Sikh had admitted, picked up his kettle of boiling water with which he was about to make tea, and stood with it over the Indian's head. The man looked up and asked him what he was doing and he said, with a cold yet gentle finality, 'There is no difference between cruelty and noncruelty.' Thereupon, the Hindu walked out into the night." [Francis Schaeffer, *The God Who Is There* (Downers Grove, Ill.: InterVarsity Press, 1968), p. 101.]

that matter and evil (including sin, disease, death) are *unreal*."[6] That is the consensus of pantheism. If God is all, and God is good, then anything evil must not really exist. After all, if it existed, it would be God. On a higher level, however, God is beyond good and evil. Those are rational opposites that cannot exist in the Absolute One. Many of the images for God in Hinduism are ugly and evil to demonstrate that truth. The goddess Kali the Destroyer is also the symbol of motherhood. The truth of her being is that she is both kind and cruel and, at the same time, neither kind nor cruel. God is beyond good and evil.

WHAT DO PANTHEISTS BELIEVE ABOUT VALUES?

Pantheist writings are filled with moral appeals to goodness and self-sacrifice. However, these only apply to the lower levels of spiritual attainment. Once an initiate moves beyond these levels, his goal is to achieve union with God and "he has no further concern with moral laws."[7] If he is to be like God, then he too must be beyond good and evil. Ethical conduct is a means for spiritual growth. There is no absolute basis for morality.

The following is a typical statement about pantheistic values:

New Age Ethics

In keeping with the idea that there are ultimately no opposites, most New Agers agree that right and wrong are not of great concern to them, but they are not amoral. They have many moral principles. Mark Satin suggests four ethical guidelines:

1. Develop yourself.
2. Work with nature's resources.
3. Be self-reliant but cooperative.
4. Be nonviolent.

However, these are not to be taken as absolutes. They are to be applied in a situational way and only for the sake of expediency. They do good because they want to avoid bad karma, or unwanted retribution. Ultimately, there is no good and no evil. "In a spiritual state, morality is impossible," because, "if you wish for something for yourself, even guidelines or principles, you've already separated yourself from the One (and besides, everything is as it should be)." All judgments of right and wrong, good and evil, belong to a lower level of consciousness which disappear when we become one with the One and all with the All. [All quotes from Mark Satin, *New Age Politics* (New York: A Delta Book, 1979), pp. 103–04, 98.]

. . . Every action [meaning any kind of action], under certain circumstances and for certain people, may be a stepping-stone to spiritual growth, if it is done in a spirit of detachment. All good and evil are relative to the individual point of growth. . . . But, in the highest sense, there can be neither good nor evil.[8]

HOW SHOULD WE RESPOND TO PANTHEISM?

Pantheism requires absolute devotion of its followers and it provides an overall view of all reality. Also it rightly stresses the fact that we cannot place the restrictions of our limited language on God. However, the basic claim of pantheism is self-defeating.

For example, the claim that reason does not apply to ultimate reality is also self-defeating. The statement, "Reason can tell us nothing about God," is either a reasonable statement (meaning it is either true or false, for that is the essence of all logic) or it is not. On the face of it, it appears to be a reasonable statement that reason gives us no information about God—*except that it just did.*

It just told us that we can't use reason. So we have to use reason to deny the use of reason, which makes logic an inescapable reality. If the pantheist avoids this by saying that it was not a reasonable statement, then we have no reason to believe it. It is simply gibberish on the order of a two-year-old's singsong.

Further, pantheists believe that there is one absolute, unchanging eality (God). They also believe that we can come to realize that we are God. However, if I *come to realize* something, then I have changed. But God cannot change. Therefore, anyone who "comes to realize that he is God" isn't! The unchanging God always knew that He is God.

Also, we must ask why the illusion of matter seems so real to us. If life in the material world is a dream of our own creation, why are we all having such a bad dream? Why are physical relations still needed to produce children? Why do devout Christian Scientists, who deny the reality of matter and renounce pain, still suffer and die in childbirth? (The childbirth sanitarium in Los Angeles was closed by the health department because of the number of deaths that occurred there.) Even devout pantheists who have supposedly mastered life in the world still live with physical limitations like eating, or moving from here to there Mark Twain pointed out this dissonance of proverb and practice in his treatise on Christian Science:

> "Nothing exists but Mind?"
> "Nothing," she answered. "All else is substanceless, all else is imaginary."
> I gave her an imaginary check, and now she is suing me for substantial dollars. It looks inconsistent.[9]

The lack of moral foundation in pantheism is quite unsatisfying. It not only leaves one with no rule to guide his actions, but actually promotes cruelty in the name of spiritual expansion. This is seen quite graphically in the traditional lack of social concern in India. If people suffer because of their *karma* (the law of cause and effect that determines destiny, not to be confused with moral guilt), then to help that individual would be working against God. It would stop him from working off his own karmic debt, and it would show that I am still attached to the world rather than indifferent to it. Hence, it is better to ignore all suffering than do anything to alleviate it. Action beyond good and evil equates evil with goodness.

PANENTHEISM—WHAT IF THE WORLD IS GOD'S BODY?

A view that is halfway between pantheism and theism is panentheism, also known as process theology. It says that God is to the world as a soul is to a body. As in theism, the world needs God to exist but, like pantheism, God also needs the world to express Himself. So, while God is beyond the world in one sense, He also is the world in another sense. What is beyond the world actualizes itself (makes itself real) in the world. So God is always changing as the world changes. He is in the *process* of becoming all that He can be. This is a recent view developed by twentieth-century philosophers Alfred North Whitehead, Charles Hartshorne, Schubert Ogden, and others, but it is based on ideas found in Plato. No major religion subscribes to it, but it is currently being taught in some Christian seminaries, the feminist movement has given it some endorsement, and it is used in the Liberation theology of Marxists in South America and South Africa.

PANTHEISM	PANENTHEISM
God is the universe	God is in the universe
God is not personal	God is personal
God is infinite	God is actually finite
God is eternal	God is actually temporal
God is unchanging	God is actually changing
God and creatures are identical	God and creatures are not identical

WHAT DO PANENTHEISTS BELIEVE ABOUT GOD AND THE WORLD?

God has two poles: a *primordial* pole, which is eternal, unchanging, ideal, and beyond the world; and a *consequent* pole, which is temporal, changing, real, and identical to the world. The primordial nature of God is His **potential** pole—what He can be; the consequent nature is what He **actually** is at the moment. So the world is not different from God; it is one of God's poles. His potential pole inhabits the world just like a soul inhabits a body. There it becomes actualized or real. So what the world is, is what God has become. As such God is never actually perfect; He is only striving toward perfection. For God to become more perfect, He needs our help. As Hartshorne has written:

> God, in his latest concrete state, is jointly "made" or produced by God and the world in prior states of each. We are not simply co-creators, with God, of the world, but in the last analysis, co-creators with him, of himself.[10]

Much like the Maxwell Escher lithograph on page 49 of two hands drawing each other, the world creates God just as much as God creates the world. They are two poles of the same being. This situation is eternally the case. For neither pole could exist without the other at any time and the potential pole, being infinite, can never become completely actualized in a finite realm. So God is "as it was in the beginning, is now, and ever shall be, world without end."

Process Thought and Evangelicals

Panentheism is not simply a scholarly discussion that has no effect on normal people. Its effect is already being felt in the Christian community. The Perkins School of Theology at Southern Methodist University, where Schubert Ogden teaches, is devoted to process theology, as is Clairmont School of Theology where John Cobb and David Griffin teach. In the evangelical community, several important thinkers have concluded that God is not timeless and eternal, but everlastingly in time. This view has been published by Nicholas Wolterstorff, Clark Pinnock, and J. Oliver Buswell. While these writers have not accepted a complete panentheistic worldview, they have made an important concession to it by allowing change in God. For if He has any potential for change, then He cannot be the necessary Being that we spoke of in chapter 2.

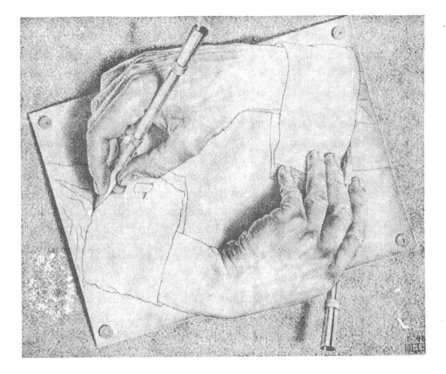

WHAT DO PANENTHEISTS BELIEVE ABOUT EVIL?

Because of limitations in His actual pole, God is not omnipotent. He directs the world only through influence. But not all of the world recognizes or is controlled by His influence, so evil exists. God simply can't control it, nor can He guarantee that it ever will be eliminated. However, they believe that evil opens new possibilities for the self-realization of God and presents new opportunities for growth to become more perfect, so it is not necessarily undesirable. There are some senses in which God does not want to do away with evil.

WHAT DO PANENTHEISTS BELIEVE ABOUT VALUES?

Like theists, process thinkers hold that values are rooted in the nature of God. But just as the nature of God is different in the two views, so is the nature of their values. Since God is constantly changing, so are values. There may be some ideal good in the primordial nature of God, but what must concern us is that we create beauty in our lives in the real world, without reference to some imagined future state of things. We can never expect to create perfection, but only strive to do more good. Values, then, can only be defined in general terms, and the term most often used is beauty or aesthetics. As Hartshorne writes, "The only good that is intrinsically good, good in itself, is good experience, and the criteria for this are aesthetic. Harmony and intensity come close to summing it up . . . *to be ethical is to seek aesthetic optimization of experience for the community.*"[1] By this standard, we are to avoid disputes and boredom in the community as well as for ourselves. Kindness brings about beauty and harmony while cruelty brings on ugliness and discord. Concern breeds intensity, and apathy is its opposite. All moral standards must be derived from these principles and suited to influence the present experience for the better.

HOW SHOULD WE RESPOND TO PANENTHEISM?

Panentheism views God as having an intimate relation to the world, and it is able to incorporate modern scientific thought into its system easily. But one must ask the simple question of how the whole system got going. It's like asking, "Which came first: the chicken or the egg?" If the potential pole came before the actual, then how was anything ever actualized? The actual pole could not have come first, because it had no potential to become. Panentheists would say that they always existed together, but then we have to face the fact that time cannot go back into the past forev-

THEISM	PANENTHEISM
God is creator of the world	God is director of the world
World is different from God	World is the same as God's body
God is in control of the world	God cooperates with the world
God is independent of the world	God is interdependent with the world
God is unchanging	God is continually changing
God is absolutely perfect	God is constantly being perfected
God is infinite and eternal	God is actually finite and temporal
God is absolutely one	God has two poles

er. The only answer can be that something else created the whole ball of wax. It took a creator beyond the process, like Maxwell Escher, to draw the hands that are eternally drawing each other. It took a transcendent God to create a chicken who would lay eggs.

Also, how can one know that everything is changing if there is not some unchanging standard by which to measure change? Because we are moving along with it, we don't notice that the world is rotating on its axis or revolving around the sun. It feels like we are standing still. The same thing happens if we toss a ball straight up in the air in an airplane. We don't realize that the ball is really traveling at 500 miles per hour because we are moving at the same speed. We can only be sure that something is moving when we measure it by something that is not moving. So how can we know that everything is changing unless we can look at something that is not changing? Panentheism has no explanation for this because it holds that even God is constantly changing.

FINITE GODISM—WHAT IF GOD IS NOT ALL-POWERFUL?

Panentheism is not the only view that holds that God is subject to limitations. Finite godism holds that God is very much like the Christian God, but He is not perfect; He is limited in His power and His nature. This view has been held by many individuals, from Plato to the present, but was never adopted by any particular religion. It was recently popularized by Rabbi Kushner in his book *When Bad Things Happen to Good People*. In wrestling with the premature death of his son, Rabbi Kushner concluded, "God wants the righteous to live peaceful, happy lives, but sometimes He can't bring that about . . . there are some things God does not control."[12]

WHAT DO FINITE GODISTS BELIEVE ABOUT GOD?

They basically agree with the theist that God is beyond the world and has created it. They simply cannot affirm that He is perfect or infinite in either His nature or power. Finite godists argue that a finite universe only needs a finite cause and that the imperfection of the universe demands an imperfect source.

ANCIENT POLYTHEISM

This chart shows the similarities between the gods of three different cultures. The Romans simply adapted the Greek mythology to themselves, but the Norse gods were created independently and are not entirely equivalent to the others. It is interesting to note that each has a Father, Mother, and favorite Son, who embodies all of the ideals of their culture.

Realm	Greek	Roman	Norse
Father God	Zeus	Jupiter	Odin
Mother	Hera	Juno	Frigga
Light, truth	Apollo	Apollo	Balder
Hunt, crops	Artemis	Diana	Freyer
Beauty, love	Aphrodite	Venus	Freya
Messenger	Hermes	Mercury	Heimdall
Sea	Poseidon	Neptune	------
War	Ares	Mars	Tyr

WHAT DO FINITE GODISTS BELIEVE ABOUT THE WORLD?

They believe that the world was created by God either from nothing or from some preexisting matter. However, they do not believe that the design of the world is perfect. Nature seems to have violent upheavals of chaos built into it, like volcanoes, tornadoes, and earthquakes. These are natural evils that God, apparently, just couldn't work out of the system. Most finite godists do not believe that God performs miracles.

WHAT DO FINITE GODISTS BELIEVE ABOUT EVIL?

The existence of evil is the primary reason for the existence of this worldview. Pantheism's rejection of the reality of evil is repugnant to them, and Leibniz's explanation that this is the best of all possible worlds leads them to conclude, "If this is the best God can do, then He must have some real problems." As Peter Bertocci has stated:

If God is omnipotent, and therefore the creator of so much evil, how can He be good? Or if He is good, and did not intend evil, can He be omnipotent in the sense defined? Must there not be something beyond the control of His good will which is the source of evil in the world?[13]

This appears to them to be the only way of understanding evil: that God cannot control it.

WHAT DO FINITE GODISTS BELIEVE ABOUT VALUES?
There is no consensus on this matter in their writings. Plato believed in intrinsic values and absolute morality. William James was the father of American pragmatism and to him, whatever was expedient was right. There is no necessary connection between values and this view of God, because God may or may not have established a moral order. That, i.e., establishing a moral order, may or may not be within His limitations.

HOW SHOULD WE RESPOND TO FINITE GODISM?
This view has a realistic approach to evil and asks a very good question, "How can the presence of evil be reconciled with the existence of an all-powerful and all-loving God?" However, just like any other finite thing, a finite god would need a cause. Also, it seems that an imperfect god would not be worthy of worship. A perfect and infinite God, however, does not have these problems and is able to overcome evil since He has both the desire and the ability to do it (see chap. 4 for a full discussion).

POLYTHEISM—WHAT IF THERE ARE MANY GODS?
Polytheism says that there are many finite gods who reign over separate realms of the universe. The gods of ancient Greece, Rome, and Norway are good examples of these. Each god had a certain domain and was worshiped as supreme in that respect only. For instance, in Greece, Poseidon was the god of the sea and one would pray to him for safe travel. But for victory in war prayers must be offered to Aries. Polytheism is not confined to antiquity. David L. Miller, a professor of religion at Syracuse

University, has said that the West is no longer looking for a single uniting principle and, "The death of God has given rise to the birth of the gods."[14] He cites the growing interest in the ancient polytheistic traditions, which is sometimes called the new paganism. One such group, in Breckenridge, Texas has patterned their worship after the Norse gods in the 1959 Kirk Douglas movie *The Vikings*. The largest and fastest-growing polytheistic religion in America today is Mormonism. Though their P.R. would lead us to believe that they are just another Christian denomination, their doctrine says something different:

> God himself once was as we are now, and is an exalted man, and sits enthroned in yonder heavens! . . . Here then is eternal life—to know the only wise and true God; and you have got to learn how to be gods yourselves . . . the same as all gods have done before you.[15]

WHAT DO POLYTHEISTS BELIEVE ABOUT GOD?

Polytheists reject the idea of a single God ruling over all things. Instead, they focus on the multiplicity and chaos of the world to show that there are many gods with sometimes discordant plans. Some polytheists say that the gods arose from nature, while others claim that the gods were once men. The Mormons posit an infinite regress of gods begetting gods, so that all gods were "spirit children of an Eternal Father" and "the offspring of an Eternal Mother,"[16] yet there was no first cause for their existence. All gods have a beginning, but they have no end. In the case of the ancient deities, their behavior does not always live up to their exalted status, as they are typically seen quarreling, seeking revenge, and deceiving both gods and men.

WHAT DO POLYTHEISTS BELIEVE ABOUT THE WORLD?

According to polytheists, the universe is either eternal or made out of eternal matter. The Mormon *Book of Abraham* says, "And then the Lord said: Let us go down. And they went down at the beginning, and they, that is the gods, organized and formed the heavens and the earth" (4:1). The material used to form the earth is called by Joseph Smith, Jr., *element,* which is chaotic matter that "had no beginning, and can have no end."[17] Nature is usually seen to have its own life principle, which explains why it is possible for it to give birth to the gods (e.g., Aphrodite arising from the sea-foam). But this vivifying principle also explains the chaos of nature as different forces war with one another.

WHAT DO POLYTHEISTS BELIEVE ABOUT EVIL?
For polytheists, evil is a necessary part of nature. The Greeks saw evil in the first power struggle between the gods which resulted in Creation, so that the world was a mixture of good and evil from the beginning. Mormonism says that evil is necessary for the progress and existence of all things, for without opposition there is no challenge to overcome in moral choices.

WHAT DO POLYTHEISTS BELIEVE ABOUT VALUES?
Some polytheists say that the moral laws are given by the gods, and that the gods punish whoever breaks their laws. Others say that the whole idea of absolute laws comes from monotheism and is foreign to this many-oriented system. These, like David Miller, prefer a relativistic ethic. Values cannot be absolute, he says, because, "truth and falsity, life and death, beauty and ugliness, good and evil are forever and inextricably mixed together."[18] In either case, the main motivation for doing good is self-interest.

HOW SHOULD WE RESPOND TO POLYTHEISM?
The multiplicity of the world and its forces, which polytheism stresses, are very real; some wonderful imagery and expressions of man's struggles with these forces have been developed. Polytheism runs aground on its own principles, however. If the gods are not eternal, but come from nature, then they are not the ultimate. Why worship something that is not of ultimate value? It would be better to worship nature itself which gave the gods birth; however, that would be pantheism (Hinduism is really a polytheistic religion which admits an ultimate unity beyond the gods). There is also a problem with the notion of an eternal universe. The evidence for a beginning of the universe is given in chapters 2 and 10. Finally, the anthropomorphic nature of the polytheistic gods is

questionable. Some resemblance between God and man is to be expected, but should we impose human imperfections on God too? This would seem to lower His worthiness and deem Him unfit to be worshiped. This aspect makes the gods seem very much to be made in the image of man.

These six worldviews represent six different ways of looking at reality. For their adherents, they are a grid through which to interpret everything around them. Just as a person with rose-colored glasses sees everything in pink, so all that we see is colored by our worldview. We have shown some reasons for rejecting each of the six worldviews covered in this chapter, but that doesn't make Christianity true by default. The argument presented in chapter 2 establishes the existence of the Christian God and His creation (both are needed to distinguish it as theism). In chapter 5, we will add the other distinctive mark of theism, miraculous intervention; but first we must deal with one of the most common objections to theism—the problem of evil.

NOTES

1. Friedrich Nietzsche, *Joyful Wisdom*, trans. by Thomas Common (New York: Frederick Unger Publishing Co., 1960), section 125, pp. 167–168.

2. See *Marx and Engels on Religion*, ed. by Reinhold Niebuhr (New York: Schocken, 1964), p. 295.

3. Thomas Jefferson, *Jefferson Bible*, ed. by Douglas Lurton (New York: Wilfred Funck, 1943), p. 132.

4. "Kena," *The Upanishads: Breath of Eternal*, trans. by Swami Prabhavananda and Frederick Manchester (New York: Mentor Books, 1957), pp. 30–31.

5. D.T. Suzuki, *Zen Buddhism*, ed. by William Barrett (Garden City, N.J.: Doubleday Anchor Books, 1956), p. 88.

6. Mary Baker Eddy, *Miscellaneous Writings* (Boston: Trustees

under the Will of Mary Baker G. Eddy, 1924), p. 27.

7. Swami Prabhavananda, *The Spiritual Heritage of India* (Hollywood: Vedanta Press, 1963), p. 65.

8. Swami Prabhavananda and Christopher Isherwood, "Appendix II: The Gita and War," in Bhagavad Gita (Bergerfield, N.J.: The New American Library, Inc., 1972), p. 140.

9. Mark Twain, *Christian Science* (New York: Harper and Brothers Publishers, n.d.), p. 38.

10. Charles Hartshorne, *A Natural Theology of Our Times* (La-Salle, Ill.: The Open Court Publishing Co., 1967), pp. 113–114.

11. Charles Hartshorne, "Beyond Enlightened Self-Interest: A Metaphysics of Ethics," *Ethics* 84 (April 1974): 214.

12. Harold S. Kushner, *When Bad Things Happen to Good People* (New York: Avon Books, 1981), pp. 43, 45.

13. Peter Bertocci, *Introduction to Philosophy of Religion* (New York: Prentice Hall, Inc., 1953), p. 398.

14. David L. Miller, *The New Polytheism: The Rebirth of Gods and Goddesses* (New York: Harper and Row, 1974), p. 4.

15. Joseph Smith, Jr., *The History of the Church of Jesus Christ of Latter-day Saints* (Salt Lake City: Deseret Book Co., 1976), 6:305–306.

16. Bruce R. McConkie, *Mormon Doctrine—A Compendium of the Gospel,* rev. ed. (Salt Lake City: Bookcraft, 1966), p. 516.

17. Joseph Smith, Jr., *Teachings of the Prophet Joseph Smith,* ed. by Joseph Fielding Smith, 4th ed. (Salt Lake City: The Deseret News Press, 1938), p. 345.

18. Miller, op. cit., p. 29.

4

QUESTIONS ABOUT EVIL

> Sooner or later I must face the question in plain language. What reason have we, except our own desperate wishes, to believe that God is, by any standard we can conceive, "good"? Doesn't all the *prima facie* evidence suggest exactly the opposite? What have we to set against it?
>
> We set Christ against it. But how if He were mistaken? Almost His last words have a perfectly clear meaning. He had found that the Being He called Father was horribly and infinitely different from what He had supposed. The trap, so long and carefully prepared and so subtly baited, was at last sprung, on the cross. The vile practical joke had succeeded. . . . Step-by-step we were "led up the garden path." Time after time, when He seemed most gracious He was really preparing the next torture.[1]

Those words did not come from an atheist or a skeptic attempting to shake anyone's faith in God. They came from one of the great defenders of Christianity, C.S. Lewis. He wrote them while he was still grieving over the loss of his wife to cancer. Such a response points out the fact that sooner or later each of us must deal with the problem of pain—that is, the problem of evil.

If God did not claim to be good, then the problem would be simple; but He does. If He were not all-powerful, as the finite godists say, there would not be a problem. If evil were not real, we could escape the problem. But such is not the case. The problem is very real—especially to those in pain—and even if we can't give an answer for each individual situation, we can find some general principles about evil. We can at least show that the idea of a good and powerful God is not irreconcilable to the existence of evil.

WHAT IS EVIL?

What is the nature of evil? We talk about evil acts (murder), evil people (Charles Manson), evil books (pornography), evil events (tornadoes), evil sicknesses (cancer or blindness), but what makes all of these things evil? What is evil when we look at it by itself? Some have said that evil is a substance that grabs hold of certain things and makes them bad (like a virus infecting an animal) or that evil is a rival force in the universe (like the dark side of Luke Skywalker's Force). But if God made all things, then that makes God responsible for evil. The argument looks like this:

1. God is the author of everything.
2. Evil is something.
3. Therefore, God is the author of evil.

Augustine vs. Manichaeus

Manichaeus was a third-century dualist who claimed that the world was made of uncreated matter which was, in itself, evil. Hence, all physical existence was evil; only spiritual things could be good. Augustine wrote a great deal to show that all that God created was good, but evil was not a substance.

"What is evil? Perhaps you will reply, Corruption. Undeniably this is a general definition of evil; for corruption implies opposition to nature; and also hurt. But corruption exists not by itself, but in some substance which it corrupts; for corruption itself is not a substance. So the thing which it corrupts is not corruption, is not evil; for what is corrupted suffers loss of integrity and purity. So that which has no purity to lose cannot be corrupted; and what has, is necessarily good by the participation of purity. Again, what is corrupted is perverted; and what is perverted suffers loss of order; and order is good. To be corrupted, then does not imply the absence of good; for in corruption it can be deprived of good, which could not be if there was the absence of good." [*On the Morals of the Manichaens, 5.7.*]

The first premise is true. So it appears that in order to deny the conclusion we have to deny the reality of evil (as the pantheists do). But we can deny that evil is a thing, or substance, without saying that it isn't real. It is a lack in things. When good that should be there is missing from something, that is evil. After all, if I am missing a wart on my nose, that is not evil because the wart should not have been there in the first place. However, if a man lacks the ability to see, that is evil. Likewise, if a person lacks the kindness in his heart and respect for human life that should be there, then he may commit murder. Evil is, in reality, a parasite that cannot exist except as a hole in something that should be solid.

In some cases, though, evil is more easily explained as a case of bad relationships. If I pick up a good gun, put in a good bullet, point it at my good head, put my good finger on the good trigger and give it a good pull . . . a bad relationship results. The things involved are not evil in themselves, but the relationship between the good things is definitely lacking something. In this case, the lack comes about because the things are not being used as they ought to be. Guns should not be used for indiscriminate killing, but are fine for recreation. My head was not meant to be used for target practice. Similarly, there is nothing wrong with strong winds moving in a circle, but a bad relationship arises when the funnel of wind goes through a mobile home park. Bad relationships are bad because the relationship is lacking something, so our definition of evil still holds. Evil is a lack of something that should be there in the relationship between good things.

WHERE DID EVIL COME FROM?

In the beginning, there was God and He was perfect. Then the perfect God made a perfect world. So how did evil come into the picture? Let's summarize the problem this way:

1. Every creature God made is perfect.
2. But perfect creatures cannot do what is imperfect.
3. So, every creature God made cannot do what is imperfect.

But if Adam and Eve were perfect, how did they fall? Don't blame it on the snake because that just backs the question up one step; didn't God make the snake perfect too? Some have concluded that there must be some force that is equal with God or beyond His control. Or maybe God just isn't good after all. But maybe the answer lies in the idea of perfection itself.

1. God made everything perfect.
2. One of the perfect things God made was free creatures.
3. Free will is the cause of evil.
4. So, imperfection (evil) can arise from perfection (not directly, but indirectly through freedom).

One of the things that makes men (and angels) morally perfect is freedom. We have a real choice about what we do. God made us that way so that we could be like Him and could love freely (forced love is not love at all, is it?). But in making us that way, He also allowed for the possibility of evil. To be free we had to have not only the opportunity to choose good, but also the ability to choose evil. That was the risk God knowingly took. That

TWO KINDS OF DEPRAVITY

Metaphysical	Moral
In matter.	In intention or will.
Lack of being or powers.	Lack of good purpose.
Effects what it is.	Effects what one does.
Leads to nonexistence.	Leads to wicked acts.
Totally depraved car is a rust spot on the road.	Totally depraved person is one who has no intention to do good.

Defining Free Will

There are several points on which there is confusion about what is meant by free will. Some have said that it refers to the ability to *desire*. But a better definition is that it is the ability to *decide* between alternatives. Desire is a passion, an emotion; but will is a choice between two or more desires. Also, some think that to be free means that there can be no limitation of alternatives—one must be able to do whatever he wants. But the opposite of freedom is not fewer alternatives, it is being forced to choose one thing and not another. Freedom is not in *unlimited options*, but in *unfettered choice* between whatever options there are. As long as the choosing comes from the individual rather than an outside force, the decision is made freely. Free will means the ability to make an **unforced decision** between two or more alternatives.

doesn't make Him responsible for evil. He created the **fact** of freedom; we perform the **acts** of freedom. He made evil **possible**; men made evil **actual**. Imperfection came through the abuse of our moral perfection as free creatures.

As for the snake, the same answer applies. God made Satan the most beautiful of all creatures with the perfection of free will. Satan rebelled against God, and that became the first sin and the pattern for all sin that followed. Some people ask, "What made Satan sin?" That is like asking what caused the first cause; nothing outside his own free will caused him to sin. He was the first cause of his sin and you can't go back any farther than that. When we sin, ultimately we (by our wills) are the cause of the evil we do.

WHY CAN'T EVIL BE STOPPED?

The classic form of this argument has been rattling through the halls of college campuses for hundreds of years.

1. If God is all-good, He *would* destroy evil.
2. If God is all-powerful, He *could* destroy evil.
3. But evil is not destroyed.
4. Hence, there is no such God.

Why hasn't God done something about evil? If He could and

would do something, why do we still have evil? Why is it so persistent? And it doesn't even seem to be slowing down!

There are two answers for this question. First, evil cannot be destroyed without destroying freedom. As we said before, free beings are the cause of evil, and freedom was given to us so that we could love. Love is the greatest good for all free creatures (Matt. 22:36-37), but love is impossible without freedom. So if freedom were destroyed, which is the only way to end evil, that would be evil in itself, because it would deprive free creatures of their greatest good. Hence, to destroy evil would actually be evil. If evil is to be overcome, we need to talk about it being defeated, not destroyed.

The argument against God from evil makes some arrogant assumptions. Just because evil is not destroyed right now does not mean that it never will be. The argument implies that if God hasn't done anything as of today, then it won't ever happen. But this assumes that the person making the argument has some inside information about the future. If we restate the argument to correct this oversight in temporal perspective, it turns out to be an argument that vindicates God.

1. If God is all-good, He will defeat evil.
2. If God is all-powerful, He can defeat evil.

Pierre Bayle (1647–1706) was one of the most influential skeptics of the seventeenth century. His writings, and particularly his *Dictionary* which states this argument, had a profound effect on the later Enlightenment writers Hume, Voltaire, Berkeley, and Diderot. In it he attempted to confront every mistake ever made by philosophers, and in doing so, provided grounds for doubting virtually everything. He wished to show that all human reasoning is "big with contradiction and absurdity." In another series of articles he shows that Christians cannot refute the Manichaen doctrine of two gods, one good and one evil. However, Bayle claimed to be a Christian and a defender of Calvinism. In one of his last messages, he wrote, "I am dying as a Christian philosopher, convinced of and pierced by the bounties and mercies of God, and I wish you a perfect happiness." It is unclear how he reconciled these beliefs.

3. Evil is not *yet* defeated.
4. Therefore, God can and *will one day* defeat evil.

The very argument used against the existence of God turns out to be a vindication of God in the face of the problem of evil. There is no question here that if it has not yet happened and God is as we suppose Him to be, that we simply haven't waited long enough. God isn't finished yet. The final chapter has not been written. Apparently God would rather wrestle with our rebellious wills than to reign supreme over rocks and trees. Those who want a quicker resolution to the conflict will have to wait.

WHAT IS THE PURPOSE OF EVIL?

The question that roars in the minds of those who suffer is, "*WHY?*" "Why did I lose my leg?" "Why did our church burn down?" "Why did my little girl have to die?" "*WHY?*" Unfortunately, we can't always give an answer that satisfies the souls of those who hurt and makes sense of their pain. But to those who use this as a reason to deny God's existence or goodness, we can give an answer. Their argument is this:

1. There is no good purpose for much suffering.
2. An all-good God must have a good purpose for everything.
3. So, there cannot be an all-good God.

We can deal with this problem in two ways. First, we need to make a distinction. There is a difference between our knowing the purpose for evil and God having a purpose for it. Even if we don't know God's purpose, He may still have a good reason for allowing evil in our lives. So we can't assume that there is no good purpose for something just because we don't know what it could be.

Furthermore, we do know some of God's purposes for evil. For instance, we know that God sometimes uses evil to warn us of greater evils. Anyone who has raised a child has gone through the months of fearing that the baby would touch a hot stove for the first time. We hate the thought of it, but we know that once she does it, she won't do it again. She will instantly have an existential awareness of the meaning of the word "hot" and will obey our warning readily when we use it. That first small pain is allowed to avoid the danger of bigger ones later.

Pain also keeps us from self-destruction. Do you know why lepers lose their fingers, toes, and noses? Usually, it has nothing directly to do with the leprosy itself. Rather, the disease causes them to lose feeling in their extremities, and they literally destroy themselves. They can't feel the pain when they touch a hot pan, so they hang on to it until it burns them. Without feeling things that they are about to bump into, they hit them full force without slowing down. Without the sensation of pain, they do tremendous damage to themselves and don't even realize it.

While it may seem like a high price to pay, some evil helps to bring about greater good. The Bible gives several examples of this in men like Joseph, Job, and Samson. Each went through real suffering. How would the nation of Israel have survived the famine and had a refuge in which to grow if Joseph had not been sold

---

The Gift of Pain

Dr. Paul Brand, a leading researcher and therapist of Hansen's disease, expressed significant insights on the problem of pain. Having just examined three patients, Lou—who may lose his thumb to infection from playing the autoharp, Hector—who can't feel the damage he is doing to his hand while mopping, and Jose—who is unwilling to wear special shoes to prevent the loss of the nubs that were once his feet, Dr. Brand says this:

Pain—it's often seen as the great inhibitor which ropes off certain activities. But I see it as the great giver of freedom. Look at these men. Lou: we're desperately searching for a way to give him simple freedom to play an autoharp. Hector: he can't even mop a floor without harming himself. Jose: too proud for proper treatment, he's given a makeshift shoe which may keep him from losing even more of his feet. He can't dress nicely and walk normally: for that, he would need the gift of pain. [From *Where Is God When It Hurts?* by Philip Yancey (Grand Rapids: Zondervan, 1977), p. 37]

into slavery by his brothers and imprisoned unjustly? Would Job have been able to make his marked spiritual growth had he not suffered first? (Job 23:10) What kind of leader would the Apostle Paul have been if he had not been humbled after his exalted revelations of God? (2 Cor. 12) Joseph summarized the matter when he told his brothers, "You meant evil against me, but God meant it for good" (Gen. 50:20).

Finally, permitting some evil actually helps defeat evil. One of the first steps in some of the substance abuse rehabilitation programs (alcohol, tobacco, marijuana, cocaine) is to give the patient all that he can stand of the substance until he gets sick of it. It's easier to quit once you've had a bad experience. Projects like the "Scared Straight" program at Rahway Prison have stopped many young people from following a life of crime, but the convicts who tell them about prison life have both caused suffering and are suffering. And then there is the ultimate example: the Cross. It seems that there an infinite injustice was wrought on an innocent Man so that good might come to all. The evil that He endured as our substitute allows us free access to God without fear, because

---

On the Cross
Why would God allow His own Son to suffer and die a cruel and violent death as a criminal when He had done nothing wrong and, by nature, had no need to die? This injustice is very hard to explain unless there is some greater good accomplished by Christ's death which overshadows the evil of it. Jesus' own explanation was that He had come "to give His life [as] a ransom for many" (Mark 10:45) and saying, "Greater love has no one than this, that one lay down his life for [on behalf of] his friends" (John 15:13). Hebrews 12:2 states the purpose of Jesus, "who for the joy set before Him endured the cross, despising the shame," meaning that the reconciliation of sinners was worth the suffering. As Isaiah says, "He was pierced through for our transgressions, He was crushed for our iniquities; the chastening for our well-being fell upon Him, and by His scourging we are healed" (53:5). The higher purpose and greater good derived from Christ's death as our substitute for the penalty of our sins is more important than the evil inherent in the process.

our guilt and punishment have been taken away.

C.S. Lewis said, "God whispers to us in our pleasures, speaks in our conscience, but shouts in our pains: it is His megaphone to rouse a deaf world."[2] In some sense, we need pain so that we are not overcome by the evil that we would choose were it painless. He alerts us to the fact that there are better things than misery.

DOES THERE HAVE TO BE SO MUCH EVIL?

The extent of evil poses a problem. Surely there doesn't have to be this much evil to fulfill God's purposes. Couldn't there have been one less rape, one less drunk driver? That would have made the world better. And, of course, that "one-less" theory can be extended until there is no evil at all. This can even be taken to the extreme case: What about hell? Wouldn't it be better to have one less person in hell? Since both of these questions have the same answer, lets deal with the extreme case.

1. The greatest good is to save all men.
2. Even one person in hell would be less than the greatest good.
3. Therefore, God cannot send anyone to hell.

To answer this objection, we go back to the subject of free will. It is true that God desires all men to be saved (2 Peter 3:9), but that means that they have to choose to love Him and believe in Him. Now, God can't force anyone to love Him. Forced love is a contradiction in terms. Love must be free: it is a free choice. So in spite of God's desire, some men do not choose to love Him (Matt. 23:37). All who go to hell do so because of their free choice. They may not want to go to hell (who would?), but they do will it. They make the decision to reject God, even though they don't desire punishment. People don't go to hell because God sends them; they choose it and God respects their freedom. "There are two kinds of people in the end: those who *say* to God, 'Thy will be done,' and those to whom God *says*, in the end, '*Thy* will be done.' All that are in hell, chose it."[3]

Now if that is how eternal destiny is decided, then it is not one person in hell that is evil; it is one more than is really necessary

Men Choose Hell

John 3:18—"He who believes in Him is not judged; he who does not believe has been judged already, because he has not believed."

John 3:36—"He who believes in the Son has eternal life; but he who does not obey the Son shall not see life, but the wrath of God abides on him."

John 5:39-40—"You search the Scriptures, because you think that in them you have eternal life; and it is these that bear witness of Me; and you are unwilling to come to Me, that you may have life."

John 8:24—"Unless you believe that I am He, you shall die in your sins."

John 12:48—"He who rejects Me, and does not receive My sayings, has one who judges him; the word I spoke is what will judge him at the last day."

Luke 10:16—"The one who listens to you [disciples] listens to Me, and the one who rejects you rejects Me; and he who rejects Me rejects the One who sent Me."

(i.e., one who did choose God but was sent to hell anyway). Granted, a world in which some men go to hell is not the best of all conceivable worlds, but it may be the best of all achievable worlds if free will is to be maintained. Likewise, the world might be made better by one less crime, but it must be left to the would-be criminal to make that choice. Whether we are talking about daily sins along the way, or the biggest sin of all (rejecting God), the answer for the question is the same.

COULDN'T GOD MAKE A WORLD WITHOUT EVIL?

The last objection that we need to deal with is that God could have done a better job designing the world in the first place. It is possible that He could have created a world that did not have evil. Here is the argument:

1. God knows everything.
2. So God knew evil would occur when He created the world.
3. God had other nonevil possibilities. God could have:
   a. not created anything,

     b. created a world without free creatures,

     c. created free creatures that would not sin,

     d. created free creatures who would sin but would all be saved in the end.

   4. Hence, God could have created a world that did not include either evil or hell.

That seems like a pretty strong argument, since God did have all those options. The question is, "Are those options really better than the world we have?" Let's examine them one at a time.

GOD COULD HAVE NOT CREATED ANYTHING

This argument wrongly implies that nothing is better than something. It suggests that it would have been better for nothing ever to have existed than for some evil to exist. But that overlooks the fact that the things created were good and it was good for them to merely exist. That good could not have been if God had not created. Besides this, the objection really makes no sense. It says, in effect, "It would have been *morally* better for God to have made a *nonmoral* world." But what has no morality attached to it cannot

Possible Worlds

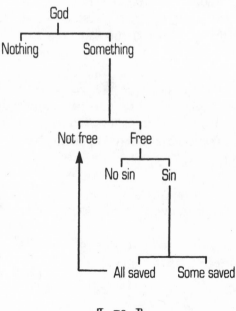

be either better or worse. It has no moral status; it doesn't even have any reality status. This isn't even like comparing apples and oranges because they both exist. Here the comparison is nothing with something.

GOD COULD HAVE CREATED A WORLD WITHOUT FREE CREATURES

It is possible that God could have inhabited the earth with all animals or robots who would only do His will. But this option runs into the same problem as the first: it is a nonmoral option. That is, a nonmoral world cannot be a morally good world. Again, we can't compare what is nongood (i.e., morally neutral) to what is bad. There is an insurmountable difference between what has *no* moral value and what has *some* moral value, however much it is. Also, even if there were no moral corruption in such a world, there could still be physical corruption. Animals would still degenerate physically and decay. So just because there are no free creatures does not mean that there could be no physical evil. Hence, it would just be trading one form of evil for another.

GOD COULD HAVE CREATED FREE CREATURES THAT WOULD NOT SIN

It is logically possible to have free will and not sin. Adam did it before the Fall. Jesus did it throughout His whole life (Heb. 4:15). The Bible says that there will someday be a world in heaven where everyone has free will but there won't be any sin (Rev. 21:8, 27). There is no problem with the idea of such a world, but not everything that is logically possible becomes actually real. It is logically possible that the United States could have lost the Revolutionary War, but that is not what actually happened. In the same way, it is conceivable that free creatures would never sin, but getting it to happen is another matter. How could God have guaranteed that they would never sin? One way would be to tamper with their freedom. He could have set up some mechanism so that just when they were about to choose something evil, a distraction would come along to change their decision. Or maybe He could have programmed creatures to only do good things. But are such creatures really free? It's hard to call a choice free if it was

There is an old story about an Irish priest who had just delivered a strong message denouncing sin and was greeting his congregation at the close of the service. Among those congratulating him for his boldness was an old widow who cheerfully clasped his hand and said, "Father, I was so glad to hear your message today and I'll have you to know that I've been living a holy life for some time now. Why, I haven't sinned in the last thirty years." The priest, only slightly taken back by this boast, replied, "Well keep it up, Darlin'; another three years and you'll beat the record!" Sin may be inevitable in attitudes even when it is not evident to us.

programmed so that there was no alternative. And if our actions are merely diverted from doing evil, aren't there already evil motives in the decision that we were about to make? So a world where no one sins may be conceivable, but it is not actually achievable.

Beyond all of this, a world of freedom without evil would actually be morally inferior to the present world. In this world, men are challenged to do good and noble things and to overcome evil tendencies. That could not happen in a world without evil. The highest virtues and the greatest pleasures are impossible to achieve if there is not opposition as a precondition. Courage can only occur where there is a real fear of danger. Self-sacrifice is only noble where there is need and an opposing selfishness to overcome. As the adage says, "No pain, no gain." It is better to have the opportunity to reach the highest good rather than be confined to achieving lesser goods with no opposition.

GOD COULD HAVE CREATED FREE CREATURES WHO WOULD SIN, BUT WOULD ALL BE SAVED IN THE END

This option makes the same error as the one before it in assuming that God can manipulate human freedom to choose good. Some people say that God will never stop pursuing a person until he makes the right choice. But this view does not take seriously the biblical teaching that hell is real for some. Such a view suggests that God will save individuals no matter what He has to do. But we must remember that He cannot force them to love Him.

Forced love is rape; and God is not a divine rapist. He will not do anything to coerce their decision. God will not save men at any cost. He respects their freedom and concurs with their choice. He is not a puppet master, but a lover wooing men to Himself.

THEN WHY DID GOD CHOOSE THIS WORLD?

Is this the best world God could have made? This may not be the best of all possible worlds, but it is the **best way** to the best world. If God is to both preserve freedom and defeat evil, then this is the best way to do it. Freedom is preserved in that each person makes his own free choice to determine his destiny. Evil is overcome in that, once those who reject God are separated from the others, the decisions of all are made permanent. Those who choose God will be confirmed in it, and sin will cease. Those who reject God are in eternal quarantine and cannot upset the perfect world that has come about. The ultimate goal of a perfect world with free creatures will have been achieved, but the way to get there requires that those who abuse their freedom be cast out. God has assured us that as many as possible will be saved—all who will believe (John 6:37). And God has provided for the salvation of all in Christ (1 John 2:2). He waits patiently, desiring all men to be saved (2 Peter 3:9) but, as Jesus said mourning over Jerusalem,

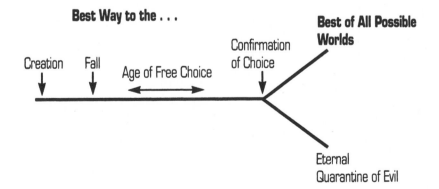

"How often I wanted to gather your children together, the way a hen gathers her chicks under her wings, and you were unwilling" (Matt. 23:37). As atheist Jean-Paul Sartre noted in his play *No Exit*, the gates of hell are locked from the inside by man's free choice.

NOTES

1. C.S. Lewis, *A Grief Observed* (New York: Bantam Books, Inc., 1976), pp. 33–35.

2. ———, *The Problem of Pain* (New York: Macmillan, 1962), p. 93.

3. ———, *The Great Divorce* (New York: Macmillan, 1946), p. 69.

5

QUESTIONS ABOUT MIRACLES

The Bible is laced with miracles. From the Creation to the Second Coming, from Moses at the burning bush to Daniel in the lions' den, from the Virgin Birth to the Resurrection, miraculous happenings seem to fill the pages of Scripture. To the believer, these are a wonderful confirmation of the power and message of God, but to the unbeliever, miracles are a stumbling block—a proof that religion is just a bunch of fairy tales after all. In the world that he lives in, there is no divine intervention, no interruptions to the normal order; there is only natural law. Fire consumes when it burns; lions eat whatever is available; pregnancy only happens when male sperm unite with female ova, and the dead stay dead. As far as they are concerned, the miracles of the Bible could no more be true than Mother Goose.

The purpose of this chapter is not to give a complete explanation of how each miracle occurred. Neither will we attempt to convince anyone that miracles should be considered part of the normal operations of the universe. Our objective is to convince people that the naturalistic attitude toward miracles which has been fostered for over 200 years goes against simple common sense. Rather, this naturalistic attitude is based on faulty logic and unsound thinking that has decided what it is going to find long before it finds anything. The chapter may be thought of as addressing three pairs of questions. The first two questions deal with the believability of miracles (possibility and credibility). The second pair show that miracles do not violate modern methods of study (scientific and historical). The third set answers the commonly asserted religious grounds for explaining miracles (namely, myth and pantheistic claims). The final section begins to establish grounds for accepting biblical miracles as actual events.

One naturalistic thinker said, "The first step in this, as in all other discussions, is to come to a clear understanding as to the meaning of the term employed. Argumentation about whether miracles are possible and, if possible, credible, is mere beating the air until the arguers have agreed what they mean by the word 'miracle.' "[1] A miracle is divine intervention into, or interruption of, the regular course of the world that produces a purposeful but unusual event that would not have occurred otherwise. By this definition, then, natural laws are understood to be the normal, regular way the world operates. But a miracle occurs as an unusual, irregular, and specific act of a God who is beyond the universe. This does not mean that miracles are violations of natural law or even opposed to them. As the famous physicist Sir George Stokes has said, "It may be that the event which we call a miracle was brought on not by a suspension of the laws in ordinary operation, but by the super addition of something not ordinarily in operation."[2] In other words, miracles don't violate the regular laws of cause and effect, they simply have a cause that transcends nature.

ARE MIRACLES POSSIBLE?

The most basic question to ask about miracles is, "Are miracles possible?" If they are not possible, we can wrap up our discussion early and go home. If they are possible, then we need to address the argument that gave us the idea that they are absurd. We find the root of this argument in the writings of Benedict de Spinoza. He developed the following argument against miracles.

1. Miracles are violations of natural laws.
2. Natural laws are immutable.
3. It is impossible for immutable laws to be violated.
4. Therefore, miracles are not possible.

He was bold in his assertion that "nothing then, comes to pass in nature in contravention to her universal laws, nay, nothing does not agree with them and follow from them, for . . . she keeps a fixed and immutable order."[3]

Certainly we can't argue with the third step in that argument, for what is immutable can't be set aside. But are natural laws immutable? And does he have a correct definition of a miracle? It seems that Spinoza has stacked the deck. He built into his premises his own view that nothing exists beyond the universe (and that God is the universe). So once he has defined natural law as "fixed and immutable," it is impossible for miracles to occur. He had gotten the idea that natural laws were fixed from the Newtonian physics that were the latest rage in his day. But today scientists understand that natural laws don't tell us what *must* happen, but only describe what usually *does* happen. They are statistical probabilities, not unchangeable facts. So we can't rule out the possibility of miracles by definition.

The definition he uses also carries his antisupernatural bias. It assumes that there is nothing *beyond* nature that could act *in* nature. This follows from Spinoza's pantheism. As long as God is limited to staying inside nature's boundaries, or is nonexistent, then a miracle can only be seen as a violation of order. The bottom line of the matter is that if God exists, then miracles are possible. If there is anything beyond the universe which might cause something to happen in the universe, then there is a chance that it will do so. Now most scientists will want some evidence to show them that God exists, and that can be found in chapter 2.

Benedict de Spinoza (1632–1677) was one of the modern rationalist philosophers. Rationalism believed that all truth could be deduced from self-evident principles without examining factual evidence. Spinoza's background was Jewish, but he was expelled from the synagogue at age twenty-four for his unusual views. He was convinced that there could only be one infinite substance and nothing else, so he concluded that God is the universe (pantheism). Natural laws, then, were the laws of God. Given this starting point, miracles are automatically eliminated. If the supernatural is identical to nature, then there is nothing beyond nature to intervene. Anything beyond nature must be greater than God, and that is absurd.

But once we have established that a theistic God exists, miracles cannot be ruled out.

ARE MIRACLES CREDIBLE?

Some people don't deny the possibility of miracles; they just can't see any justification in believing in them. To these, the miraculous is not absurd; it is just incredible. The great English skeptic David Hume advanced this very famous argument against believing in miracles.

1. A miracle is a violation of the laws of nature.
2. Firm and unalterable experience has established these laws.
3. A wise man proportions his belief to the evidence.
4. Therefore, a uniform experience amounts to a proof; there is here a direct and full proof, from the nature of the fact, against the existence of any miracle.[4]

Some see this argument as saying that miracles can't occur, but that would easily be refuted by showing that he is begging the question when he defines miracles as impossible. It seems that his real point is that no one should believe in miracles because all of our experience suggests that they don't happen. That is certainly

---

David Hume (1711–1776) was a Scottish philosopher and historian born and raised in Edinburgh. Shortly after earning a law degree, he decided not to practice law and took up a study of philosophy. Unlike Spinoza, Hume was an empiricist who held that knowledge comes only by examining and ordering the factual and historical evidence. Natural law became the backbone of order in his philosophical system, so he was antagonistic to any thought that allowed for God and miracles. While Spinoza was dogmatic about his views, Hume was skeptical about all beliefs, doubting that any certainty was possible. Though he did not deny causality, he claimed that we can never be certain what caused any given effect. The best we can say is that so-and-so type of effect is usually caused by such-and-such type of cause.

the point that we all learned in school, even if we didn't study Hume.

Instead of begging the question in his definition, Hume does so in his evidence. He presumes to know that all experience is uniformly against miracles before he looks at the evidence. How can he know that all possible past and future experience will support his naturalism? The only way to be sure is to know in advance that miracles do not occur. On the other hand, he might be saying that the uniform experience of some, or even most, people is against miracles. But what about the other people—the ones who have experienced miracles? Then he is selecting only the evidence that he likes and leaving out the rest. Either way, he has made a fundamental error in logic.

As to Hume's first maxim, that "a wise man always proportions his belief to the evidence," we would certainly agree. However, for Hume, "greater evidence" means "that which is repeated more often." So any rare event can never have as much evidence as common events. Hume has stacked the deck here too. That means that no miracle can ever have enough evidence for a reasonable person to believe it. Hume doesn't really *weigh* the evidence at all; he just *adds* up the evidence against miracles. Since death happens to almost everyone and there are only a few stories about resurrections from the dead, he simply adds all the deaths and decides that those stories about resurrection must be false. Even if a few people

---

Richard Whately made fun of Hume's ideas in a pamphlet called *Historical Doubts Concerning the Existence of Napoleon Bonaparte*. He traced all of the amazing exploits of Napoleon's career and showed that they are so fantastic and so unprecedented that no intelligent person should believe that such a man ever existed. We should put him in the same category as Paul Bunyan and Pecos Bill. His point is to show that if the skeptic does not deny the existence of Napoleon, he "must at least acknowledge that they do not apply to that question the same plan of reasoning which they have made use of in others." [Richard Whately, *Historical Doubts Concerning the Existence of Napoleon Bonaparte* in *Famous Pamphlets*, 2nd ed., ed. by Henry Morley (London: George Routledge and Sons, 1880), p. 290.]

really were raised from the dead, no one should believe it because the number of deaths overshadow them. That is like saying that you shouldn't believe it if you won the lottery because of all the thousands of people who lost. It equates evidence with probability and says that you should never believe that long shots win. The odds of being dealt a perfect bridge hand (which has happened) are 1,635,013,559,600 to 1. But according to Hume, if you get it, you better fold your hand and ask for a redeal because you should never believe that such an outrageous thing could happen.

It is odd that the scientist objects to miracles on such grounds as these, for his own study is not conducted in this way. If a scientist knew in advance how an experiment would turn out on the basis of known natural laws, he would not go to the trouble of doing the experiment. Hume even admitted that nothing can be known concerning the future just by looking at past experience. Likewise, the scientist is constantly trying to expand and refine our understanding of natural law by revising those laws as new evidence is found. Hume's principles for miracles would make that kind of scientific progress impossible because the researcher would never believe his data. It could never overcome past uniform experience.

ARE MIRACLES SCIENTIFIC?

Many people refuse to believe in miracles because they feel that if God were allowed to intervene in nature, then there could be no scientific method. This method is built on the principles of uniformity and regularity, and any irregular causes would make science impossible. As Dr. Allan Bloom has written, "Scientists are to a man against creationism, recognizing rightly that, if there is anything to it, their science is wrong and useless. . . . Either nature has a lawful order or it does not; either there can be miracles or there cannot. Scientists do not prove there are no miracles, they assume it; without this assumption there is no science."[5]

There are several arguments used to show that miracles are contrary to the scientific method, but we will look at the one used by Patrick Nowell-Smith. He objects to the supernaturalist using miracles as an explanation for things, for science might find a natural explanation in the future. His objection can be summa-

Patrick Nowell-Smith is a graduate of Harvard and Oxford and accepted a chair as professor of philosophy at York University in Toronto in 1969. In his essay "Miracles," he objects to the supernaturalist using God as an explanation for any unusual event. "We may believe him [the supernaturalist] when he says that no scientific method or hypothesis known to him will explain it." But "to say that it is inexplicable as a result of natural agents is already beyond his competence as a scientist, and to say that it must be ascribed to supernatural agents is to say something that no one could possibly have the right to affirm on the basis of the evidence alone." [Patrick Nowell-Smith, "Miracles" in *New Essays in Philosophical Theology*, ed. by Antony Flew and Alasdair MacIntyre (New York: Macmillan, 1955), pp. 245–46.]

rized as follows:

1. Only what has predictive capabilities can qualify as an explanation for an event (such as natural laws).
2. A miracle cannot be predicted.
3. Therefore, a miracle does not qualify as an explanation of any event.

In short then, only scientific explanations for things will do, and all other explanations must conform to science or be silent.

While Nowell-Smith claims that the scientist should keep an open mind and not reject evidence that ruins his preconceived theories, it is clear that he has closed his mind to the possibility of any supernatural explanations. He arbitrarily insists that all explanations must be natural ones or they do not really count. He makes the grand assumption that all events will ultimately have a natural explanation, but doesn't offer any proof for that assumption. The only way that he can know this is to know beforehand that miracles cannot occur. It is a leap of naturalistic faith!

Scientists claim that explanations must have some predictive value, but there are many events in the natural world that cannot be predicted. No one can predict if or when an automobile accident might happen, or when a house might be robbed, but no one claims that it is a miracle when it happens. Even the naturalist admits that he cannot always predict events in practice, only in principle. No weatherman in his right mind would claim otherwise. The supernaturalist makes the same claim: *a miracle occurs whenever God deems it necessary*. If we had all the evidence (if we knew all that God knows), we could predict when God was going to intervene as well as the scientist can predict natural events.

But miracles do have some explanatory value in the scientific method. Some events can easily be explained by natural forces. It is easy to see that the Grand Canyon was caused by erosion and wind as the river cut through the rock. Natural forces that we know well can explain how that was caused. But what about Mount Rushmore? Is there any natural force that can explain how the faces of our first, third, sixteenth, and twenty-sixth Presidents emerged out of the rock suddenly between 1927 and 1941? Obviously, it needed an intelligent cause. In the same way, certain events are clearly purposeful and have meaning when understood in their context, like giving someone a hug. These are also caused by intelligent causes. Miracles belong to this class of events. God doesn't intervene just to play around and confuse us; He has a purpose and communicates something with each miracle. Moses' miracles confirmed that God had sent him and mocked the Egyptian gods whose domain the miracles overcame (Ex. 7:14–12:36). Elijah didn't call down fire for nothing (1 Kings 18:16-40). The whole day had been spent waiting for Baal to do something, but Elijah's God acted immediately, proving His reality and power. These kinds of events call for an intelligent cause, and this is a principle that is both regular and uniform. So when an event occurs which is purposeful, like the Red Sea parting so that the Israelites can escape from Pharaoh, the scientific method tells us that we should not look for a natural cause, but for an intelligent cause. Miracles do not destroy science. But trying to explain miracles by means of natural causes is definitely unscientific! Science actually points to an intelligent cause for these events.

ARE MIRACLES HISTORICAL?

Science is not the only discipline that rejects miracles. The study of history also claims that miracles cannot be included in its method. If they were to occur, the historian could never know them or believe them. Antony Flew develops the argument in this way:

All critical history depends on the validity of two principles:
1. The remains of the past can be used as evidence for reconstructing history only if we presume the same basic regularities of nature held then as now.
2. The critical historian must use his present knowledge of the possible and probable as criteria for knowing the past.
But belief in miracles is contrary to both of these principles. Therefore, belief in miracles is contrary to critical history.

The historian must reject all miracles. Anyone who believes in miracles is naive and uncritical in his thinking. This argument does not say that miracles are not possible; they are just *unknowable* by any objective study of history.

Like David Hume, whose thought he attempts to refine, Antony Flew makes the error of adding evidence rather than weighing it. He will not accept any evidence for events in *particular,* but only for events in general. So whatever is common and repeated should

---

Antony Flew (1923–   ) has been a lecturer in philosophy at three major universities in England and has authored and edited numerous books on philosophical theology, making him an important figure in today's world on questions about God. He is especially noted for his article in the *Encyclopedia of Philosophy* on "Miracles." The argument he gives there is more closely aligned with Hume's argument. It goes like this:
1. Every miracle is a violation of natural law.
2. The evidence against any violation of natural law is the strongest possible evidence.
3. Therefore, the evidence against miracles is the strongest possible evidence.
Not only does this fall subject to the same criticisms as Hume's argument, but it violates Flew's own principle of falsifiability. Under no circumstances would Flew ever admit that a miracle occurred. But in practice if his view could not be false in any conceivable circumstance, then how can he claim that it is true about the way the world really is?

be believed, but what is uncommon and unique should be rejected. So we should believe that a peasant woman washed her clothes
in the river (though we have no direct evidence of it) but reject
the idea that Alexander the Great conquered Egypt (for which we
have massive evidence).

Flew's two principles of history are really just a restatement of
Hume's maxims that "uniform experience amounts to a proof"
and "the wise man proportions his belief to the evidence." But
assuming absolute uniformity sets his bias against any supernatural
occurrence. It hinders the search for truth rather than helping it
because it *legislates* the meaning that can be found instead of *looking* for it. And wise men do not proportion their belief to mere
probabilities, but to the *facts*. This recycling of Hume's argument
does nothing to advance historical study and suffers from the same
naturalistic bias that its predecessor had.

The significance of refuting this objection is that there is no
reason that miraculous events cannot be examined and verified by
the historical method. The miracles recorded in the Scripture are
as open to investigation as any event recorded in ancient history.

ARE MIRACLES MYTHOLOGICAL?

One of the most influential theologians of this century, Rudolf
Bultmann, has said:

> Man's knowledge and mastery of the world have advanced to
> such extent through science and technology that it is *no longer
> possible* for anyone seriously to hold the New Testament view of
> the world—in fact, there is hardly anyone who does. . . . The
> *only* honest way of reciting the creeds is to strip the mythologi-
> cal framework away from the truth they enshrine.[6]

For Bultmann, modern science has eliminated miracles. The
only way to reconcile this with faith is to recognize all supernatural elements as myths that have grown up around the kernel
of truth that we must live by. To understand the Bible and Jesus'
real message, we must weed out the myths to find the truth. If we
can get behind the minds of the early Christians, we might even

be able to understand what circumstances and needs were present that caused such a myth to arise. That would lead us to a truth on another level which we can accept by faith. His argument might be stated like this:

1. Myths are by nature more than objective truths; they are transcendent truths of faith.
2. But what is not objective cannot be a part of a verifiable space-time world.
3. Therefore, miracles (myths) are not part of the objective space-time world.

This not only eliminates the need to believe in miracles, but makes it impossible to evaluate them in any sense. But does this argument hold up? Are miracles only myths?

First, it does not follow that because an event is *more than* objective and factual that it must be *less than* historical. Certainly miracles point to something *beyond* the world, but that does not mean that they don't happen *in* the world. If they are more than objective and factual, then they must be *at least* objective space-time events.

Also, Bultmann has clearly concluded beforehand that miracles cannot occur. He would make the same conclusion no matter what the evidence says. He calls miracles "incredible," "irrational," "no longer possible," "meaningless," "utterly inconceivable," and "intolerable." These are not the words of a man open to looking at

---

Rudolf Bultmann (1884–1976) pioneered the method of interpreting the Bible by "demythologizing" it. Following the thought of phenomenologist Martin Heidegger, Bultmann sought to make the Bible existentially relevant to modern men by separating the core truths of Christianity from the first-century worldview, which confuses us and is not part of our lives. The means of doing this is to strip away the myth (supernatural elements) from the existential reality of the story. This higher and spiritual truth can be translated to any worldview and understood by men of any time. Unfortunately, it also destroys the historicity of the Christian faith and the authority of the Bible.

the evidence. This is the language of someone who does not want to be "confused" by the facts.

But if miracles are not objective and historical, then they are neither verifiable nor falsifiable. You can't prove they happened, *but no one can disprove them either.* This appeals to some Christians because it removes the need for defending their beliefs and calls people to "simply believe" without evidence. However, it also makes us fall victim to a valid criticism from Antony Flew.

> Now often it seems to people who are not religious as if there was no conceivable event or series of events the occurrence of which would be admitted by sophisticated religious people to be a sufficient reason for conceding "There wasn't a God after all." . . . What would have to occur or to have occurred to constitute for you a disproof of the love of, or of the existence of, God?[7]

In plain language, if a belief could never under any circumstance be false, then how can you say that it is really true? It has left the realm of true and false and simply exists as opinion. For Bultmann, someone could deliver the corpse of Jesus Christ to his office in a wheelbarrow and it would not falsify his faith in the Resurrection. The Apostle Paul, on the other hand, said that "if Christ has not been raised, your faith is worthless; you are still in your sins" (1 Cor. 15:17). This religious attempt to preserve Christianity from attack by modern science has left us with an empty faith that prevents us from ever calling our beliefs true.

ARE MIRACLES DEFINABLE?

There are a lot of religions that claim to be "proven" by miraculous deeds. Moses' rod became a serpent in Judaism; Jesus walked on water in Christianity; Islam's Mohammed moved a mountain; and Hindu gurus claim to levitate themselves and others. This is no less true today when some pantheistic groups claim that they are performing miracles daily. New Age prophet Benjamin Creme has said this of what he calls "the Christ," meaning a spirit of power and divination which "overshadowed" Jesus and is now available to the followers of "the Christ":

> It is this which has enabled them to perform what at that time were called miracles, which today are called spiritual or esoteric healings. Daily, all over the world, there are miracles of healing being performed. . . . these miracles are now being performed by men and women in the world all the time.[8]

And to make matters more complicated, there are many Christians making very similar claims today and, while some are valid, some have been exposed as frauds. Even the loose way we use the word shows our confusion. Some say it's a miracle when a baby is born and some say it's a miracle when they pass an examination.

How can you tell what is truly miraculous and what is not? Is it possible to define a miracle in such a way that false claims and other kinds of unusual events are eliminated from the definition?

The main threat to defining miracles today comes from the pantheistic New Age movement. Pantheists say that there is no God beyond the universe. They agree that all events in the universe must have natural causes. As Jesus supposedly said in the Aquarian Gospel, a psychically obtained account of Jesus' alleged psychic training, "All things result from natural law."[9] Even Christian Science says that a miracle is "that which is divinely natural, but must be learned humanly; a phenomenon of Science."[10] So instead of saying that there are no miracles, pantheists redefine miracles as a manipulation of natural law, much like Luke Skywalker had to learn to use the Force (natural law) to do his incredible deeds. Pantheists have even tried to incorporate advanced physics into their framework to explain the supernormal. Fritjof Capra's book, *The Tao of Physics*, is an updated version of the pantheistic doctrine that all matter is at heart mystical.

> The basic oneness of the universe is not only the central characteristic of the mystical experience, but is also one of the most important revelations of modern physics. It becomes apparent at the atomic level and manifests itself more and more as one penetrates deeper into matter, down into the realm of subatomic particles.[11]

This then, not an all-powerful God beyond the universe, is the source of pantheistic miracles. They are not really supernatural; they are only *supernormal*.

Now Christians don't deny that such supernormal events take place, but we do deny that they fit the definition of a miracle. That definition has three basic elements that are reflected in the three words associated with miracles in the Bible: power, sign, and wonder. The *power* of miracles comes from a God who is beyond the universe. The nature of miracles is that they are *wonders*, which inspire awe in those who see them because they are astonishing. The word *sign* tells us the purpose of miracles: they confirm God's message and His messenger. The theological dimension of this definition is that miracles imply that there is a God beyond the universe who intervenes in it. Morally, because God is good, miracles only produce and/or promote good. In their doctrinal dimension, miracles tell us which are true prophets and which are false.

"Sign," "Wonder," and "Power"

These are the three words used in both the Old and New Testaments to describe miracles.

In the Old Testament:

Sign—Confirm Moses' authority (Ex. 3:12; 4:3-8); Confirm God's message (Jud. 6:17; Isa. 38:7; Jer. 44:29)

Wonder—Used with sign (Ex. 7:3; Deut. 26:8); Signs called wonders (Ex. 4:21)

Power—To create (Jer. 10:12); To defeat enemies (Ex. 15:6-7; Num. 14:17); To rule (1 Chron. 29:12); Used with signs and wonders (Ex. 9:16)

In the New Testament:

Sign—Jesus' miracles (John 2:11; 6:2; 9:16; 11:47); Apostles' miracles (Acts 2:43; 4:16, 30; 8:13; 14:3); Resurrection (Matt. 12:39-40)

Wonder—Used sixteen times and always with the word "sign" (Matt. 24:24; John 4:48; Acts 6:8; 14:3)

Power—Of Satan (Luke 10:19; Rom. 8:38); Of miracles (Matt. 11:20; 13:58; Luke 1:35; 1 Cor. 12:10); Of the Gospel (Rom. 1:16)

And teleologically, miracles are never performed for entertainment, but have the distinct purpose of glorifying God and directing men to Him.

Pantheistic miracles, however, don't meet this definition because their power is not from God. In fact, New Age writer David Spangler has identified the source of miracles for pantheists when he wrote, "Christ is the same force as Lucifer but moving in seemingly the opposite direction. Lucifer moves in to create the light within . . . Christ moves out to release that light."[12] So the power for supernormal events in pantheism comes from Lucifer, or Satan, even though it is called Christ when it goes out from the individual.

From a biblical perspective, Lucifer, also called the devil and Satan, is not the same as God or even equal to God. In the beginning, God created everything good: the earth (Gen. 1:1), man (vv. 27-28), and angels (Col. 1:15-16). One of the angels was named Lucifer (Isa. 14:12), and he was very beautiful. But he was "lifted up with pride" (1 Tim. 3:6, KJV) and rebelled against God, saying, "I will make myself like the Most High" (Isa. 14:14). In doing so, he also led many other angels to follow him, so that one third of all the angels left their home with God (Rev. 12:4). These beings are now known as Satan and his angels (v. 7; Matt. 25:41). They do have unusual powers and are said to be currently "working [energizing] in the sons of disobedience" (Eph. 2:2). Satan is able to disguise "himself as an angel of light" (2 Cor. 11:14) and appear to be on God's side, but it is only a disguise. Satan is always working against God.

How can we tell whether it is Satan or God at work? The Bible gives us some tests so that we can know who is a true prophet and who is false. The key is to distinguish miracles from magic. Miracles are God-ordained supernatural interventions; human magic is man's manipulation by normal or supernormal forces. The chart on page 90 summarizes these differences.

One of the key distinctions between miracles and magic is the use of occult means to perform its acts. These are practices which claim to conjure powers from the spirit realm. In many cases they do just that; but it is demonic power, not divine. Some of the practices directly linked to demonic power in the Bible are:

1. Witchcraft (Deut. 18:10)
2. Fortune-telling (Deut. 18:10)
3. Communicating with spirits (Deut. 18:11)
4. Mediums (Deut. 18:11)
5. Divination (Deut. 18:10)
6. Astrology (Deut. 4:19; Isa. 47:13-15)
7. Heresy (false teaching) (1 Tim. 4:1; 1 John 4:1-2)
8. Immorality (Eph. 2:2-3)
9. Self-deification (Gen. 3:5; Isa. 14:13)
10. Lying (John 8:44)
11. Idolatry (1 Cor. 10:19-20)
12. Legalism and self-denial (Col. 2:16-23; 1 Tim. 4:1-3)

Miracles	Magic
Under God's control	Under man's control
Not available on command	Available on command
Supernatural power	A natural (mystical) power
Associated with good	Associated with evil
Associated only with truth	Associated also with error
Can overpower evil	Cannot overpower good
Affirm Jesus is God in the flesh	Denies Jesus is God in the flesh
Prophecies always true	Prophecies sometimes false
Never associated with occult practices	Often associated with occult practices

Many of those who practice and teach pantheistic "miracles" not only admit that they use these occult practices, but recommend them for others also. These characteristics show that such claims to miraculous powers are demonic.

What if we apply these tests to one of the many self-proclaimed prophets of our time, Jeane Dixon? First, let's check her track record. Even her biographer, Ruth Montgomery, admits that Dixon has made false prophecies. "She predicted that Red China would plunge the world into war over Quemoy and Matsu in

October of 1958; she thought that labor leader Walter Reuther would actively seek the presidency in 1964."[13] On October 19, 1968 she assured us that Jacqueline Kennedy was not considering marriage; the next day, Mrs. Kennedy wed Aristotle Onassis. She also said that World War III would begin in 1954, the Vietnam War would end in 1966, and Castro would be banished from Cuba in 1970. A study of prophecies made by psychics in 1975 and observed until 1981, including Mrs. Dixon's projections, showed that of the seventy-two predictions, only six were fulfilled in any way. Two of these were vague and two others were hardly surprising—the U.S. and Russia would remain leading powers and there would be no world wars. With only a 6 percent accuracy rate, how serious can we take these claims?

Her most noted prophecy was to predict the death of her friend John F. Kennedy. We must face the fact that some psychic prophecies come true. Sometimes this is because they are so general that they can be interpreted to fit many situations. Others simply offer common sense, like a horoscope that says, "Careful investments will secure your financial future." But some are specific and accurate, and these can be accounted for in three ways: the prophet is of God (that means 100 percent accuracy though), has demonic

---

Dixon Prophesies Kennedy Assassination
The May 13, 1956 edition of *Parade* magazine published this prediction from Jeane Dixon:

"As to the 1960 election, Mrs. Dixon thinks it will be dominated by labor and won by a Democrat. But he will be assassinated or die in office, though not necessarily in his first term."

Facts
1. The election was not dominated by labor.
2. In January 1960, she said, "The symbol of the Presidency is directly over the head of Vice President Nixon." There was a 100 percent chance that the '56 or '60 prediction would be right.
3. Three of the ten Presidents who had served in this century had died in office and two others were critically ill at the end of their terms. The odds against her were not too bad.

influence, or they just made a lucky guess. Just exactly what is the source of Jeane Dixon's power?

An accuracy rate around 6 percent could easily be explained by chance and general knowledge of circumstances. But there may be more to it. Montgomery also tells us that Dixon uses a crystal ball, astrology, and telepathy, and that her gift of prophecy was given to her by a gypsy fortune-teller when she was a little girl.[14] Even her prophecy of Kennedy's death is vague, wrong in some aspects (she said that the 1960 election would be dominated by labor, which it was not), and contradicted by her other prophecies—she also said Nixon was supposed to win!

But the Bible allows no room for such things. All forms of divination are prohibited. More important, no error is allowed for a prophet of God. Deuteronomy 18:22 says that he must be 100 percent accurate.

> When a prophet speaks in the name of the Lord, if the thing does not come about or come true, that is the thing which the Lord has not spoken. The prophet has spoken it presumptuously; you shall not be afraid of him.

That last phrase, being interpreted, means that it is all right to stone him. If God has spoken, it will come about. There is no need for a second chance.

But the demonic is not the only source of power found in such miracles. Some claims to supernormal powers have been shown to be nothing more than illusions and sleight-of-hand tricks. Danny Korem, a professional magician who has written a book to expose such frauds, says, "Given the proper circumstances, anyone can be made to believe he has witnessed something which never took place."[15]

One example of this is the "psychic" Uri Geller, who claims to have the power to bend metal objects without touching them, as well as telepathy and clairvoyance. He even received some support from a Stanford Research Institute report. But the editors of the magazine also noted that the men who had refereed the tests felt that "insufficient account had been taken of the established methodology of experimental psychology. . . . Two referees also felt

Psychic Confessions

In his book *Powers: Testing the Psychic and Supernatural,* Danny Korem exposes a leading psychic and leads him to make a filmed confession that he was doing all of his tricks by illusion rather than supernormal powers. James Hydrick had developed quite a reputation and following by such powers as psychically moving a piece of paper inside an inverted aquarium and turning pages of a book without touching it. After Korem found a slight gap on one end of the aquarium and developed special breath control, he was able to duplicate the trick and Hydrick confessed. "See, it takes so many years of practice in getting this down pat . . . to where you can't see my mouth move when I blow . . . and in my practice—you know, I spent a year and six months in solitary confinement. All the time I thought and thought, and finally said to myself, 'That's it. That's what I'm going to do.' " He told of making prison guards think someone was behind them and converting inmates to Christ by saying, "Father, in the name of Jesus Christ make these pages move." Then he would turn several pages with an imperceptible burst of air.

that the authors had not taken into account the lessons learned in the past by parapsychologists researching this tricky and complicated area."[16] Their skepticism proved to be well-founded, as *New Science* magazine recorded "at least five people claim to have seen Geller actually cheat." One woman observing him in a television studio said that "she actually saw Geller bend—by hand, not by psychic powers—the large spoon."[17] Another of Geller's tricks is to take his picture with a camera while the lens cap is on. But this has been duplicated by a photographer using a wide angle lens and with the cover not quite closed. Geller's success also seems to drop dramatically when the controls are tightened. On television shows, he liked to pick an object from one of ten film cans.

On the Merv Griffin show on US TV, Geller did the trick successfully, but some people thought they saw Geller jarring the table so that the cans would shake and he could tell which was heaviest. On the Johnny Carson Tonight show on 1 August, 1973, therefore, special precautions were taken and Geller was not permitted to get near enough to the table to jar it or touch the cans. He failed.[18]

It is hard to avoid the conclusion of one critic who said flatly that "the SRI paper simply does not stand up against the mass of circumstantial evidence that Uri Geller is simply a good magician."[19] Magician Andre Kole enlightens us:

What most people do not realize about Uri Geller—what he has tried to suppress in his publicity—is that he studied and practiced magic as a youth in Israel. But he quickly realized that he attracted a far greater following by claiming paranormal powers than he did as a conjurer. In fact, most of what he does would be rather insignificant coming from a magician.[20]

In contrast to this, we see the superiority of biblical miracles. The magicians of Egypt tried to reproduce Moses' works by means of illusions and had some success at first (Ex. 7:19ff; 8:6ff), but when God brought forth gnats from the dust, the sorcerers failed and exclaimed, "This is the finger of God" (v. 19). In the same way, Elijah silenced all claims of the prophets of Baal when

---

Geller Proves His Powers

Andre Kole relates a story from Persi Diaconis, who once drove Geller to the airport.

"While waiting for his flight, the psychic expressed disappointment that the professor remained a skeptic, and offered to provide conclusive proof of his powers. He then asked Diaconis to reach into his coat pocket, grab his keys, and concentrate on a key that could be bent. The professor says, "I opened my hand and the key I was thinking of was bent. For about five minutes I was as badly fooled as I've ever been in my life."

Diaconis solved the mystery by reviewing the trip to the airport. Geller had insisted on sitting in the back seat, where Diaconis' coat lay. At the airport parking lot, he insisted that he bring the coat "in case it gets too cool." The key ring contained four keys, only one of which could be bent easily. When he further examined his coat, he discovered an envelope turned inside out, and each of his pens' tops bent and twisted. Geller apparently had prepared several "proofs" of his power. [Andre Kole, *Miracles or Magic?* (Eugene: Harvest House, 1987), p. 28.]

he called down fire from heaven when they could not (1 Kings 18). Moses' authority was vindicated when Korah and his followers were swallowed up by the earth (Num. 16). And Aaron was shown to be God's man for the priesthood when his rod budded (Num. 17).

Jesus healed the sick (Matt. 8:14-15), made the blind to see (Mark 8:22-26), reached down and embraced lepers to heal them (1:40-45), and raised people from death (Luke 8:49-56). His pattern continued in the apostles after He was gone as we see Peter healing the beggar at the temple gate (Acts 3:1-11) and raising Dorcas from the dead (9:36-41). Hebrews 2:4 tells us the purpose of these miracles: "God [was] also bearing witness with them, both by signs and wonders and by various miracles and by gifts of the Holy Spirit according to His own will." As far as purposefulness, goodness, and confirmation of God's message, these miracles are in an entirely different class to bending spoons and pointing to film cans. There is no comparison.

Biblical prophecy is also unique in that, while most predictions are vague and often wrong, the Scriptures are remarkably precise and accurate. In them, God foretold not only the coming of the destruction of Jerusalem (Isa. 22:1-25), but the name of the Persian ruler who would return them (44:28; 45:1) 150 years before it all happened. The very place of Jesus' birth is cited in about 700 B.C. (Micah 5:2). His triumphal entry into Jerusalem was predicted by Daniel to the day in 538 B.C. (Dan. 9:24-26). No fortune-teller can boast of anything like this accuracy or consistency.

Finally, Christ predicted His own death (Mark 8:31), the means of death (Matt. 16:24), that He would be betrayed (26:21), and that He would rise from the dead on the third day (12:39-40). There is nothing like this anywhere in the occult prophecies or miracles. The resurrection of Jesus stands alone as the unique and unrepeatable event of history

ARE MIRACLES VALUABLE?

We have shown that miracles are possible, believable, and historical. They don't violate science, are not mere myths, and can be distinguished from even supernormal events. This is all fine in

---

Nostradamus
Also called Michel de Notredame (1503–1566), this physician and astrologer became famous for the prophecies in his book *Centuries,* named for the fact that it contains rhymed quatrains in sets of 100. Some of these prophecies are said to have come true. The following is said to have predicted the rise of Adolf Hitler:
  "Followers of sects, great troubles are in store for the Messenger. A beast upon the theater prepares a scenical play. The inventor of that wicked feat will be famous. By sects the world will be confused and divided."
  While this may truly be a prophecy, it is so vague that it might be fulfilled by many events of history. But a Christian need only look to Nostradamus' source to discredit him. One quatrain tells of him using occult practices to contact demons. He practiced astrology, alchemy, magic, and used the kabbala (an ancient Jewish mystical tradition). The Bible prohibits such practices. [Andre Lamont, *Nostradamus Sees All* (Philadelphia: W. Foulsham Co., 1942), p. 252, 71.]

---

principle, but what good are they? Can we really believe miraculous reports? Besides, where would we be if we believed every story about miracles? Jesus, Mohammed, and Buddha can't all be right! What value can miracles have if we don't know which ones to believe?

David Hume stated a second objection; that the historical evidence is never enough to justify the belief in miracles (even though he thought he had eliminated the possibility of miracles with his first argument). He gave four reasons to reject the evidence for any miracle:

1. There is never a sufficient number of witnesses of good character.
2. Human nature is to exaggerate and find wonder in things.
3. Miracles abound among the ignorant.
4. Miracles have a self-canceling nature.

When we examine Hume's objections, we find some problems. First, though he implies that if a miracle was witnessed by a good number of people, who were upstanding citizens (Objection 1), sober-minded (Objection 2), well educated and in a modern city (Objection 3), then he would believe it. Hume himself admits that the Jansenist miracles, occurring in his time in Paris among the upper-middle class, do meet these criteria, but he says, "And what have we to oppose to such a cloud of witnesses but the *absolute impossibility* or miraculous nature of the events which they relate?"[21] (emphasis added) So in practice, Hume would never accept any evidence as sufficient to support a miracle. His real objection is that miracles are impossible, and we have shown this to be false several times already. It does no good to look at historical evidence if the final judgment has already been made in favor of naturalism.

But Hume's last objection actually supports the case we have been making. He said that all religions, even non-Christian religions, use miracles to support their claims. But if the same kind of evidence supports all religions, they cancel each other and can't count for any of them. So miracles, he concludes, cannot support any religion. However, as we have seen earlier, Christian miracles are not of the same kind as those in other religions. The miracles that support Christianity are unique. This changes the way Hume's argument looks. We can agree with him about miraculous claims in non-Christian religions and state the argument this way:

1. All non-Christian religions are supported by the same kind of "miracles."
2. But such "miracles" have no evidential value because they are self-canceling.
3. Therefore, no non-Christian religion is supported by "miracles."

This opens the way for a second argument:

1. Only Christianity has unique miraculous confirmation of its truth claims.
2. What has unique miraculous confirmation of its claims is true.
3. Therefore, Christianity is true (and all opposing views are false).

So Hume's principals have led us straight to the confirmation of Christianity through its miracles. Where there is valid testimony and superior miracles, miracles have great value. We find that Christianity has better evidence and more witnesses writing closer to the time of the events than any other religion. Besides this, no religion offers the kind of miracles that Christianity can claim. No other religion has the record of specific prophecy or divine deliverance that the Bible gives. And no other religion has any miracle that can be compared to the resurrection of Jesus Christ in its grandeur or its testimony. The specific historical evidence for this event becomes the focus of our next chapter.

NOTES

1. Thomas Huxley, *The Works of T.H. Huxley* (New York: Appleton, 1896), p. 153.

2. As quoted in the *International Standard Bible Encyclopedia* (Grand Rapids: Eerdmans, 1939), p. 2036.

3. Benedict de Spinoza, *Tracatus Theologico-Politicus*, in *The Chief Works of Benedict de Spinoza*, trans. by R.H.M. Elwes (London: George Bell and Sons, 1883), 1:83.

4. David Hume, *An Inquiry Concerning Human Understanding*, ed. by C.W. Hendel (New York: Bobbs-Merrill, 1955), sec. 10, pt. 1, pp. 122, 118, 123.

5. Allan Bloom, *The Closing of the American Mind* (New York: Simon and Schuster, Inc., 1987), p. 182.

6. Rudolf Bultmann, *Kerygma and Myth: A Theological Debate*, ed. by Hans Werner Bartsch, trans. by Reginald H. Fuller (London: Billing and Sons, 1954), p. 4.

7. Antony Flew, "Theology and Falsification" in *The Existence of God*, ed. by John Hick (New York: Macmillan, 1964), p. 227.

8. Benjamin Creme, *The Reappearance of Christ* (Los Angeles: Tara Center, 1980), p. 136.

9. "Levi," Levi H. Dowling, *The Aquarian Gospel of Jesus the*

Christ (Santa Monica: DeVorss & Co., Publishers, 1907 and 1964), p. 227.

10. Mary Baker Eddy, *Science and Health with Key to the Scriptures* (Boston: The Christian Science Publishing Society, 1973), 591:21–22.

11. Fritjof Capra, *The Tao of Physics* (New York: Bantam Books, 1984), p. 117.

12. David Spangler, *Reflections on the Christ* (Findhorn Lecture Series, 1978), p. 40.

13. Ruth Montgomery, *A Gift of Prophecy* (New York: William Morrow & Company, 1965), p. viii.

14. Ibid., p. 15.

15. Danny Korem, *The Fakers* (Grand Rapids: Baker, 1980), p. 19.

16. *Nature,* Oct. 18, 1974, p. 55.

17. *New Science,* Oct. 17, 1974, p. 174.

18. Ibid., p. 174.

19. Ibid., p. 185.

20. Andre Kole and Al Janssen, *Miracles or Magic?* (Eugene, Ore.: Harvest House, 1987), p. 27.

21. Hume, *op. cit.,* p. 133.

6

QUESTIONS ABOUT JESUS CHRIST

Thomas Paine, one of early America's influential thinkers and author of *Common Sense* and *The Age of Reason,* said of Jesus Christ, "There is no history written at the time Jesus Christ is said to have lived that speaks of the existence of such a person, even such a man."[1]

In his famous essay *Why I Am Not a Christian,* Bertrand Russell wrote, "Historically it is quite doubtful whether Christ ever existed at all, and if He did we know nothing about Him."[2] As to Christ's character, he said:

> I cannot myself feel that either in the matter of wisdom or in the matter of virtue Christ stands quite as high as some other people known to history. I think I should put Buddha and Socrates above Him in those respects.[3]

The truth of Christianity depends entirely on the truth and truthfulness of Jesus Christ. Did He exist? How can we know anything about His life? Who was He? Why should we believe in Him above all others? Without positive answers to these questions, the truth-claims of Christianity are void.

This chapter will present the historical evidence and reason that Jesus not only existed, but that He was God in the flesh. The outline of this argument goes like this:

1. The New Testament documents are historically reliable evidence.

2. The historical evidence of the New Testament shows that Jesus claimed to be God and confirmed that claim by miraculous signs culminating in His resurrection.
3. Therefore, there is reliable historical evidence that Jesus Christ is God.

Before we begin looking at this evidence, though, there are two big objections that could be raised to this approach. The first is that historical evidence is relative and cannot give objective knowledge about the events of the past. If "objective" means "absolute," they are right; but there is no reason that historical evidence cannot give us a fair but revisable account of the events. Some say that historians never record what really happened because they can only see an event from their own perspective. But the very assertion, "All statements about history are relative," if it is true, is itself a relative statement because it is a statement about history. But if it is relative, then it is not objectively true; it is just a subjective opinion about historical studies. If there are claims that it is objectively true, we find such claims contradicting the asser-

---

Four Modern Views of Christ
1. Jesus never lived—Those who hold this view say that Paul invented the idea of Jesus from ancient myths, and the Gospels were written later to create the illusion that He was a real person.
2. Jesus without theology or miracles—Some believe that Jesus did indeed live, but we can't know anything about Him from the New Testament. After stripping away all the supernatural aspects of Jesus' life they found that there was no history left.
3. Jesus mythologized—Rudolf Bultmann developed a system of interpretation that eliminates all supernatural elements by calling them myth. To get to the true Jesus, he tried to strip away the myth and find out what kinds of needs people had that would make them invent such a story.
4. It doesn't matter—Some scholars say that the Resurrection may or may not have happened, but it doesn't matter. What matters is that we believe. Truth, they say, is only what you believe to be true.

tions. The objectivity of history is inescapable. Why else would historians be constantly rewriting history books if they did not think they could come closer to an ideal 100 percent objective accuracy?

The second objection is that we are suddenly saying that the New Testament is a historical document, not just a religious book. True, the Bible is a source of religious knowledge and it would be unreasonable to expect an unbeliever to accept what it says as such. However, there can be no objection to accepting what the Bible says about historical events if we can show that the New Testament is also a historical record. Consider this:

1. Gospel records were written by eyewitnesses within forty years of the events described. This gives their account credibility and assures a fair degree of accuracy.
2. The Bible is not one account of those events, but at least four accounts which agree in the main facts.
3. The account given in the New Testament agrees with the evidence from secular and Jewish historians of the first and second centuries. This evidence can be found in chapter 9 of this book.
4. The Bible has proven to be remarkably accurate in what it says about the ancient world. For example, in citing thirty-two countries, fifty-four cities, nine islands, and several rulers, Luke never made a mistake.

So there is no reason that the New Testament should not be accepted as a reliable historical document which gives us valuable information about the life and death of Jesus of Nazareth.

WHO WAS JESUS?

The Nicene Creed (A.D. 325) states the uniform belief of all orthodox Christianity that Christ was fully God and fully Man. All heresies regarding Christ deny one or the other of these. This portion of the chapter will show that Jesus was fully human, claimed to be God, and offered more than adequate evidence to support that claim.

HIS HUMANITY

While some have insisted that Jesus was only a man, others have said that He only appeared to be human. In reality, they say, He was a phantom—an apparition with no physical substance—pure Spirit with the illusion of material form. This doctrine is called Docetism. If this is so, then Christ was not really tempted as we are and did not really die because a spirit can do neither of these things. Hence, He was not really "one of us" and cannot be our substitute in atoning for our sins. Also, His resurrection was nothing more than a return to His natural state, and it has no implications for us as to our future. Because of this teaching that Christ's feet never quite touched the ground, it is necessary to show that Jesus was fully human.

His development

Jesus went through all the normal processes of human development. He was conceived in His mother's womb by the Holy Spirit (Matt. 1:18, 20; Luke 1:34-35). He was born of a woman who

	God	Angels	Man
Kind of being	Infinite	Created	Created
Limits	None	Finite	Finite
Nature	Spirit	Spirits	Spirit-body
Duration	Eternal	Temporal	Temporal
Space/time	Above it and cannot be in it	Above it, but *can* be in it	In it by nature
Nature/will	Neither can change	Only *will* can change	Both can change
Redemption	Source of redemption	Unredeemable	Redeemable

had carried Him to full term (2:6-7). He grew up as a normal Boy, developing physically, mentally, and emotionally (vv. 40-52). He aged so that while He was in His early thirties the crowd in Jerusalem said, "You are not yet fifty years old" (John 8:57).

His affections

Jesus displayed all of the traits of humanity in His needs. Physically, He hungered (Matt. 4:2), thirsted (John 19:28), became tired (Mark 4:38), and breathed (Luke 23:46) as a human. Emotionally, He expressed sorrow (Matt. 26:38), wonder (Mark 6:6), anger and grief (3:5), and compassion (1:41). He was also tempted to sin, though He did not yield to the temptation (Matt. 4:1-11; Mark 1:12-13; Luke 4:1-13; Heb. 2:18; 4:15). The shortest verse in the Bible speaks profoundly of Jesus' humanity in His inner life: "Jesus wept" (John 11:35).

His death

There is nothing more opposed to the divine nature than death, yet Jesus died a human death. It was witnessed by many people, including John, a small group of women followers, the soldiers, and the mocking crowd (Luke 23:48-49; John 19:25-27). His death was also confirmed by professional executioners of Rome (vv. 32-34). He was buried in accordance with the customs of the time and set in a grave (vv. 38-41). You can't get more human than that!

HIS DEITY

Jesus made numerous claims to be God. We will examine these claims and the evidence that He gave to support them.

Who did Jesus claim to be?

Claim to be Jehovah (Yahweh)

Jehovah or, more properly, Yahweh is the special name given by God for Himself. In the Hebrew Old Testament, it is written simply as four letters (YHWH) and was considered so holy that a devout Jew would not pronounce it. Those who wrote it would perform a special ceremony first. It is the name revealed to Moses in Exodus 3:14, when God said, "I AM WHO I AM," and the meaning of the name has to do with God's self-existence. While other titles for God may be used of men (*adonai* in Gen. 18:12) or false gods (*elohim* in Deut. 6:14), Yahweh is only used to refer to the one true God. Nothing else was to be worshiped or served (Ex. 20:5), and His name and glory were not to be given to another. Isaiah wrote, "Thus saith [Yahweh] . . . I am the first, and I am the last; and beside Me there is no God" (44:6, KJV) and, "I am [Yahweh], that is My name; and My glory I will not give to another, neither My praise to graven images" (42:8, KJV).

In light of this, it is no wonder that the Jews picked up stones and accused Jesus of blasphemy when He claimed to be Jehovah. Jesus said, "I am the Good Shepherd" (John 10:11), but the Old Testament said, "[Yahweh] is my shepherd" (Ps. 23:1). Jesus claimed to be the judge of all men (Matt. 25:31ff; John 5:27ff), but the Prophet Joel quotes Yahweh as saying, "For there I will sit to judge all the surrounding nations" (Joel 3:12). Jesus prayed, "Father, glorify Thou Me with Thine own Self with the glory which I had with Thee before the world was" (John 17:5, KJV). But Yahweh of the Old Testament said, "I will not give My glory to another" (Isa. 42:8). Likewise, Jesus spoke of Himself as the "Bridegroom" (Matt. 25:1) while the Old Testament identifies Yahweh in this way (Isa. 62:5; Hosea 2:16). The risen Christ says, "I am the first and the last" (Rev. 1:17)—precisely the words used by Yahweh in Isaiah 42:8. While the psalmist declares, "[Yahweh] is my light" (Ps. 27:1), Jesus said, "I am the light of the world" (John 8:12). Perhaps the strongest claim Jesus made to be Yahweh is in verse 58, where He says, "Before Abraham was born, I AM." This statement claims not only existence before Abraham, but equality with the "I AM" of Exodus 3:14. The Jews

---

Overview of Jesus' Claims
To be Yahweh—John 8:58
Equality with God—John 5:18
To be Messiah—Mark 14:61-64
Accepts worship—Matthew 28:17
Equal authority with God—Matthew 28:18
Prayer in His name—John 14:13-14

around Him clearly understood His meaning and picked up stones to kill Him for blaspheming (cf. John 8:58; 10:31-33). The same claim is made in Mark 14:62 and John 18:5-6.

Claim to be equal with God

Jesus claimed to be equal with God in other ways too. He not only assumed the titles of Deity, but claimed for Himself the prerogatives of God. He said to a paralytic, "My son, your sins are forgiven" (Mark 2:5ff). The scribes correctly responded, "Who can forgive sins but God alone?" So, to prove that His claim was not an empty boast He healed the man, offering direct proof that what He had said about forgiving sins was true also.

Another prerogative that Jesus claimed was the power to raise and judge the dead: "Truly, truly, I say to you, an hour is coming and now is, when the dead shall hear the voice of the Son of God; and those who hear shall live . . . and shall come forth; those who did the good deeds, to a resurrection of life, those who committed the evil deeds to a resurrection of judgment" (John 5:25-29). He removed all doubt about His meaning when He added, "For just as the Father raises the dead and gives them life, even so the Son also gives life to whom He wishes" (v. 21). But the Old Testament clearly taught that only God was the giver of life (1 Sam. 2:6; Deut. 32:39); the One to raise the dead (1 Sam. 2:6; Ps. 49:15) and the only Judge (Joel 3:12; Deut. 32:35). Jesus boldly assumed for Himself powers that only God has.

But Jesus also claimed that He should be honored as God. He said that all men should "honor the Son, even as they honor the Father. He who does not honor the Son does not honor the Father" (John 5:23). The Jews listening knew that no one should claim to be equal with God in this way, and again they sought to kill Him (v. 18).

Claim to be Messiah-God

The teaching of the Old Testament is clear that the coming Messiah who would deliver Israel would be God Himself. When Jesus claimed to be that Messiah, He was also claiming to be God. For example, the famous Christmas text (Isa. 9:6) calls the Messiah, "Mighty God, the everlasting Father." The psalmist wrote of

What Is Messiah?

The word Messiah comes from the Hebrew word meaning "Anointed One." In a general sense, the word is used of Cyrus the Persian (Isa. 45:1) and the king of Israel (1 Sam. 26:11). After the death of David, Israel began looking for a king like him because of the promise of 2 Samuel 7:12-16. But prophecies of a coming Saviour/Prophet/King go back as far as Genesis 3:15 and Deuteronomy 18. Many passages describe the coming King. He is said to be of David's seed (Jer. 33), and born in Bethlehem (Micah 5:2). His acts are to include making the blind see, releasing captives, and proclaiming the Gospel (Isa. 61:1). His kingdom is described in Zechariah 9 and 12. In the period between the Testaments, two ideas of Messiah arose: one political, one spiritual. Both were expected to be found in the same Person.

Messiah, "Thy throne, O God, is forever and ever" (Ps. 45:6; cf. Heb. 1:8). Psalm 110:1 records a conversation between the Father and the Son: "[Yahweh] says to my Lord, 'Sit at My right hand.'" Jesus applied this passage to Himself in Matthew 22:43-44. In the great messianic prophecy of Daniel 7, the Son of man is called the "Ancient of Days" (v. 22), a phrase used twice in the same passage of God the Father (vv. 9, 13). Throughout His ministry, the title Son of man was Jesus' favorite way of referring to Himself, making clear illusion to this passage. But Jesus also quoted it directly at His trial before the high priest. When asked, "Are You the Christ [Greek for Messiah], the Son of the Blessed One?" Jesus responded, "I am; and you shall see the Son of man sitting at the right hand of power, and coming with the clouds of heaven." At this, the high priest tore his robe and said, "What further need do we have of witnesses? You have heard the blasphemy!" (Mark 14:61-64) There was no doubt that in claiming to be Messiah, Jesus also claimed to be God.

Claim by accepting worship

The Old Testament forbids worshiping anyone other than God (Ex. 20:1-5; Deut. 5:6-9). The New Testament agrees, showing that men refused worship (Acts 14:15) as did angels (Rev. 22:8-9). But Jesus accepted worship on numerous occasions. A healed leper worshiped Him (Matt. 8:2), and a ruler knelt before Him with a request (9:18). After He stilled the storm, "those who were in the boat worshiped Him saying, 'Truly You are the Son of God' " (14:33, NIV). A group of Canaanite women (15:25), the mother of James and John (20:20), the Gerasene demoniac (Mark 5:6), all worshiped Jesus without one word of rebuke (cf. Rev. 22:8-9). A blind man said, " 'Lord, I believe.' And he worshiped Him" (John 9:38). But Christ also elicited worship in some cases, as when Thomas saw the risen Christ and cried out, "My Lord and my God!" (20:28) This could only be done by a Person who seriously considered Himself to be God.

Claim to equal authority with God

Jesus also put His words on a par with God's. "You have heard that the ancients were told. . . . But I say to you" (Matt. 5:21-22) is repeated over and over again. "All authority has been given to Me in heaven and on earth. Go therefore and make disciples of all the nations" (28:18-19). God had given the Ten Commandments to Moses, but Jesus said, "A new commandment I give to you, that you love one another" (John 13:34). Jesus said, "Until heaven and earth pass away, not the smallest letter or stroke shall pass away from the Law" (Matt. 5:18), but later Jesus said of His own words, "Heaven and earth will pass away, but My words shall not pass away" (24:35). Speaking of those who reject Him, Jesus said, "The word I spoke is what will judge him at the last day" (John 12:48). There is no question that Jesus expected His words to have equal authority with God's declarations in the Old Testament.

Claim by requesting prayer in His name

Jesus not only asked men to believe in Him and obey His commandments, but also He asked them to pray in His name. "Whatever you ask in My name, that I will do. . . . If you ask Me anything in My name, I will do it" (John 14:13-14). "If you abide in Me, and My words abide in you, ask whatever you wish, and it shall be done for you" (15:7). Jesus even insisted, "No one comes to the Father, but through Me" (14:6). In response to this the disciples not only prayed in Jesus' name (1 Cor. 5:4), but prayed to Christ (Acts 7:59). Jesus certainly intended that His name be invoked both before God and as God in prayer.

So Jesus claimed to be God in several ways. He claimed equality with God in prerogatives, honor, worship, and authority. He claimed to be Yahweh of the Old Testament by applying truths about Yahweh to Himself and by claiming to be the promised Messiah. Finally, He claimed to be the only way to approach God in prayer and requested prayer to Himself as God. The reactions of the Jews around Him show that they clearly understood these things to be blasphemous claims for a mere man to make. Any unbiased observer studying this historically reliable record of Jesus' teaching must agree that He claimed to be equal with Yahweh of the Old Testament.

WHAT CLAIMS DID THE DISCIPLES MAKE ABOUT JESUS?

Along with Jesus' own claims to be God, we should consider what His disciples believed about Him. It is one thing to claim to be God; it is quite another to get other monotheistic Jews to believe it. However, we find that the followers of Jesus believed in His deity very strongly.

THEY ATTRIBUTED TO JESUS THE TITLES OF DEITY

In agreement with their Master, the apostles called Him "the first and the last" (Rev. 1:17; 2:8; 22:13), "the true light" (John 1:9), their "rock" or "stone" (1 Cor. 10:4; 1 Peter 2:6-8; cf. Pss. 18:2; 95:1), the "Bridegroom" (Eph. 5:28-33; Rev. 21:2), "the chief Shepherd" (1 Peter 5:4), and "the Great Shepherd" (Heb. 13:20).

Claims of Jesus' Disciples
Titles of Deity—Revelation 1:17
Messiah—Philippians 2:10
Powers of God—Colossions 1:16-17
Association with God—Galatians 1:3
Prayer to Jesus—Acts 7:59
Called God—Titus 2:13
Superior to angels—Hebrews 1:5-6

He is seen as the forgiver of sins (Acts 5:31; Col. 3:13; cf. Jer. 31:34; Ps. 130:4) and "Saviour of the world" (John 4:42; cf. Isa. 43:3). The apostles also taught that "Jesus Christ . . . is to judge the living and the dead" (2 Tim. 4:1). All of these titles are given to Yahweh in the Old Testament and to Jesus in the New.

THEY CONSIDERED HIM TO BE MESSIAH—GOD
The New Testament opens with a passage concluding that Jesus is Immanuel (God with us), which refers to the messianic prediction of Isaiah 7:14. The very title "Christ" carries the same meaning as the Hebrew appellation "Messiah" (Anointed). In Zechariah 12:10, Yahweh says, "They will look on Me whom they have pierced." But the New Testament writers apply this passage to Jesus twice (John 19:37; Rev. 1:7) as predicting His crucifixion. Paul interprets Isaiah's message, "For I am God, and there is no other. . . . To Me every knee will bow, and every tongue will swear" (Isa. 45:22-23) as applying to his Lord, "at the name of Jesus every knee should bow . . . and every tongue should confess that Jesus Christ is Lord, to the glory of God the Father" (Phil. 2:10-11). The implications of this are strong, because Paul says that all created beings will call Jesus both Messiah (Christ) and Yahweh (Lord).

THEY ATTRIBUTED THE POWERS OF GOD TO JESUS
Some things only God can do, but these very things are attributed to Jesus by His disciples. He is said to be able to raise the dead (John 11) and forgive sins (Acts 5:31; 13:38). Moreover, He is said to have been the primary agent in creating the universe (John 1:3; Col. 1:16) and in sustaining its existence (v. 17). Surely only God can be said to be the Creator of all things, but the disciples claim this power for Jesus.

THEY ASSOCIATED JESUS' NAME WITH GOD'S
Their use of Jesus' name as the agent and recipient of prayer has been noted (1 Cor. 5:4; Acts 7:59). Often in prayers or benedictions, Jesus' name is used alongside God's, as in, "Grace to you and peace from God our Father, and the Lord Jesus Christ" (Gal. 1:3; Eph. 1:2). The name of Jesus appears with equal status to God's

in the so-called trinitarian formulas. For example, the command to go and baptize "in the name of the Father and the Son and the Holy Spirit" (Matt. 28:19). Again this association is made at the end of 2 Corinthians, "The grace of the Lord Jesus Christ, and the love of God, and the fellowship of the Holy Spirit be with you all" (13:14). If there is only one God, then these Three must be equated.

THEY CALLED HIM GOD DIRECTLY

Thomas saw His wounds and cried, "My Lord and my God!" (John 20:28) Paul calls Jesus, the One in whom "all the fullness of Deity dwells in bodily form" (Col. 2:9). In Titus, Jesus is called "our great God and Saviour" (2:13), and the writer to the Hebrews says of Him, "Thy throne, O God, is forever" (1:8). Paul says that before Christ existed in the "likeness of man," which clearly refers to being really human, He existed in the "form of God" (Phil. 2:5-8). The parallel phrases suggest that if Jesus was fully human, then He is also fully God. A similar phrase, "the image of the invisible God," is used in Colossians 1:15 to mean the manifestation of God Himself. This description is strengthened in Hebrews where it says, "He is the radiance of His glory and the exact representation of His nature, and upholds all things by the word of His power" (Heb. 1:3). The prologue to John's Gospel states, "In the beginning was the Word, and the Word was with God, and the Word was God" (1:1).

THEY SAID HE WAS SUPERIOR TO ANGELS

The disciples did not simply believe that Christ was more than a man; they believed Him to be greater than any created being, including angels. Paul said Jesus is "far above all rule and authority and power and dominion, and every name that is named, not only in this age, but also in the one to come" (Eph. 1:21). The demons submitted to His command (Matt. 8:32) and even angels that refused to be worshiped are seen worshiping Him (Rev. 22:8-9). The author of Hebrews presents a complete argument for Christ's superiority over angels saying, "For to which of the angels did He ever say, 'Thou art My Son, today I have begotten Thee'? . . . And when He again brings the firstborn into the world, He says,

'And let all the angels of God worship Him'" (Heb. 1:5-6). There could be no clearer teaching that Christ was not an angel, but God whom the angels were to worship.

There is testimony from Jesus Himself and from those who knew Him that Jesus claimed to be God and that His followers believed Him. He claimed the titles, powers, prerogatives, and activities that are proper only to God for Himself, a carpenter of Nazareth. Whether or not this was the case, there is no doubt that this is what they believed and what Jesus thought of Himself. As C.S. Lewis observed, when confronted with the boldness of Christ's claims, we are faced with distinct alternatives.

> I am trying here to prevent anyone saying the really foolish things that people often say about Him: "I'm ready to accept Jesus as a great moral teacher, but I don't accept His claim to be God." That is the one thing we must not say. A man who was merely a man and said the sort of thing Jesus said would not be a great moral teacher. He would rather be a lunatic—on a level with the man who says he is a poached egg—Or else he would be the Devil of Hell.[4]

WHAT EVIDENCE DID JESUS GIVE TO SUPPORT HIS CLAIMS?

To say that Jesus made such claims proves nothing by itself. The claims might not be true, in which case He was either a liar or a lunatic. The real question is whether or not there is any good reason to believe that the claims are true. What kind of evidence did Jesus offer to support His claims to Deity? He offered supernatural confirmation of His claims to be a supernatural Being. The logic of this argument goes like this:

1. A miracle is an act of God that confirms the truth of God associated with it.
2. Jesus offered three lines of miraculous evidence to confirm His claim to be God—His fulfillment of prophecy, His sinless life and miraculous deeds, and His resurrection.
3. Therefore, Jesus' miracles confirm that He is God.

Possible Objections
Several objections might be raised by this type of argument. For instance, how do we know that there is a God or that He performs miracles or that Jesus' miracles aren't just fairy tales? But we have already established all of these things before we got to this point. If this is a theistic universe (chaps. 2–3), then miracles are possible (chap. 5). The reliability of the New Testament as a historical document describing the teachings and activities of Jesus is addressed in chapter 7. So there is no reason to doubt that if we look at the record of Jesus' life we can see if His claims are given a miraculous confirmation.

FULFILLMENT OF MESSIANIC PROPHECIES

There were dozens of prophecies in the Old Testament regarding the Messiah. Some of these passages may not have been recognized as predictive when they were written, such as the ones that say He would be a Nazarene (see Matt. 2:23) or that He would flee to Egypt (see v. 15). But other passages can only make sense if they refer to Messiah God. In this latter category, here are a few of the most significant prophecies which Christ fulfilled, and the New Testament passage showing that completion.

1. Born of a woman (Gen. 3:15; Gal. 4:4)
2. Born of a virgin (Isa. 7:14; Matt. 1:21ff)
3. He would be "cut off" 483 years after the declaration to reconstruct the temple in 444 B.C. (Dan. 9:24ff) (see Harold W. Hoehner's *Chronological Aspects of the Life of Christ*, pp. 115–138)
4. Of the seed of Abraham (Gen. 12:1-3; 22:18; Matt. 1:1; Gal. 3:16)
5. Of the tribe of Judah (Gen. 49:10; Luke 3:23, 33; Heb. 7:14)
6. Of the house of David (2 Sam. 7:12ff; Matt. 1:1)
7. Born in Bethlehem (Micah 5:2; Matt. 2:1; Luke 2:4-7)
8. Anointed by the Holy Spirit (Isa. 11:2; Matt. 3:16-17)
9. Heralded by the messenger of the Lord (John the Baptist) (Isa. 40:3; Mal. 3:1; Matt. 3:1-2)
10. Would perform miracles (Isa. 35:5-6; Matt. 9:35)
11. Would cleanse the temple (Mal. 3:1; Matt. 21:12ff)

12. Rejected by Jews (Ps. 118:22; 1 Peter 2:7)
13. Die a humiliating death (Ps. 22; Isa. 53) involving:
    a. rejection (Isa. 53:3; John 1:10-11; 7:5, 48)
    b. silence before His accusers (Isa. 53:7; Matt. 27:12-19)
    c. being mocked (Ps. 22:7-8; Matt. 27:31)
    d. piercing His hands and feet (Ps. 22:16; Luke 23:33)
    e. being crucified with thieves (Isa. 53:12; Matt. 27:38)
    f. praying for His persecutors (Isa. 53:12; Luke 23:43)
    g. piercing His side (Zech. 12:10; John 19:34)
    h. buried in a rich man's tomb (Isa. 53:9; Matt. 27:57-60)
    i. casting lots for His garments (Ps. 22:18; John 19:23-24)
14. Would rise from the dead (Ps. 16:10; Mark 16:6; Acts 2:31)
15. Ascend into heaven (Ps. 68:18; Acts 1:9)
16. Would sit down at the right hand of God (Ps. 110:1; Heb. 1:3)

It is important to understand that these prophecies were written hundreds of years before Christ was born. No one could have been reading the signs of the times or just making intelligent guesses, like the "prophecies" we see in the check-out line at the supermarket. Even the most liberal critics admit that the prophetic books were completed some 400 years before Christ, and the Book of Daniel by about 167 B.C. Though there is good evidence to date most of these books much earlier (some of the psalms and earlier prophets were in the eighth and ninth centuries B.C.), what difference would it make? It is just as hard to predict an event 200 years in the future as it is to predict one that is 800 years in the future. Both feats would require nothing less than divine knowledge. Even using the later dates, the fulfillment of these prophecies is just as miraculous and points to the divine confirmation of Jesus as the Messiah.

Some have suggested that there is a natural explanation for what seems to be prophetic fulfillment. One explanation is that the prophecies were accidentally fulfilled in Jesus. In other words, He happened to be in the right place at the right time. But what are we to say about the prophecies involving miracles—"He just happened to make the blind man see"? "He just happened to be resurrected from the dead"? These hardly seem like chance events. If there is a God who is in control of the universe, as we have said, then chance is ruled out. Logically, it is possible for chance to have caused all these things to converge on one man, but it is certainly not probable. Mathematicians[5] have calculated the probability of sixteen predictions being fulfilled in one man at 1 in 10^{45}. If we go to forty-eight predictions, the probability is 1 in 10^{157}. It is almost impossible for us to conceive of a number that big. But it is not the logical improbability that rules out this theory; it is the moral impossibility of an all-powerful and all-knowing God letting things get out of control so that all His plans for prophetic fulfill-ment are ruined by someone who just happened to be in the right place at the right time. God cannot lie, nor can He break a promise (Heb. 6:18), so we must conclude that He did not allow His prophetic promises to be thwarted by chance. All the evidence points to Jesus as the divinely appointed fulfillment of the messianic prophecies. He was God's man confirmed by God's signs.

MIRACULOUS AND SINLESS LIFE

The very course of Christ's life demonstrates His claim to Deity. To live a sinless life does not prove Deity by itself (though only Jesus has managed to do it), but to claim to be God and offer a sinless life as evidence is another matter. Some of Jesus' enemies

---

The Great Pretender
Another hypothesis set forth by Schoenfield in *The Passover Plot* is that Jesus manipulated things to make it look like He fulfilled the prophecies. But how does one manage to manipulate his place of birth, or his family lineage, the time he would enter the world, or the way the Jewish nation would react to him? Many of the prophecies were simply beyond the control of any mere man. How can a man arrange to be born of a virgin? Or to be born in Bethlehem in a certain year? Besides this, to imagine and carry out such a deceptive and cunning plot is against everything we know about Jesus' character.

brought false accusations against Him, but the verdict of Pilate at
His trial has been the verdict of history: "I find no guilt in this
Man" (Luke 23:4). A soldier at the cross agreed, saying, "Certainly this Man was innocent" (v. 47), and the thief on the cross next
to Jesus said, "This Man has done nothing wrong" (v. 41). But
the real test is what those who were closest to Jesus said of His
character. His disciples had lived and worked with Him for several
years at close range, yet their opinions of Him are not diminished
at all. Peter called Christ "a Lamb without blemish or defect"
(1 Peter 1:19, NIV) and added, "Nor was any deceit found in His
mouth" (2:22). John called Him "Jesus Christ the righteous"
(1 John 2:1; cf. 3:7). Paul expressed the unanimous belief of the
early church that Christ "knew no sin" (2 Cor. 5:21), and the
writer of Hebrews says that He was tempted as a man "yet without sin" (4:15). Jesus Himself once challenged His accusers,
"Which one of you convicts Me of sin?" (John 8:46) but no one
was able to find Him guilty of anything. This being the case, the
impeccable character of Christ gives a double testimony to the
truth of His claim. It provides supporting evidence as He suggested, but it also assures us that He was not lying when He said
that He was God.

Beyond the moral aspects of His life, we are confronted with
the miraculous nature of His ministry. He turned water to wine
(2:7ff), walked on water (Matt. 14:25), multiplied bread (6:11ff),
opened the eyes of the blind (9:7ff), made the lame to walk (Mark
2:3ff), cast out demons (3:11ff), healed the multitudes of all kinds
of sickness (Matt. 9:35), including leprosy (Mark 1:40-42), and
even raised the dead to life on several occasions (John 11:43-44;
Luke 7:11-15; Mark 5:35ff). When asked if He was the Messiah,
He used His miracles as evidence to support the claim, saying,
"Go and report to John the things which you hear and see: the
blind receive sight and the lame walk, lepers are cleansed and the
deaf hear, and the dead are raised up" (Matt. 11:4-5). This special
outpouring of miracles was a special sign that Messiah had come
(see Isa. 35:5-6). Nicodemus even said, "Rabbi, we know that
You have come from God as a Teacher; for no one can do these
signs that You do unless God is with Him" (John 3:2). To a first-
century Jew, miracles such as Christ performed were clear indica-

tions of God's approval of the performer's message. In Jesus' case, part of that message was that He is God in human flesh. His miracles verify His claim to be true Deity.

HIS RESURRECTION

The third strand of evidence supporting Jesus' claim to be God is the grandest and greatest of them all. Nothing like it is claimed by any other religion, and no miracle has as much historical evidence to confirm it. Jesus Christ rose from the dead to a transformed body on the third day after His death. In this resurrected state He appeared to more than 500 of His disciples on at least eight different occasions over a forty-day period; He conversed with them, ate with them, let them touch Him, and cooked breakfast for them. The fact that both the Old Testament and Jesus Himself predicted that He would rise from the dead makes this miracle even stronger in its significance. When dealing with people who refused to believe in spite of His miracles, Jesus rested the case for His deity on the Resurrection alone. Since we know the New Testament provides accurate historical information, all we need to do here is examine that evidence and answer some of the objections that have been raised to explain away the Resurrection.

OLD TESTAMENT AND THE RESURRECTION

The Old Testament predicted the Resurrection both in specific statements and by logical inference. First, there are specific pas-

---

The Earliest Creed

First Corinthians 15:3-5 may be the earliest formulated creed of Christianity. The style seems to indicate it is to be understood as a kind of creed. It contains two declarations, each followed by a supporting piece of evidence: Christ's death (supported by His burial) and His resurrection (supported by His appearances). These are the central and most important teachings of Christianity. They emphasize both the forgiveness of sins and the assurance of an afterlife in which we remain "ourselves." Both of these aspects of the Gospel are to be preached and both are confirmed by the historical fact of a literal resurrection.

sages that the apostles cited from the Old Testament as applying to the resurrection of Christ. Peter says that, since we know that David died and was buried, he must have been speaking of the Christ when he said, "Thou wilt not abandon My soul to Hades, nor allow Thy Holy One to undergo decay" (Ps. 16:8-11, quoted in Acts 2:25-31). No doubt it was passages like this that Paul used in the Jewish synagogues when "he reasoned with them from the Scriptures, explaining and proving that the Christ had to suffer and rise from the dead" (Acts 17:2-3).

Also, the Old Testament teaches the Resurrection by logical inference. There is clear teaching that the Messiah was to die (cf. Ps. 22; Isa. 53) and equally evident teaching that He is to have an enduring political reign from Jerusalem (Isa. 9:6; Dan. 2:44; Zech. 13:1). There is no way to reconcile these two teachings unless the Messiah who dies is raised from the dead to reign forever. Jesus died before He could begin to reign. Only by His resurrection could the prophecies of a messianic kingdom be fulfilled.

JESUS PREDICTED HIS OWN RESURRECTION

Jesus also predicted His own resurrection on several occasions. Even in the earliest part of His ministry, He said, "Destroy this temple [of My body] and in three days I will raise it up" (John 2:19). In Matthew 12:40, He said, "As Jonah was three days and three nights in the belly of the sea monster, so shall the Son of man be three days and three nights in the heart of the earth." To those who had seen His miracles and still stubbornly would not believe, He often said, "An evil and adulterous generation craves for a sign; and yet no sign shall be given to it but for the sign of Jonah" (v. 39; 16:4). After Peter's confession, "He began to teach them that the Son of man must suffer many things . . . and be killed, and after three days rise again" (Mark 8:31), and this became a central part of His teaching from that point until His death. Further, Jesus taught that He would raise Himself from the dead, saying, "I have authority to lay it [My life] down, and I have authority to take it up again" (John 10:18).

Philosopher Karl Popper has argued that whenever a "risky

prediction" is fulfilled, it counts as confirmation of the theory that comes with it.[6] What could be riskier than predicting your own resurrection? If a man will not accept that as evidence of a truth claim, then he has a bias that will not accept anything as evidence. Jesus was willing to let the decision of who He is ride on whether or not this prediction came true.

JESUS ACTUALLY DIED ON THE CROSS

Before we can show that Jesus rose from the dead, we need to show that He really did die. The Koran claims that Jesus only pretended to be dead (Surah IV:157), and many skeptics have said that He appeared to be dead, possibly being drugged, but revived while in the tomb. It is no miracle for a live man to walk out of a tomb. For the Resurrection to have any significance, Jesus had to be dead first.

To show this, there are several points that must be considered.

1. There is no evidence to suggest that Jesus was drugged. He turned down the common painkiller that was usually given to crucifixion victims (Mark 15:23). Just before death, He was given a sip of sour wine to relieve His parched throat, but not enough to intoxicate (v. 36). The obvious agony and His death cry do not fit the picture of a man who is about to pass out in a drug-induced state.

2. The heavy loss of blood makes death highly probable. While praying in the Garden, His extreme emotional state caused Him to "sweat, as it were, great drops of blood" (Luke 22:44). He had been beaten and whipped repeatedly the night before His crucifixion with a Roman scourge (a three-lash whip with pieces of bone or metal on the ends) which tore the flesh of the skeletal muscles and set the stage for circulatory shock. A crown of thorns had been pushed onto His skull. He was probably in serious to critical condition before they crucified Him. Then He suffered five major wounds between nine in the morning and just before sunset (Mark 15:25, 33). Four of these were caused by nails used to fix Him to the cross. We know

from remains of Palestinian crucifixion victims that these nails were five to seven inches long and about three eighths inch square.

3. When His side was pierced with a spear, water and blood flowed out. The best evidence suggests that this was a thrust given by a Roman soldier to insure death. The spear entered through the rib cage and pierced His right lung, the sack around the heart, and the heart itself, releasing both blood and pleural fluids. Jesus was unquestionably dead before they removed Him from the cross and probably before this wound was inflicted. The wounds in both His wrists and feet would have severed the major nerves. The final wound to His side would have been fatal in itself (John 19:34).

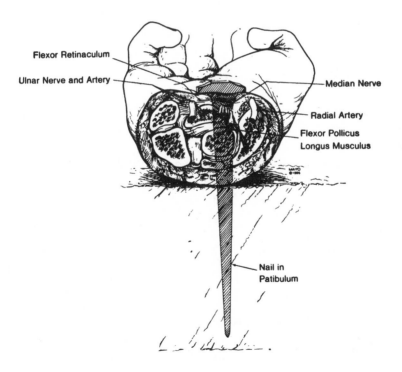

Flexor Retinaculum

Ulnar Nerve and Artery

Median Nerve

Radial Artery

Flexor Pollicus Longus Musculus

Nail in Patibulum

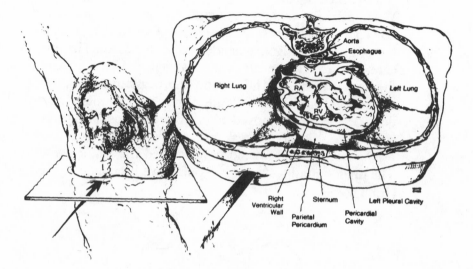

Right Lung — Aorta — Esophagus — LA — RA — LV — RV — Left Lung — Right Ventricular Wall — Sternum — Parietal Pericardium — Pericardial Cavity — Left Pleural Cavity

4. The standard procedure for crucifixion was to break the victim's legs so that he could not lift himself to exhale. The victim would then be asphyxiated as his lungs filled with carbon dioxide. Be clear on this: they broke everyone's legs. Yet, the professional Roman executioners declared Christ dead without breaking His legs (v. 33). There was no doubt in their minds.

5. Jesus was embalmed in about 75–100 pounds of spices and bandages and laid in a guarded tomb (vv. 39-40). Even if He had woken up in the tomb, He could not have unwrapped Himself, rolled the stone back up the side of its carved-out track, overcome the guards, and escaped unnoticed (Matt. 27:60).

6. Pilate asked for assurance that Jesus was really dead before releasing the body for burial.

7. If Jesus had managed all this, His appearance would have

been more like a resuscitated wretch than a resurrected Saviour. It is not likely that it would have turned the world upside down.

8. In the article "On the Physical Death of Jesus Christ" the *Journal of the American Medical Society* concluded: "Clearly, the weight of historical and medical evidence indicates that Jesus was dead before the wound to His side was inflicted and supports the traditional view that the spear, thrust between His right ribs, probably perforated not only the right lung but also the pericardium and heart and thereby ensured his death. Accordingly, interpretations based on the assumption that Jesus did not die on the cross appear to be at odds with modern medical knowledge." (March 21, 1986, p. 1463)[7]

JESUS ROSE BODILY FROM THE GRAVE

Not only did Jesus really die, but He also rose in the same physical body in which He died. There are many alternate explanations for the resurrection of Christ, but none of them satisfy the facts of the case. Many skeptics have become Christians while trying to refute the Resurrection. If we look at the other explanations, we will have an opportunity to also see the evidence that conclusively shows that only Resurrection can explain all the facts.

"JOSEPH OF ARIMATHEA TOOK THE BODY"

The problems of this theory boil down to "why, when, and where?" Why would he take the body? Joseph really had no reason. It could not be to prevent the disciples from stealing it; he was a disciple (Luke 23:50-51). If he had not been a follower of Christ, he could have produced the body and squelched the whole story. When could he have taken it? Joseph was a devout Jew and would not have broken the Sabbath, especially at Passover (see vv. 50-56). At night, because of the torches, he would have been seen. The day after the Sabbath there was a Roman guard posted in front of the tomb (Matt. 27:62-66). The following morning the women came by dawn (Luke 24:1). There was simply no opportunity. And if he had taken it, where did he put it? The body was

The Passover Plot

In 1965, Dr. Hugh Schonfield published a book called *The Passover Plot* which claims to shed new light on the history of Jesus. In it, he said that Jesus had instructed Joseph of Arimathea to remove the body from the tomb so that He could appear to be the Messiah. The Resurrection appearances are explained as cases of mistaken identity. The boldness of the disciples after the Resurrection is due to the fact that the hoax had fooled them and they didn't know any better.

never found even though almost two months elapsed before the disciples began preaching. This was plenty of time to expose a fraud if there was one. There is no motive, opportunity, or method to support this theory, and it gives no explanation of the appearances of Christ in His resurrected body.

"THE ROMAN OR JEWISH AUTHORITIES TOOK THE BODY"

This theory doesn't even make sense. If they had the body, why did they try to accuse the disciples of stealing it? (Matt. 28:11-15) Besides, they could have stopped the Resurrection story cold by simply bringing the body forth. Instead, they continually resisted the apostles' teaching, but never attempted to refute it. Again, this theory does not explain the Resurrection appearances in that very same physical body.

"THE DISCIPLES STOLE THE BODY"

This does not fit with what we know about the lives of these men. These were not dishonest men. They all taught that honesty was a great virtue. Peter later denied the charge that they followed cleverly devised tales (2 Peter 1:16). Neither were they clever men trying to make Christ's predictions come true. On the night of His arrest, they did not even understand that He was going to die, let alone be raised (John 13:36). They did not know what to think when they first saw the empty tomb (20:9). They hid because they were afraid of the Jews (v. 19). Are these the kind of men who would boldly steal the body from a heavily guarded tomb? If this hypothesis were true, then we must also believe that the apostles persisted in this hoax and died for what they knew to be false.

"THE TOMB WAS NEVER VISITED"

Some say that in the two months after Jesus' death He appeared spiritually to some of the disciples, and they preached the Resurrection based on this. But they never visited the tomb to see if His body was there. But the Gospels clearly say that several people went to the tomb. First, the women who came to finish burial procedures (Mark 16:1) saw the stone rolled away and the empty tomb. John was next to reach the grave site, and he saw the burial clothes. He was followed by Peter who entered the tomb and saw the same plus a facecloth (a strip wrapped around the head to keep the jaw closed) lying separately (John 20:3-8). Also, there is no reason to believe that the guards did not make a thorough search of the tomb before they reported to the Jewish leaders (Matt. 28:11ff). These guards would not have agreed to lie if they could have offered some reasonable explanation for the unusual disappearance of the body. This theory cannot explain the Resurrection appearances, the transformation of the disciples, or the mass conversions of people only a few weeks later.

"THE WOMEN WENT TO THE WRONG TOMB"

Some suggest that the women went to the wrong tomb, saw it empty, and thought He had risen. This is too simplistic. If it was so dark, why did Mary think Jesus was the gardener? (John 20:15) Why did Peter and John make the same mistake in broad daylight? (v. 6) And especially, why didn't the authorities just go to the right tomb and show the body? That would have easily disproved all claims to a resurrection. This theory offers no explanation of the physical appearances of Jesus in the same material body of flesh and bones that had been crucified.

JESUS APPEARED IN A RESURRECTED BODY

The most outstanding proof that Jesus rose from the dead is that He was seen by more than 500 people on twelve different occasions. The creed-like statements recorded in 1 Corinthians 15:3-5 are from very early in the life of the church, being formulated within a few years of the death of Jesus. Hence, it has great historical reliability.[8]

Kirsopp Lake's Theory

A famous liberal theologian, Kirsopp Lake, presented the theory that the women had gone to the wrong tomb. He suggested that the women went to the tomb early Sunday morning and asked the gardener where Jesus was laid. The gardener then responded, "He is not here," and the women rushed off to preach the Resurrection before the gardener could turn to point and say, "He is over there."

He rose bodily, not just spiritually. When Paul uses the term "spiritual body" in verse 44, it means a spirit-dominated or supernatural body in contrast to the "natural" body we now possess. It certainly was not an immaterial body, since the same word is used to describe a material rock (10:4), literal food (v. 3), and a physical human being (2:15). Paul uses the phrase much like we say, "Paul is a spiritual man," or "The Bible is a spiritual book."

Jesus had flesh and bones (Luke 24:39), ate fish (vv. 42-43), and challenged doubters to touch Him and see (v. 39). To Thomas, He said, "Put your finger here; see My hands. Reach out your hand and put it into My side" (John 20:27, NIV). This kind of contact makes it impossible to suggest that the disciples saw a spirit or an illusion. The Bible even makes it clear that there is a

---

12 RESURRECTION APPEARANCES

1. To Mary Magdalene (John 20:11)

2. To the other women (Matt. 28:9-10)

3. To Peter (Luke 24:34)

4. To two disciples (Luke 24:13-32)

5. To ten apostles (Luke 24:33-49)

6. To Thomas and the other apostles (John 20:26-30)

7. To seven apostles (John 21)

8. To all the apostles (Matt. 28:16-20)

9. To all the apostles (Acts 1:4-9)

10. To 500 brethren (1 Cor. 15:6)

11. To James (1 Cor. 15:7)

12. To Paul (1 Cor. 15:7)

---

difference between seeing a vision (where there is no real manifestation in the world, but only in the mind [cf. Acts 7:54-58; 2 Cor. 12:1-4]) and an appearance of Jesus where everyone around saw or heard something with their physical senses.

Beyond this several people saw Him on more than one occasion, some alone, and some with large groups; sometimes at night and sometimes in daylight. Paul challenges any who doubt the report to simply ask any of the witnesses who were still alive to be questioned (1 Cor. 15:6). Also, the appearances were long enough to be sure of the identity of the Man. He walked and talked with some (Luke 24:13ff), ate with others (John 21:1ff), and stayed long enough to teach them concerning God's kingdom (Acts 1:3). With this kind of testimony, there can be no doubt as to its truth.

SUMMARY AND CONCLUSION

At the beginning of the chapter we said that we would prove that Jesus Christ is God. First we answered the objection that we can't really know anything about history. Then we mentioned that the New Testament documents are not only religious writings, but are also reliable as historical documents. They originate from the first-century eyewitnesses and are confirmed by other historical data of the time. Finally, we saw that Jesus claimed to be Yahweh God in several direct and indirect ways and gave three lines of evidence to support this claim: fulfillment of prophecy, a sinless and miraculous life, and His resurrection. Inasmuch as there is solid historical evidence to confirm each of these claims, there is no escaping the conclusion that Jesus' claim to be God is true. It is confirmed by reliable historical evidence from eyewitnesses and by God through the miracles performed. The convergence of these lines of evidence in one Man show that Jesus alone is the unique Son of God, for He alone claimed and proved to be Deity. One former atheist, now a famous scholar, who examined the evidence for the Resurrection, came to this conclusion:

The resurrection of Jesus acquires such decisive meaning, not merely because someone or anyone has been raised from the dead, but because it is Jesus of Nazareth, whose execution was instigated by the Jews because He had blasphemed against God. If this Man was raised from the dead, then that plainly means that the God whom He supposedly blasphemed has committed Himself to Him.[9]

The same logic is seen in a letter in *Time* magazine regarding a Jewish rabbi who has recognized the historicity of the Resurrection:

Pinchas Lapide's logic escapes me. He believes it is a possibility that Jesus was resurrected by God. At the same time he does not accept Jesus as the Messiah. But Jesus said that He was the Messiah. Why would God resurrect a liar?[10]

That is a very good question. If we are honest about the evidence, we should fall on our knees with Thomas and cry out, "My Lord and my God!"

WHY IS JESUS BETTER THAN OTHER TEACHERS?
Does Christianity really offer anything which is superior to other religions? Is Jesus Christ superior to other religious or philosophical leaders? Let us look at the claims and fundamental teachings of some of the founders of world religions and philosophical schools to see how they compare with Christ.

MOSES
Being a Jew Himself, Jesus had no argument with Moses, the prophet who brought the Jewish Law and led the Israelites out of Egyptian bondage to freedom as an independent nation. Moses and Jesus were prophets of the same God, and Jesus even said that He did not come to abolish the Law (Moses' writings) but to fulfill it (Matt. 5:17). Jesus implies that Moses' words are God's words (cf. 19:4-5 with Gen. 2:24). However, in many respects, we find that Jesus is superior to Moses.

Moses predicted Jesus' coming
In Deuteronomy 18:15-19, Moses predicted that God would

raise up a Jewish Prophet with a special message from God. Anyone who did not believe this Prophet would be judged by God. This passage has been traditionally interpreted as referring to Messiah. Genesis 3:15 is also understood by many to refer to Jesus as the seed of the woman who would crush the head of the serpent.

Jesus had a superior revelation

"The Law was given through Moses; grace and truth were realized through Jesus Christ" (John 1:17). While Moses set up the moral and social structures which guided the nation, the Law could not save anyone from the penalty of their sins, which is death. As Paul says, "By the works of the Law no flesh will be justified in His sight; for through the Law comes the knowledge of sin" (Rom. 3:20). The revelation which came through Jesus, though, was one in which the sins which the Law made known are forgiven, "being justified as a gift by His grace through the redemption which is in Christ Jesus" (v. 24). Christ's revelation builds on the foundation of Moses by solving the problem of which the Law made us aware.

Jesus has a superior position

Moses is the greatest of the Old Testament prophets, but Jesus was more than a prophet. As the Book of Hebrews says, "Moses was faithful *in* all His house as a servant, for a testimony of those things which were to be spoken later; but Christ was faithful as a Son *over* His house" (Heb. 3:5-6, italics added). While Moses served God, Jesus was declared to be the Son of God with the right to rule over all servants.

Moses: The Lawgiver
Moses is not the founder of Judaism. The Jewish nation began with Abraham (ca. 2000 B.C.) about 600 years before Moses. Moses was born into a Hebrew family in Egypt and raised by Pharaoh's daughter to be a prince. After learning of his Hebrew heritage, he killed a man and fled Egypt to become a shepherd until God called him to free his people. He wrote the first five books of the Old Testament (Genesis, Exodus, Leviticus, Numbers, and Deuteronomy), which are known as the Pentateuch or Torah.

Jesus' miracles were superior

Moses certainly performed great miracles of the same kind that Jesus performed, but Christ's miracles were greater in degree. Moses lifted the bronze serpent to give healing to those who would look, but he never made the blind to see or the deaf to hear. Also, there is nothing in Moses' ministry to compare with the Resurrection.

Jesus' claims were superior to Moses

Simply put, Moses was not God; Jesus is. Moses never made a claim to be God and did nothing other than fulfill his role as a prophet. Jesus did claim to be God and provided miraculous evidence to prove it.

MOHAMMED

The founder of Islam, Mohammed, would agree with Jesus and Moses that God is one, that He created the universe, and that He is beyond the universe. In fact there is a great amount of agreement over the events of the first sixteen chapters of Genesis, to the point where Hagar was cast out from Abram's house. After this, the Bible focuses on Isaac while Islam is concerned with what happened to their forefather Ishmael. The teaching of Mohammed may be summarized in five doctrines. (1) Allah is the one true God. (2) Allah has sent many prophets, including Moses and Jesus, but Mohammed is the last and greatest of all. (3) The Koran is the supreme religious book, taking priority over the Law, the Psalms, and the Injil (Evangel) of Jesus. (4) There are many intermediate beings (angels) between God and us, some of whom are good and others are evil. (5) Each man's deeds will be weighed on a balance to determine if he will go to heaven or hell in the resurrection. The way to gain salvation includes reciting the Shahadah several times a day ("There is no God but Allah; and Mohammed is his prophet."), prayer five times a day, a month of fasting each year, almsgiving, and a pilgrimage to Mecca.

But we find that Jesus offers a superior message in many respects.

Jesus offers a better way of salvation

Unlike the God of Islam, the God of the Bible has reached out to us in a special way by sending His Son to earth to die for our

Mohammed: Prophet of Allah
Mohammed was born in Mecca in A.D. 570 and died in A.D. 632. Originally named Abu'l Kassim, he was orphaned at an early age and raised by his uncle, who took him on many long journeys with trade caravans. At twenty-five years of age, he married his employer, quit working, and spent his time meditating and reflecting on life. When he was forty, he began having visions accompanied by violent convulsions during which he received his revelation from Allah. Due to persecution, he and his followers fled Mecca to Yathrib, which he renamed Medina, and this is the official beginning of Islam. The next ten years were marked by almost constant fighting to gain new converts and new territory for his religion until Mecca was finally won. His writings are called the Koran, which he claims were dictated to him by the Angel Gabriel.

sins. Mohammed offered no sure hope for salvation, only guidelines for how to work our way into Allah's favor. Christ provided all that is needed to get us to heaven in His death. "For Christ also died for sins once for all, the just for the unjust, in order that He might bring us to God" (1 Peter 3:18).

Jesus offers a superior life
Mohammed spent the last ten years of his life at war. He was a polygamist, exceeding even the number of wives (four) he had prescribed for his religion. It is reported that he also violated his own law by plundering caravans coming to and from Mecca, some of whom were probably coming for their pilgrimage.

Jesus offers superior miracles
The stories of Mohammed moving the mountain and his military conquests do not compare to the miracles of Christ. The evidence for them is neither as early nor from eyewitnesses. There is no inherent goodness and compassion in them, as we see in Christ's miracles. And none of them can be likened to Jesus' resurrection for its power and uniqueness.

Jesus offers superior claims
Mohammed never claimed to be God. The doctrine of the Trinity, which explains how Jesus can be God, is misunderstood by

Islam as polytheism. Mohammed only claimed to be a prophet, but Jesus claimed to be God. Not only did He make that claim, but He proved it by rising from the dead.

HINDU GURUS

In the Hindu religion, there are a great number of sects and differences of opinion, so no generalizations apply to all Hindus, but the doctrines mentioned here are foundational to Hinduism. Guru means teacher, and these men are essential to Hinduism because the Hindu scriptures cannot be understood by reading; they must be learned from a guru. These men are considered holy and worshiped even after their deaths. What they teach is that man needs liberation from the endless cycle of reincarnation *(samsara)* which is brought on by karma, the effects of all words, deeds, and actions in the present and all former lives. Liberation *(moksha)* is obtained when the individual expands his being and consciousness to an infinite level and realizes that atman (the self) is the same as Brahman (the One absolute being from which all else proceeds). In other words, each Hindu must realize that he is God. Such a realization can only be achieved by following one of the following disciplines: (1) Jnana Yoga—salvation by knowledge of the ancient writings and inward meditation, (2) Bhakti Yoga—salvation by devotion to one of the many Hindu deities, (3) Karma Yoga—salvation by works, such as ceremonies, sacrifices, fasting, and pilgrimages, which must be done without thought of their rewards. Each of these methods will to some extent include Raja

---

The Beginnings of Hinduism
The Hindu religion had its earliest stages about 2000 B.C. The tribes living in the Indus Valley of northern India had a polytheistic religion that was primarily occult. These tribes were later conquered by armies from central Asia who combined their Vedic religion, which emphasized nature more than gods, with that of the Indus Valley tribes. This made a complete chain of gods and goddesses. The final period became more philosophical as writings called the Upanishads began to focus on one single principle to tie all reality together. This pantheistic principle is called Brahman. This period also introduced the idea of reincarnation.

Yoga, a meditation technique involving control over the body, breathing, and thoughts. This is what Hinduism is ideally. Hinduism as it is actually practiced consists largely of superstition, legendary stories about the gods, occult practices, and demon worship.

The teaching of Jesus Christ is superior to Hinduism in several significant ways.

Jesus teaches a superior worldview

In chapter 3 we discussed the problems with an atheistic worldview and concluded that theism was a superior view. As we said in evaluating pantheism, it is impossible to meaningfully say, "I came to realize I am God," since God always knew He was God. Yet the claim of godhood is the heart of all Hindu thought and religion.

Jesus is morally superior to the gurus

Classical Hinduism insists that suffering people be left to suffer because it is their destiny as determined by karma. Jesus said, "Love your neighbor as yourself," and He defined neighbor as anyone in need of help. John said, "But whoever has the world's goods, and beholds his brother in need and closes his heart against him, how does the love of God abide in him?" (1 John 3:17) Also, many, if not most, gurus use their esteemed position to exploit their followers financially and sexually. The Bagwan Sri Rajneesh accumulated dozens of Rolls Royces as gifts from his followers. The Beatles became disenchanted with the Maharishi Mahesh Yogi when they learned that he was much more interested in the body of one of the ladies in their party than with the spirits of any of them, and they admitted, "We made a mistake.

Jesus gives a superior method for spiritual enlightenment

While the gurus are necessary to understand the Bhagavad Gita and the Upanishads, the Bible can be understood by anyone. There is no esoteric or hidden truth there that must be explained apart from ordinary reasoning. Furthermore, Christian meditation is not an effort to empty the mind, but rather to fill it with the truth of scriptural principles (Ps. 1). Inward meditation is like peeling an onion; you keep tearing off layer after layer until, when you reach the middle, you find that there is nothing there. Meditation on God's Word begins with contentful sayings and opens up the meaning until it yields contentment of the soul.

Jesus teaches a better way of salvation

The Hindu is lost in the karmic cycle of reincarnation until he reaches *moksha*, and he is left alone to work his own way out. Jesus promised that we would be saved by faith and could know that our salvation is guaranteed (Eph. 1:13-14; 1 John 5:13).

BUDDHA

Siddhārtha Gautama (Buddha is a title meaning "enlightened one") developed a religion that is quite different from Judaism and Christianity. Buddhism began as a reformation within Hinduism, which had become a system of speculation and superstition. To correct this, Gautama rejected the rituals and occultism and developed an essentially atheistic religion (though later forms of Buddhism return to the Hindu gods). His basic beliefs are summed up in the Four Noble Truths: (1) Life is suffering, (2) Suffering is caused by desires for pleasure and prosperity, (3) Suffering can be overcome by eliminating desires, (4) Desire can be eliminated by the Eightfold Path. This Path is both a system of religious education and the moral precepts of Buddhism. It includes right knowledge (Four Noble Truths), right intentions, right speech, right conduct (no killing, drinking, stealing, lying, or adultery), right occupation (none which cause suffering), right effort, right mindfulness (denial of the finite self), and right meditation (Raja Yoga). The goal of all Buddhists is not heaven or being with God, for there is no God in Gautama's teaching. Rather they seek nirvana, the elimination of all suffering, desires, and the illusion that the self exists. While a more liberal branch of Buddhism now exists which has deified Gautama and thinks of him as a savior (called Mahayana Buddhism), Theravada Buddhism stays closer to Gautama's teachings and maintains that he never claimed divinity. As to being a savior, it is reported that Buddha's last words were, "Buddhas do but point the way; work out your salvation with diligence.'

Buddha: The Enlightened One

Siddhārtha Gautama was born around 560 B.C. to an upper-class family. His early years were very comfortable and sheltered, so he was in his twenties before he realized that there was great suffering in the world. He studied with Hindu masters and practiced asceticism for a time, then realized that both extremes (indulgence and asceticism) were futile. He chose the middle path of meditation. While meditating under a fig tree one day, he is said to have gained enlightenment and reached nirvana. The writings and sayings attributed to Buddha were written about 400 years after his death, so there is no way of knowing how reliable they are. He died of food poisoning about 480 B.C.

As a variant form of Hinduism, Buddhism is subject to all of the criticisms mentioned before, and Jesus' teaching seems superior in these ways also.

Jesus teaches hope in life

While Buddhism sees life only as suffering, and selfhood as something to be eradicated, Jesus taught that life is a gift of God to be enjoyed (John 10:10) and that the individual is to be honored supremely (Matt. 5:22). Furthermore, He promised hope in the life to come (John 14:6). Surely this is better than the elimination of desire and self that Gautama taught.

Jesus teaches a better way of salvation

The Buddhist also teaches reincarnation as the means of salvation. However, in this form the self or individuality of the soul is eradicated at the end of each life. So even though you live on, it is not you as an individual who has any hope of attaining nirvana. Jesus promised an individual hope to each man as an individual (John 14:3) and said to the thief on the cross beside Him, "Today you shall be with Me in paradise" (Luke 23:43).

Jesus teaches His own deity

Again, the last word on the subject is spoken by an empty tomb which proves Jesus' claims to be God in the flesh. Gautama made no such claim and offered no proof that it was the case. He simply wanted to point the way for others to follow him to nirvana.

SOCRATES

Socrates didn't leave any writings, but Plato, his disciple, wrote a great deal about him, though these accounts may reflect as much Plato's thought as Socrates'. Plato presents Socrates as a man convinced that God has appointed him the task of promoting truth and goodness by making men examine their words and deeds to see if they are true and good. Vice, in his opinion, was merely ignorance, and knowledge led to virtue. He is credited as the first man to recognize a need to develop a systematic approach to discovering truth, though the system itself was finally formulated by Aristotle—a disciple of Plato's. Like Christ, Socrates was condemned to death on the basis of false accusations from authorities who were threatened by his teaching. He could have been acquitted if he had not insisted on making his accusers and judges examine their own statements and lives, which they were unwilling to do. He was content to die, knowing that he had carried out his mission to the end, and that death, whether a dreamless sleep or a wonderful fellowship of great men, was good.

However, Jesus is clearly superior in many respects. For example:

Jesus had a superior basis for truth

Jesus, like Socrates, often used questions to make men examine themselves, but His basis for knowing the truth about men and God was rooted in the fact that He was the all-knowing God. He said of Himself, "I am the way, and the truth, and the life" (John 14:6). He was, in His very being, the fount from which all truth ultimately flowed. Likewise, as God, He was the absolute good-

---

Socrates: The Father of Reason

Socrates was born about 470 B.C. when the Greek Empire was flourishing. His parents were wealthy and he was well educated in philosophical matters. He began his campaign to teach truth and right when he heard from the Oracle at Delphi that he was the wisest man in the world. Socrates was sure that this could not be true, but after speaking with many other wise men, he concluded that it must be true because he was the only one who knew that he was not the wisest man in the world.

ness by which all other goodness is measured. He once asked a young man to examine his words by saying, "Why do you call Me good? No one is good except God alone" (Mark 10:18). Jesus was the very truth and good which Socrates wanted to understand.

Jesus gave a more certain knowledge of the truth
While Socrates taught many true principles, he often was left to speculate about many important issues, such as what happens at death. Jesus, on the other hand, gave a sure answer to such questions because He had sure knowledge of man's destination. Where reason (Socrates) has insufficient evidence to make a definite conclusion, revelation (Jesus) gives answers that otherwise would not be known.

Jesus' death was more noble
Socrates died for a cause and did so with courage, which is certainly to be commended. However, Jesus died as a substitute for others (Mark 10:45) to pay the penalty that they deserved. Not only did He die for those who were His friends, but also for those who were and would remain His enemies (Rom. 5:6-7). Such a demonstration of love cannot be equaled by any philosopher.

Jesus' proof of His message is superior
Rational proofs are good when there is sound evidence for their conclusions. But Socrates cannot support his claim to be sent by God with anything that compares to the miracles of Christ and His resurrection. In these acts there is a superior proof that Jesus' message was authenticated by God as true.

LAO-TZU (TAOISM)
Modern Taoism is a threefold religion of witchcraft, superstition, and polytheism, but it was originally a system of philosophy, and that is how it is being presented to Western culture today. Lao-tzu (if he ever existed) built this system around one principle which explained everything in the universe and guided it all. That principle is called the Tao (pronounced *dow*). There is no simple way to explain the Tao. The world is full of conflicting opposites,

like good and evil, male and female, light and dark, yes and no, etc. All oppositions are manifestations of the conflict between yin and yang. But in ultimate reality, yin and yang are completely intertwined and perfectly balanced. That balance is the mystery called the Tao. To understand the Tao is to realize that all opposites are one and that truth lies in contradiction, not in resolution. Taoism goes beyond this to say that man should live in harmony with the Tao. He should enter a life of complete passiveness and reflection on questions like, "What is the sound of one hand clapping?" or "If a tree falls in the forest when no one is there to hear it, does it make a sound?" One should be at peace with nature and avoid all forms of violence. This system of philosophy has many similarities to Zen Buddhism.

Christ is superior in the freedom that He brings to man.

Jesus allows man the freedom to be reasonable

We have said before that it is impossible to meaningfully say, "Reason does not apply to reality," because the statement itself is a reasonable statement about reality (it is either true or false about the way things really are). You would have to use reason to deny that reason is valid! But this is what the Tao does. It says that all truth lies in contradiction: the very thing reason says is impossible.

Lao-tzu: The Old Master
Legend has it that Lao-tzu was the keeper of the royal archives before he decided to travel to the unexplored West. As he was going, a gatekeeper persuaded him to write down the great wisdom he had gained in his occupation, so he wrote a book containing 5,000 characters in 81 brief paragraphs which elaborated his philosophy. That book is the *Tao Te Ching*. Though his dates are usually said to be in the sixth century B.C., virtually all the information we have about him is as legendary as this story. It is likely that these legends began developing in the time of the great Taoist philosopher, Chuang Tzu, who lived in the fourth and third centuries B.C. The writing of the *Tao Te Ching* can also be dated to this time. Chuang Tzu's commentary on the Tao is called the Tao Tsang. It has more than 1,100 volumes and is also considered scripture.

Truth is not only beyond reason, but says, "Love the Lord your God with all your heart, and with all your soul, and with all your mind. This is the great and foremost commandment" (Matt. 22:37-38). The God of the Old Testament even says, "Come now, and let us reason together" (Isa. 1:18). Jesus gives man the freedom to use reason to evaluate truth claims.

Jesus allows man the freedom to choose

Taoism asks man to set his will on the shelf, to give up the power to change things around him. Jesus says that man has a choice, and that his choice makes all the difference in the world. Man has a choice to believe or not believe (John 3:18), to obey or disobey (15:14), to change the world or be changed by it (Matt. 5:13-16).

Jesus allows man the freedom to be saved

Taoism offers only a way to resign oneself to the way things are. Christ offers a way to change both who we are and what we are, so that we might know the joys of life. Rather than accepting death as an inevitable end, Christ provides a way to conquer death by His resurrection. Lao-tzu could make no such boast.

So Jesus can be found to be superior to other teachers for many reasons. No other teacher has made the claims to be God that Jesus has. Even when the followers of some prophet deified their teacher, there is no proof given for that claim that can be compared to the fulfillment of prophecy, the sinless and miraculous life, and the Resurrection. No other teacher offered salvation by faith, apart from works, based on what they had already done for us. Most notably though, no religious or philosophical leader has displayed the love for people that Jesus did in dying for the sins of the world (John 15:13; Rom. 5:6-8). Jesus is truly worthy of supreme devotion.

NOTES

1. Calvin Blanchard, ed., *The Complete Works of Thomas Paine* (Chicago: Belford, Clark & Company, 1885), p. 234.

2. Bertrand Russell, *The Basic Writings of Bertrand Russell*, Rob-

ert Egner and Lester Denonn, eds. (New York: Simon & Schuster, 1961), p. 62.

3. Ibid., p. 594.

4. C.S. Lewis, *Mere Christianity* (New York: The Macmillan Co., 1943), pp. 55–56.

5. Peter W. Stoner, *Science Speaks* (Wheaton, Ill.: Van Kampen Press, 1952), p. 108.

6. Karl Popper, *Conjectures and Refutations* (New York: Harper and Row, 1963), p. 36.

7. William D. Edwards, M.D., et al. "On the Physical Death of Jesus Christ," *Journal of the American Medical Association,* 255:11, March 21, 1986, p. 1463.

8. Gary R. Habermas, *Ancient Evidence for the Life of Jesus* (Nashville: Thomas Nelson, Inc., 1984), pp. 125–126.

9. Wolfhart Pannenburg, cited by William Lane Craig in *The Son Rises* (Chicago: Moody Press, 1984), p. 141.

10. *Time,* June 4, 1979.

7

QUESTIONS ABOUT THE BIBLE

The Bible has many faces. It can be studied as literature and explored as a set of stories and poetic expressions, or viewed as history which tells us of the beginnings and growth of God's people. For some it is a guide to archeology, pointing the way to buried civilizations. There is a place and a purpose for each of those aspects, but at the basis of all, the Bible is the Word of God. It is God's message to a rebelling world of how it can return to Him. It is a love letter from God to us. But do we take this claim seriously? Or are we interested only in one aspect?

How important is the Bible? The earlier chapters of this book have shown that we can know that God exists, what He is like, how He can overcome evil, that He can perform miracles, and that Jesus is God without ever referring to the Bible as a sacred book. However, it must be said that while these arguments don't rely on the Bible, they are guided by it. They take the path of reason to reach these conclusions, but they are directed by the revelation. Without the Word of God, there is no guarantee that anyone would ever reach these conclusions. Even if they did, there might not be many who found them, and there is no telling how long it would take or how much error might be included along the way. Also, reason can take us only one step farther. That step leads us to the Scriptures as God's Word. If we are to have any knowledge of God's saving grace and love, then we must have the Word of God. The big question is, *"Is the Bible really a revelation from God?"* That is the question we will try to answer in this chapter.

HOW DO WE KNOW THAT
THE BIBLE CAME FROM GOD?

We know that the Bible came from God for one very simple reason: Jesus told us so. It is on His authority, as the God of the universe, that we are sure that the Bible is the Word of God. He confirmed the Old Testament's authority in His teaching, and He promised an authoritative New Testament through His disciples. The Son of God Himself assures us that the Bible is the Word of God.

JESUS CONFIRMED THE AUTHORITY
OF THE OLD TESTAMENT

Jesus spoke of the whole Old Testament (Matt. 22:29), its central divisions (Luke 16:16), its individual books (Matt. 22:43; 24:15), its events (19:4-5; Luke 17:27), and even its letters and parts of letters (Matt. 5:18) as having divine authority. He called the Scriptures the Word of God (John 10:35). He said that they had been written by men moved by the Spirit when He said, "David himself said in the Holy Spirit" (Mark 12:36) and refers to events "spoken of through Daniel the prophet" (Matt. 24:15). In such statements He confirms the authorship of the most often disputed books, like Moses' writings (Mark 7·10), Isaiah (v. 6), Daniel, and the Psalms. He also refers to the very miracles which critics reject as historical events. He cites the Creation (Luke 11:51), Adam and Eve (Matt. 19:4-5), Noah and the Flood (24:37-39), Sodom and Gomorrah (Luke 10:12), and Jonah and the great fish (Matt.

Outline of Argument for the Bible
God exists (chap. 2).
The New Testament is a historically reliable document (chaps. 7, 9).
Miracles are possible (chap. 5).
Miracles confirm Jesus' claim to be God (chap. 6).
Whatever God teaches is true (Num. 23:19; Heb. 6:18; 1 John 1:5-6).
Jesus (= God) taught that the Bible is the Word of God by confirming the Old Testament and promising the New Testament.
Therefore, the Bible is the Word of God.

What Jesus Taught about the Old Testament
1. Authority—Matthew 22:43
2. Reliability—Matthew 26:54
3. Finality—Matthew 4:4, 7, 10
4. Sufficiency—Luke 16:31
5. Indestructibility—Matthew 5:17-18
6. Unity—Luke 24:27, 44
7. Clarity—Luke 24:27
8. Historicity—Matthew 12:40
9. Facticity (scientifically)—Matthew 19:2-5
10. Inerrancy—Matthew 22:29; John 3:12; 17:17
11. Infallibility—John 10:35

12:39-41). He said, "It is easier for heaven and earth to pass away than for one stroke of the letter of the Law to fail" (Luke 16:17). The fact that He considered the Scripture to be the final authority is seen clearly in His temptations, when He defends himself from Satan's attacks three times with the phrase, "It is written" (Matt. 4:4ff).

"Here," Jesus was saying, "is the permanent, unchangeable witness of the eternal God, committed to writing for our instruction." Such it appears to have been to Jesus' inmost soul, quite apart from any convenience to Him in controversy. In the hour of utmost crisis and at the moment of death, words of the Scripture came to His lips: "My God, My God, why have You forsaken Me?" (Ps. 22:1; Matt. 27:46; Mark 15:34, NIV) "Into Your hands I commit My spirit" (Ps. 31:5; Luke 23:46, NIV).[1]

JESUS PROMISED THE NEW TESTAMENT

Jesus told His disciples just before He left them, "These things I have spoken to you while abiding with you. But the Helper, the Holy Spirit, whom the Father will send in My name, He will teach you all things, and bring to your remembrance all that I said to you" (John 14:25-26). Jesus added, "When He, the Spirit of Truth, comes, He will guide you into all the truth; for He will not speak on His own initiative, but whatever He hears, He will speak; and He will disclose to you what is to come" (16:13). These statements promise that the teachings of Jesus will be remembered and understood, and that additional truths would be given to the apostles so that the church could be established. They set the stage for the apostolic era which began on the Day of Pentecost (Acts 2:1ff) and continued until the last of the apostles died (John, about A.D. 100).

During this period, the apostles became the agents of the complete and final revelation of Jesus Christ and He continued "to do and teach" through them (Acts 1:1). They were given the "keys to the kingdom" (Matt. 16:19) and by their hands did believers receive the Holy Spirit (Acts 8:14-15; 19:1-6). The early church built its doctrines and practices on "the foundation of the apostles" (Eph. 2:20). It followed the "apostles' teaching" (Acts 2:42) and was bound by decisions of the apostolic council (Acts 15). Even though Paul had received his apostleship by a revelation from God, his credentials were confirmed by the apostles in Jerusalem.

Some of the New Testament writers were not apostles, though. How can we explain their authority? They used the apostolic message which was "confirmed to us by those who heard" (Heb. 2:3). Mark worked closely with Peter (1 Peter 5:13); James and Jude were closely associated with the apostles in Jerusalem and were probably Jesus' brothers; Luke was a companion of Paul (2 Tim. 4:11) who interviewed many eyewitnesses to produce his account (Luke 1:1-4). Paul's writings are even equated with Scripture by Peter (2 Peter 3:15-16). In each case (with the exception of Hebrews; we don't know for sure who wrote that book), there is a definite link between the writer and the apostles who gave them information (cf. 2:3).

Now if Jesus, who was God in the flesh and always spoke the truth, said that the Old Testament was the Word of God and that the New Testament would be written by His apostles and prophets as the sole authorized agents for His message, then our entire Bible is proven to be from God. We have it on the best of authority—Jesus Christ Himself.

HOW WAS THE BIBLE WRITTEN?

The process by which the Bible was written is called inspiration. The term comes from 2 Timothy 3:16, which says, "All Scripture is inspired by God [literally, God-breathed] and profitable for teaching, for reproof, for correction, for training in righteousness." God is the source of all that is said in the Bible. From Moses to John, a prophet is always a man who delivers God's message to men. That message begins with a revelation from God. That revelation might be a voice from a burning bush (Ex. 3:2), a series of visions (Ezek. 1:1; 8:3; Rev. 4:1), an inner voice of the prophet's communion with God ("The word of the Lord came unto me"), or derived from some earlier prophecy (Dan. 9:1-2).

But to be Scripture, the message had to be written too. Second Peter 1:21 gives us a description of this process: "No prophecy was ever made by an act of human will, but men moved by the Holy Spirit spoke from God." That word "moved" means, literally, "to be carried along," like a ship is carried by the wind. God carried each writer along as he wrote so that the message was kept intact.

Inspiration does not mean simply that the writer felt enthusiastic, like Handel composing the *Messiah*. Nor does it mean that the writings are necessarily inspiring, like an uplifting poem. As a process, it refers to the writers and the writings being controlled by God. As a product, it refers to the writings only, as documents that are God's message.

How does inspiration work? This remains largely a mystery, but we do know that it was done through prophets, as spokesmen for God. We also know that they were not mere secretaries. The secretary model suggests that men were merely taking divine dictation as they wrote the books of the Bible. This assures that God's message comes through, but it does not explain the human elements of the Scriptures, such as style differences, personal experiences related, and different languages used. Neither were they merely witnesses to revelation. Here the human author is seen as an observer of the revelation of God who is making a record of the experience. While his words may not be inspired, the concepts he records are. However, this model tends to neglect the divine aspects of inspiration in favor of emphasizing the human contribution to it, including human error. Such a view does not take seriously what the Bible says about inspiration because it does not include God in the writing process, and it implies that not all

Human Aspects of Scripture
It is written in different human languages (such as Hebrew and Greek) that exhibit dated linguistic forms.
It was written by some thirty-five different human authors.
It reflects grammatical irregularities.
It displays different human literary styles.
It shows human interests (2 Tim. 4:13).
It utilizes fallible human memory (1 Cor. 1:15-16).
It incorporates distinct human cultures (1 Thes. 5:26).
It speaks from a human observer's perspective (Josh. 10:12-13).
It reflects common human differences of perspective (differences in Gospel accounts).
It speaks of God from a human perspective (anthropomorphisms).

Scripture comes from God. The only adequate view incorporates both divine and human factors; it is the prophet model. In this process, the human writer is seen as one who has received a revelation and actively participates in its writing, while God gives the revelation and oversees the writing. Hence, the message is wholly from God, but the humanity of the writer is included to enhance the message. Both the divine and human concur in the same words (1 Cor. 2:13).

The net result is that we have the Word of God written by men of God, inspired not only in its concepts, but in the very words used to express those concepts. The human writers are not mere secretaries, but active agents who express their own experiences, thoughts, and feelings in what they have written. It is not simply a record of revelation, but a revelation itself. It is God's message in written form (Heb. 1:1; 2 Peter 1:21).

CAN THE BIBLE BE WRONG?

Just how trustworthy is the Bible? This has been one of the great issues of this century. Is the Bible *inerrant* (meaning no errors), or is it merely an *infallible* guide in matters of faith and practice (meaning that what it says about spiritual truths is true, but there may be errors in science, geography, and history)? While there are unbiblical views that reject the authority of the Word altogether or say that it becomes God's Word as you experience it, the above stated views are the center of the current debate.

The neo-evangelical view of infallibility states that the purpose of Scripture is to lead men to salvation (2 Tim. 3:15), and that any other subject that it might touch on (like botany or cosmology) is unimportant to that purpose, so what it says about those things may not be correct. They stress that the authors did not intentionally deceive us with these false statements, because either they did not know better, or else they simply accommodated themselves to the popular views of the times so that they could get their main point across, which had to do with salvation. Jack Rogers, one of the major proponents of this view, wrote:

[It] is no doubt possible to define the meaning of biblical inerrancy according to the Bible's saving purpose and taking into account the human forms through which God condescended to reveal Himself . . . to confuse error in the sense of technical accuracy with the biblical notion of error as willful deception diverts us from the serious intent of Scripture. The purpose of the Bible is not to substitute human science. The purpose of the

TWO VIEWS CONTRASTED

Neo-evangelical	Evangelical
True in whole, but not all parts.	True in whole and in all parts.
True spiritually, but not always historically.	True spiritually and historically.
True morally, but not always scientifically.	True morally and scientifically.
True in intention, but not in all affirmations.	True in intention and all affirmations.
Bible is infallible, not inerrant.	Bible is infallible and inerrant.
Bible is God's instrument of revelation.	Bible is intrinsically a revelation.
Bible is God's record of revelation.	Bible is God's revelation.
God speaks through the words of the Bible.	God speaks in the words of the Bible.
Human language is inadequate to communicate God.	Human language is adequate but not exhaustive.
Much of higher criticism may be accepted.	None of higher criticism is accepted.
Faith is opposed to reason.	Faith is not opposed to reason.

Bible is to warn against human sin and offer us God's salvation in Christ. It infallibly achieves that purpose.[2]

From this expression of this view, several things become evident. First, truth resides in the intention or purpose of the author, not in what he actually said. The apostles did not *mean* to mislead us in matters of science or history—that was not part of their intention—so it is all right if what they said was not true by normal standards. Meaning is found in purpose, not in what is affirmed. Jesus' intended meaning was that a little faith accomplishes a great deal; so if He made a mistake by calling the mustard seed the smallest seed (when an orchid seed is really smaller), then it doesn't matter—that wasn't part of His purpose. Second, human language is not really adequate for communicating truths about God. It is limited and this-worldly, and cannot really convey the unlimited God, who is so different from us. So error is unavoidable as long as we are stuck with human language. If God is to reveal Himself to us as we read the Bible, then He must do it in our experience as we read the text. He can't communicate *in* the words, but He can work *through* them to meet us in a personal way that goes beyond language. Finally, faith is opposed to reason. Reason cannot judge what is true about faith, and faith is not subject to reason nor provable by it. The methods for determining truth about this world don't work in the other world. Hence, science is right about scientific matters, and the Bible is right about spiritual matters.

Neo-evangelicals are right in pointing out that the Bible is not meant to be a science text. They also are correct in recognizing the limitation of human language. However, if their views were accepted, the results would be devastating.

Jesus' words and actions seem to contradict many of their claims. He said, "If I told you earthly things and you do not believe, how shall you believe if I tell you heavenly things?" (John 3:12) Jesus expected His accuracy in factually testable matters to be proof that He was telling the truth about spiritual matters that cannot be tested. Again, Jesus said to the crowd, "'Which is easier, to say to the paralytic, "Your sins are forgiven"; or to say, "Arise, and take up your pallet and walk"? But in order that you may know that the Son of man has authority on earth to forgive sins,' He said to the paralytic, 'I say to you, rise, take up your pallet and go home'" (Mark 2:9-11). Jesus proved that what He said about faith and the unverifiable realm was true by giving a very verifiable and physical healing. He made a point to say that what God says about this world demonstrates His truthfulness about the other world.

And what about Jesus' resurrection? Was it mythical or historical? If it was mythical, does that mean that it may not have happened in the real world where it could be tested? If it was historical, does that mean that it has no higher, spiritual meaning? Such a distinction is impossible to make, given the kind of evidence that Jesus offered to prove His deity.

Also, Jesus had the annoying habit of affirming the very passages that higher criticism calls errors. He affirmed things like Creation (Luke 11:51), Adam and Eve (Matt. 19:4-5), Noah and the Flood (24:37-39), Sodom and Gomorrah (Luke 10:12), and Jonah and the great fish (Matt. 12:39-41). He even went so far as to say that Moses wrote the Law (rather than Ezra or a collection of scribes; see Mark 7:10; John 7:19) and that Isaiah wrote all of Isaiah (critical scholars say the last half was written centuries later; see John 12:38-41 where both halves are quoted together and each is attributed to Isaiah). These passages show that Jesus linked the historical reality of the Old Testament with the truth of His own spiritual message.

The scholars respond by saying that Jesus was only accommodating the popular views of the day so that they would understand His main point without being distracted by the new knowledge that God used evolution and that some of the miracles never occurred. There are two serious problems with this idea. First, it is not like Jesus to accommodate popular opinion. He never hesitated to confront false beliefs head-on (Matt. 5:21-22, 27-28, 31-32; 15:1-9; 22:29; 23:1ff; John 2:13ff; 3:10). That is why He was always arguing with the Pharisees and the Sadducees. Second, and more important, this would amount to moral deception on Jesus' part. As God, He knew that what He was telling them was not true, but He told them anyway.

Philosophically, the infallibility position is unsatisfying. To say that truth is in the purpose or intention does not fit with what most people call truth. We expect truth to correspond to the reality that it talks about. If truth was only a matter of intention, then we could never know whether a statement was true or false because we can't know the intent in the mind of the one who spoke it. The same goes for meaning. If we can't tell what a person means by what he says, how can we know what his intended meaning was? Even if he tells us his intention to clarify it, he is still using language, and we can't be sure that he has expressed his true intention about his intention. Meaning and truth both become impossible. Also, it is self-defeating to say that language cannot express anything about God, because it just did—it expressed the idea that nothing could be expressed. Certainly there are limits to what our language can express about the infinite, but that doesn't mean we have to give up altogether. There are some things we can say in human language about God. If there weren't, how could the neo-evangelicals say that the Bible teaches truth about spiritual matters?

The view of most evangelicals is that the Bible teaches truth about both spiritual and scientific/historical matters. The passages

WHAT THE BIBLE SAYS . . . GOD SAYS.
(and vice versa)

God said	= "Scripture said"
Gen. 12:3	Gal. 3:8
Ex. 9:6	Rom. 9:17

Bible said	= "God said"
Gen. 2:24	Matt. 19:4-5
Ps. 95:7	Heb. 3:7
Ps. 2:1	Acts 4:24-25
Isa. 55:3	Acts 13:34
Ps. 16:10	Acts 13:35
Ps. 2:7	Heb. 1:5
Ps. 97:7	Heb. 1:6
Ps. 104:4	Heb. 1:7

THE WORD OF GOD:

Incarnate	Inspired
Hidden in God from eternity — John 1:1	Eternal thoughts of God — Ps. 119:89; Eph. 3:9
Conceived by Holy Spirit — Luke 1:35	Inspired by Holy Spirit — 2 Tim. 3:16; 2 Peter 1:21
Born a common man — Phil. 2:7	Written in common language — 1 Cor. 2:4-10
Perfect, sinless — John 8:46; Heb. 4:15	Perfect, inerrant — John 17:17; Ps. 19:8
Bore witness to Scriptures — Matt. 5:17-18	Bore witness to Christ — Luke 24:27
Reveals the Father — John 1:18; Heb. 1:1-2	Reveals the Son — John 5:39

which were used in reference to inspiration seem to suggest that this is what the Bible claims for itself and the way Jesus understood it. Examination of the evidence suggests that the Bible is extremely reliable in historical and scientific matters, and its critics have been proven wrong over and over again (see chaps. 8–10). More fundamentally, if the Bible is the Word of God and God can only speak truth, then there is no way to avoid the conclusion that the Bible contains no errors. Inspiration guarantees inerrancy. Just look at the way what the Bible says and what God says are equated. Jesus said that God said, "For this cause a man shall leave his father and mother," but a close examination of Genesis 2:24 shows these were Moses' words. Likewise, Paul attributes a direct quote from God to "Scripture." Where the Bible speaks, God speaks and God cannot lie.

This does not mean that the *way* we understand the Bible is perfectly true; it means that the Bible is true when understood rightly. Nor does it mean that everything in the Scriptures must be understood literally. There are figures of speech on almost every page, but there is a big difference between telling truth in a metaphor and telling tales with a myth. Further, inerrancy does not mean that everything that is *recorded* in the Bible is true, but that what is *affirmed as true* is true. Cain said, "Am I my brother's keeper?" implying that he was not. The Bible records that he said it, but it does not endorse his attitude. After all, this came from a man who just killed his brother! The teaching of the passage is that we *are* responsible for the well-being of others.

Finally, there is an analogy between the written Word of God and the Living Word. While neo-evangelicals say that error is due to the introduction of human thought and human language, they must somehow account for the fact that Jesus Christ was both fully human and fully divine, yet without sin. In both cases the human and divine are wedded, yet the human aspects have no imperfections. This suggests that sin and error are not necessary consequences of humanity; they are only accidental. God can produce both a Person and a Book that are without error.

HOW WAS THE BIBLE PUT TOGETHER?

How do we know that the sixty-six books of the Bible are the only writings that should be included in Scripture? What about the Apocrypha, or the Gnostic gospels? Why shouldn't they be included? The answer lies in the idea of canonicity. Canon comes from Greek and Hebrew words that mean a measuring rod, and it signifies a standard that all scriptural books must meet. Several inadequate views of what that standard should be have been offered, such as age, agreement with the Torah if it was written in Hebrew, religious value, and Christian usage. But each of these makes a common mistake; they confuse God's *determination* of what is Scripture with man's *recognition* of those writings. The bottom line is that whatever God inspired is Scripture and what He did not inspire is not. When the Holy Spirit moved a man of God to write, that writing became, not only inspired, but inscripturated. God has already decided what should be included; our problem is knowing how to discover what writings God has inspired.

There are five questions that have been asked by the church in accepting and rejecting books as canonical. The first is the most basic:

Books That Were Questioned[3]

Hebrews—Because the author is unknown. Accepted as having apostolic authority, if not apostolic authorship.

James—Because of conflict with Paul's teaching about salvation by faith alone. Conflict resolved by seeing works as an outgrowth of real faith.

2 Peter—Because the style differs from 1 Peter. But Peter used a scribe to write 1 Peter (see 5:12), who may have helped him smooth out his Greek.

2 and 3 John—Because author is called "elder," not apostle. However, Peter called himself an elder too (1 Peter 5:1). They are cited in the earliest lists of canon.

Jude—Because he refers to the Book of Enoch and the Assumption of Moses. He does not call them Scripture, though, much like Paul quoting pagan poets (Acts 17:28; Titus 1:12). It had wide early acceptance.

Revelation—Because it teaches a thousand-year reign of Christ, which was taught by a certain cult. It was accepted by the earliest church fathers, though.

1. *Was it written by a* prophet *of God?* Deuteronomy 18:18 tells us that only a prophet of God will speak the Word of God. This is the way that God reveals Himself (Heb. 1:1). Second Peter 1:20-21 assures us that Scripture is only written by men of God.
2. *Was he confirmed by an* act *of God?* Hebrews 2:3-4 gives us the idea that we should expect some miraculous confirmation of those who speak for God. Moses had his rod that turned into a serpent, Jesus had the Resurrection, and the apostles continued Jesus' miracles, all to confirm that their message was from God. Many of the prophets had prophecies fulfilled shortly after they were made to confirm their authority.
3. *Does it tell the* truth *about God?* "But even though we, or an angel from heaven, should preach to you a gospel contrary to that which we have preached to you, let him be accursed" (Gal. 1:8). Agreement with all earlier revelation is essential. This dictum also rules out false prophecies made in the name of God (Deut. 18:22).

4. *Does it have the* power *of God?* Any writing that does not exhibit the transforming power of God in the lives of its readers is not from God, "For the Word of God is living and active and sharper than any two-edged sword" (Heb. 4:12).

5. *Was it* accepted *by the people of God?* Paul thanked the Thessalonians for receiving the apostles' message as the Word of God (1 Thes. 2:13). It is the norm that God's people, that is, the majority of them and not simply a faction, will initially receive God's Word as such. Moses' scrolls were placed immediately into the ark of the covenant (Deut. 31:24-26) and Joshua's writings were added in the same fashion (Josh. 24:26), as were Samuel's (1 Sam. 10:25). Jeremiah is known as the plagiarizing prophet because he quoted so many of the other prophets who had written only a few years before him, which shows that their writings had been readily accepted. Daniel is seen studying the Book of Jeremiah within fifty years after it was written (Dan. 9:2). The New Testament also shows similar acceptance in that Peter calls Paul's writings Scripture (2 Peter 3:16) and Paul quotes Luke alongside a passage from the Law (1 Tim. 5:18). We also are aware that Paul's letters were circulated among the churches (Col. 4:16; 1 Thes. 5:27). This may have been the beginning of the collection of books for the New Testament canon. Though some books were later disputed, their original acceptance speaks strongly in favor of their inclusion.

But what about the books that were left out? This question has the wrong perspective on the issue. No other books were ever accepted and there is no reason to believe that most of them were even in the running. For both the Old and New Testaments there are certain books that were accepted by everyone, some books that were later disputed, and some that were rejected by all. There is no category of books initially accepted and later thrown out. There are, however, two groups of books that many are saying should have been included. These are the Apocrypha and the Gnostic gospels.

WHAT ABOUT THE APOCRYPHA?

The Apocrypha is a set of books written between the third century B.C. and the first century A.D. It consists of fourteen books (fifteen if you divide the books differently) which are found in the several ancient copies of important Greek translations of the Old Testament and reflect some of the Jewish tradition and history that came after the time of Malachi (the last Old Testament prophet). Most of the Apocrypha was accepted as Scripture by Augustine and the Syrian church in the fourth century and was later canonized by the Catholic church. The apocryphal books are alluded to in the New Testament and by the early church fathers and have been found among the Dead Sea Scrolls at Qumran.

However, these books were never accepted by the Jews as Scripture and are not included in the Hebrew Bible. Though the New Testament may allude to them (e.g., Heb. 11:35), none of the allusions are clearly called the Word of God (Paul quotes pagan poets too, but not as Scripture). Augustine admitted that it has

WHAT IS THE APOCRYPHA?

Revised Standard Version	Douay
1. The Wisdom of Solomon (ca. 30 B.C.)	Book of Wisdom
2. Ecclesiasticus (132 B.C.)	Ecclesiasticus
3. Tobit (ca. 200 B.C.)	Tobias
4. Judith (ca. 150 B.C.)	Judith
5. I Esdras (ca. 150–100 B.C.)	(rejected)
6. I Maccabees (ca. 110 B.C.)	I Maccabees
7. II Maccabees (ca. 110–70 B.C.)	II Maccabees
8. Baruch (ca. 150–50 B.C.)	Baruch chap. 1–5
9. Letter of Jeremiah (ca. 300–100 B.C.)	Baruch chap. 6
10. II Esdras (ca. A.D. 100)	(rejected)
11. Additions to Esther (140–130 B.C.)	Esther 10:4–16:24
12. Prayer of Azariah (1st or 2nd cent. B.C.)	Daniel 3:24-90
13. Susanna (1st or 2nd cent. B.C.)	Daniel 13
14. Bel and the Dragon (ca. 100 B.C.)	Daniel 14
15. Prayer of Manasseh (1st or 2nd cent. B.C.)	(rejected)

secondary status to the rest of the Old Testament. One reason for supporting it was that it was included with the Septuagint (a Greek translation), which he considered to be inspired; but Jerome, a Hebrew scholar, made the official Latin Vulgate version of the Old Testament without the added apocryphal books. Those churches that have accepted the Apocrypha have done so long after it was written (fourth, sixteenth, and seventeenth centuries). The fathers who cited these writings are offset by others who vehemently opposed them, such as Athanasius and Jerome. In fact, these books were never officially added to the Bible until A.D. 1546 at the Council of Trent. But this is suspect in that they accepted these books on the basis of Christian usage (the wrong reason) just twenty-nine years after Martin Luther had called for some biblical support for beliefs like salvation by works and prayer for the dead (which the Apocrypha provides: 2 Maccabees 12:45-46; Tobit 12:9). As for the Qumran finds, hundreds of books have been found there that are not canonical; this offers no evidence that they accepted the apocryphal books as anything other than popular literature. Finally, no apocryphal book claims to be inspired. Indeed, some specifically deny that they are inspired (1 Maccabees 9:27). If God did not inspire it, then it is not His Word.

WHAT ABOUT THE GNOSTIC GOSPELS?

The Gnostic gospels and the writings related to them are part of the New Testament pseudepigrapha, which means "false writing." They are so called because the author has used the name of some apostle rather than his own name, for example, the Gospel of Peter and the Acts of John. These were not written by the apostles, but by men in the second century (and later) pretending to use apostolic authority to advance their own teachings. Today we call this fraud and forgery. For the people who advance these writings as legitimate Christian tradition, this poses no problem, because they think that much of the New Testament was written in the same way. The books teach the doctrines of the two earliest heresies, both of which denied the reality of the Incarnation. They said that Jesus was really only a spirit that looked like a man; so His resurrection was just a return to spiritual form. They claim to

Are the Gnostic gospels on a par with Scripture? The following is a story from the Gospel of Thomas. Read it and decide for yourself.

> But the son of Annas the scribe was standing there with Joseph; and he took a branch of a willow and (with it) dispersed the water which Jesus had gathered together. When Jesus saw what he had done he was enraged and said to him: "You insolent, godless dunderhead, what harm did the pools and the water do to you? See, now you shall wither like a tree and shall bear neither leaves nor root nor fruit." And immediately that lad withered up completely; and Jesus departed and went into Joseph's house. But the parents of him that was withered took him away, bewailing his youth, and brought him to Joseph and reproached him: "What a child you have, who does such things." [Gospel of Thomas 3:1-3]

provide information about Jesus' childhood, but the stories they record are highly unlikely and are not from eyewitnesses. No one ever accepted these as Scripture in any sense except the heretical factions which created them. They are not a legitimate part of the Christian tradition, but a record of the myths and heresies which arose outside of the mainstream of Christianity.

HOW RELIABLE ARE OUR MODERN BIBLES?

Nowhere in the Bible is there a promise of purity of the text of Scripture throughout history, but there is a great deal of evidence that suggests that the Bibles we read are extremely close to the original, inspired manuscripts that the prophets and apostles wrote. This evidence is seen in the accuracy of the copies that we have. Such reliability helps support our claim that the Bible is valuable as a historical account as well as a revelation from God. Since each testament has its own tradition, we must deal with them separately.

OLD TESTAMENT MANUSCRIPTS

If we want to know about the Old Testament, we must look to its keeper, the Jewish religion. What we find is, at first, not encouraging. Keeping a manuscript written on animal skins in good shape

History of the Masoretic Text

As a result of the destruction of Jerusalem in A.D. 70, there was a revival in Judaism. As the Bible became more important to the people, the need for a standardized Hebrew text to support the strong, oral tradition became clear. This text consisted only of the consonants, as there were no symbols for vowels. The scribes who copied the text actually counted the letters and words to make sure there were no errors. They found that the "w" in a word in Leviticus 11:42 was the middle letter of the Torah and "drsh" in 11:42 was the middle word. Markings were added around the text to show accents, weekly Scripture readings, and syntax. Vowel symbols were created which could be written under the consonants and not corrupt the text. The major work of the scribes was to transcribe the Masorah, which were marginal and endnotes about the text itself pointing out problem spots to copyists, how often a word is used, and concordance-like lists. Passing on the text of the Old Testament became a whole way of life to these men.

for 3,000–4,000 years is not easy, and the Jews did not even try. Rather, out of respect for the sacred writings, they had a tradition that all flawed and worn-out copies were to be ceremoniously buried. Also, the scribes who standardized the Hebrew text (uniting all of its oral traditions and adding vowels, which written Hebrew does not have) in the fifth century, probably destroyed all copies which didn't agree with theirs. So we only have a few manuscripts that date from the tenth century of the Christian era, and only one of these is complete. That's the bad news.

Here's the good news. The accuracy of the copies we have is supported by other evidence. First, all of the manuscripts, no matter who prepared them or where they were found, agree to a great extent. Such agreement from texts that come from Palestine, Syria, and Egypt suggests that they have a strong original tradition from way back in history. Second, they agree with another ancient source of the Old Testament, the Septuagint (Greek translation), which dates from the second and third century. Finally, the Dead Sea Scrolls provide a basis of comparison from 1,000 years before our manuscripts were written. That comparison shows an astonishing reliability in transmission of the text. One scholar observed that the two copies of Isaiah found in the Qumran caves, "proved to be word for word identical with our standard Hebrew Bible in more than 95 percent of the text. The 5 percent of variation consisted chiefly of obvious slips of the pen and variations in spelling."[3] The main reason for all of this consistency is that the scribes who made the copies had a profound reverence for the text. Jewish traditions laid out every aspect of copying texts as if it were law, from the kind of materials to be used to how many columns and lines were to be on a page. Nothing was to be written from memory. There was even a religious ceremony to perform each time the name of God was written. Any copy with just one mistake in it was destroyed. This guarantees us that there has been no substantial change in the text of the Old Testament in the last 2,000 years and evidence that there was probably very little change before that.

NEW TESTAMENT MANUSCRIPTS

For the New Testament, the evidence is overwhelming. There are 5,366 manuscripts to compare and draw information from, and some of these date from the second or third centuries. To put that in perspective, there are only 643 copies of Homer's *Iliad*, and that is the most famous book of ancient Greece! No one doubts the text of Julius Caesar's *Gallic Wars*, but we only have 10 copies

---

New Testament Textual Problems

Most of the textual difficulties in the New Testament are quite trivial, such as deciding between five different word orders for "Who are you then: Are you Elijah?" (John 1:21) all of which have the same sense. Some, however, are more important. First John 5:7 in the *Authorized Version* is omitted from the newer translations simply because there is only one Greek manuscript from 1,520 that contains it. The story of the woman caught in adultery (John 7:53–8:11) may be a later addition since all of the earliest manuscripts, translations, and church fathers omit it and even the copies that have it insert it in four different locations. The ending of Mark's Gospel (16:9-20) is probably not original, but there is little agreement about what the original ending was. This is one of the toughest textual problems in the New Testament and no certainty may ever be reached.

of it and the earliest of those was made 1,000 years after it was written. To have such an abundance of copies for the New Testament from dates within 70 years of their writing is amazing.

With all those manuscripts, there are a lot of little differences. It is easy for someone to leave the wrong impression by saying that there are 200,000 "errors" that have crept into the Bible when the word should be "variants." A variant is counted any time one copy is different from any other copy and it is counted again in every copy where it appears. So when a single word is spelled differently in 3,000 copies, that is counted as 3,000 variants. In fact, there are only 10,000 places where variants occur and most of those are matters of spelling and word order. There are less than 40 places in the New Testament where we are really not certain which reading is original, but not one of these has any effect on a central doctrine of the faith. Note: the problem is not that we don't *know what* the text is, but that we are not *certain which* text has the right reading. We have 100 percent of the New Testament and we are sure about 99.5 percent of it.

But even if we did not have such good manuscript evidence, we could actually reconstruct almost the entire New Testament from quotations in the church fathers of the second and third centuries. Only eleven verses are missing, mostly from 2 and 3 John. Even if all the copies of the New Testament had been burned at the end of the third century, we could have known virtually all of it by studying these writings.

Some people have balked that inerrancy is an unprovable doctrine because it refers only to the original inspired writings, which we don't have and not to the copies that we do have. But if we can be this certain of the text of the New Testament and have an Old Testament text that has not changed in 2,000 years, then *we don't need the originals to know what they said*. The text of our modern Bibles is so close to the original that we can have every confidence that what it teaches is truth.

SUMMARY

This chapter has shown that the Bible is the Word of God. This teaching stands on no lesser authority than Jesus Christ Himself,

who confirmed the inspiration of the Old Testament and promised the New Testament. The testimony of Jesus and the apostles
is that the Bible is inerrant in what it teaches about all matters,
down to the tenses of verbs and the very last letters of words. Also
we have a great deal of evidence to show that the Bibles we have
in our hands represent the original manuscripts with a very high
degree of accuracy, like no other book from the ancient world.
The Bible in your hand is God speaking to you.

NOTES

1. John W. Wenham, "Christ's View of Scripture" in *Inerrancy*,
   ed. by Norman L. Geisler (Grand Rapids: Zondervan, 1979),
   pp. 15–16.

2. Jack Rogers, "Church Doctrine and Biblical Inspiration" in
   Biblical Authority (Waco, Texas: Word, 1977), pp. 45–46.

3. Gleason Archer, Jr., *A Survey of Old Testament Introduction*
   (Chicago: Moody, 1964), p. 19. See also N.L. Geisler and
   W.E. Nix, *General Introduction to the Bible* (Chicago: Moody,
   1968), pp. 249–266.

8

QUESTIONS ABOUT BIBLE DIFFICULTIES

"How can you believe that stuff? Don't you know the Bible is chock-full of contradictions and mistakes?" This is the reaction some Christians have come to expect when they confront non-Christians with scriptural evidence. George Gershwin devoted an entire song in *Porgy and Bess* to the claim that "dem things that you's liable to read in the Bible, dey ain't necessarily so." Sometimes this critic can be silenced if you just say, "Name one." A great many people have only heard that there are problems in the Bible, but have never examined the evidence. However, if you try this and get an answer, you better be prepared to explain the difficulty. There are real problems in the Bible, but there are also real answers to those difficult passages.

WHAT ARE THE GUIDELINES FOR HANDLING DIFFICULT PASSAGES?

Before we start listing rules, let's talk about attitude. The burden of proof rests on the critics. We have very good reasons to believe that the Bible tells the truth since there is good evidence that the *whole* Bible is inspired by God (see chap. 7). As long as we show that there is a *possible* solution—that their objection "ain't *necessarily* so"—then the conflict has been resolved. Like any American citizen, the Bible should be presumed innocent until proven guilty. Like a reliable friend, it should be given the benefit of the doubt. A scientist always assumes that there is an explanation when faced with some unexpected and unexplained anomaly. In the same way, a Bible student assumes that there is a harmony in the Bible in light of what appear to be contradictions. The presence of these types of problems motivates the student to dig deeper and find information that otherwise he may have never come across.

BE SURE YOU KNOW WHAT THE TEXT SAYS

Often a misquoted verse will mislead someone. More often, there is a textual problem that is disguised in your English translation. Especially in the Old Testament where numbers are involved, a minor copyist's error might have been incorporated into the text. A good commentary can tell you about these things and probably answer 90 percent of the objections you will encounter. Remember that our Bibles are only inerrant inasmuch as they agree with the originals that God inspired. It is crucial that we have the right text before we try to solve any problem.

BE SURE YOU KNOW WHAT THE TEXT MEANS

That may sound redundant, but it isn't. The Bible uses some words and phrases that may not mean exactly what you expect

---

Money Is a Root of All Evil

This verse (1 Tim. 6:10) is as often misquoted as quoted and is a great illustration of the importance of knowing what the text says and what it means. What the text says is, "The love of money is a root of all sorts of evil." The love of money—not money itself—is decried. It is not the only source of evil but it is called a root. The Greek text says "all evil," but the idea of "all sorts" is implied by the phrase. That is what it says.

But what does it mean? The preceding verses introduce the subject of contentment with the essentials of life, and verse 9 says, in contrast, "Those who want to get rich fall into temptation and a snare." Verse 10 explains this by stressing the fact that there is a root which inevitably grows evil and is very hard to dig out. That root is the love of money. The phrase "all evil" is probably exaggeration for the sake of emphasis. The point in the text is that one should make sure this root does not grow into his life.

them to mean. For example, some have complained that Jesus was wrong to call the mustard seed the smallest seed when an orchid seed is really smaller. A closer examination of what Jesus *said* reveals that the word He used for "seed" *means* garden seeds that yield a crop. He says it was a seed which a man sows in the field (Matt. 13:31; Mark 4:31) and compares it to the garden plants.

Also remember that some words change meaning in different contexts. A *trunk* might belong to an elephant, a car, a salesman, or a tree: its meaning depends on the context in which it is used. In Acts 19:32, the word usually used for "church" or "congregation" is used for a "mob" in a town forum. Look closely at the context and the meaning of the words to be sure that you really understand what is meant by what is said. In this regard, the Bible is the best interpreter of itself. Clear passages often help in understanding difficult ones, and phrases are often used in other contexts that help to clarify their meaning. There is no substitute for comparing Scripture with Scripture.

DON'T CONFUSE ERROR WITH IMPRECISION

Precision with measurements is crucial for an aircraft engineer, but those requirements are not necessary in other areas. Rounded numbers do fine when trying to give a general idea of the size of an object or an army. Likewise, quotations don't have to be reproduced verbatim from their source. No one was going to grade the biblical authors on their form as if they were writing research papers. As long as it can be shown that their citation is faithful to the meaning of the text quoted, imprecision can be tolerated. This is the same standard accepted by today's media. One can be faith-

---

Measurements of the Laver

First Kings 7:23 says that the laver, a huge basin for washing, in Solomon's temple was ten cubits in diameter with a circumference thirty cubits. Now any schoolboy who's taken geometry knows that a circle with a diameter of ten cubits has a circumference of 31.4159 cubits (circumference is diameter times pi). So some critics have mentioned this as a possible problem, but round numbers are not the same thing as error. Pi (3.141) rounds off to three quite nicely and that would give an answer of thirty cubits.

ful to the idea without using the exact same words.

DON'T CONFUSE FALSITY WITH PERSPECTIVE

Just because a witness only sees part of the accident or only sees it from one angle doesn't mean that his testimony is false. So also, when a biblical writer records a part of an event which he saw and fails to mention some other part that someone else saw, his record is still true. These differences in accounts assure us that the authors did not conspire to "get their story straight."

LANGUAGE ABOUT THE WORLD IS EVERYDAY LANGUAGE

Language about the world is often expressed from human perspective. If an archeologist 2,000 years from now found a copy of the book *The Sun Also Rises,* would he be justified in concluding that our culture had no concept that the earth revolves around the sun? No, we often speak of things as they appear to us rather than as we know them to be in the bigger picture of things. The same goes for the biblical authors, who speak of the sun standing still (Josh. 10:12) and heaven being above the earth (Isa. 40:22). There is no reason to assume that the Bible is supporting any theory that the earth is the center of the universe; this is the normal way to express these ideas.

REMEMBER THAT THE BIBLE RECORDS THINGS THAT IT DOES NOT APPROVE

The Bible is largely a book of history. As such, it sometimes records things without approving them. For example, David's sins (2 Sam. 11) and Solomon's polygamy (1 Kings 11:1-8) are recorded without any sermons condemning them. It also records Satan's lie without approving it (Gen. 3:4-5). The sermons are not necessary because the condemnation is clearly stated elsewhere.

HOW CAN WE RESOLVE SOME OF THESE DIFFICULTIES?

Having set out these guidelines, let's look at a few of the problems that critics have noticed and apply our principles to real situations

It would be impossible to answer every possible question in a book like this, but there are a few very good books that answer a lot of them. These are typical and frequently raised problems. If you want to have more answers to more questions, we recommend Gleason L. Archer's *Encyclopedia of Bible Difficulties* (Grand Rapids: Zondervan, 1982). Several of the answers that follow came from there.

GENEALOGICAL PROBLEMS

Genesis 5
Some complain that the wording of the genealogy in Genesis 5 would force one to conclude that the human race began in 4004 B.C., which is at odds with the archeological evidence suggesting a much earlier appearance of man. We are aware that some Christians would dispute the archeological findings, but that is not necessary and may not be biblically correct. Luke 3:36 states very clearly that there is at least one gap in the accompanying genealogy in Genesis 10:24—Cainan the son of Arphaxad. While Genesis says that Shelah was the son of Arphaxad, Luke inserts Cainan between them. So the genealogy in Genesis 5 is not complete. There are gaps.

That sounds like an even bigger problem until you do some

The Need of the Moment
Gleason Archer's preface to his *Encyclopedia of Bible Difficulties* reads:

"The idea for this book first occurred to me in October 1978, in connection with the Summit Conference of the International Council on Biblical Inerrancy, held in Chicago. At that time it was apparent that a chief objection to inerrancy was that the extant copies of Scripture contain substantial errors, some of which defy even the most ingenious use of textual criticism. In my opinion this charge can be refuted and its falsity exposed by an objective study done in a consistent, evangelical perspective. Nothing less than the full inerrancy of the original manuscripts of Scripture can serve as the basis for the infallibility of the Holy Bible as the true Word of God."

checking on how the Bible uses the term "father." Matthew 1:8 says that Joram was the father of Uzziah, but they were separated by three generations (see 2 Kings 8–15). Jesus said that Abiathar was the high priest who gave David the showbread (Mark 2:26), but Samuel says that it was Ahimelech, Abiathar's son (1 Sam. 21:1; 2 Sam. 8:17). The point is that the Bible uses the terms "father" and "son" to denote any direct ancestry or descendance. So trying to prove that genealogies like Genesis 5 have no gaps misses the meaning of the text. Also, there is no statement at the end of this genealogy to say what the total time from Adam to Noah was, as there is for the time spent in Egypt (Ex. 12:40) and the founding of the Northern Kingdom to its exile (Ezek. 4:5).

Christ's genealogies

The two genealogies for Christ are identical between Abraham and David, then part ways after that, Matthew tracing His lineage through Solomon, and Luke following it through Nathan. The objection is that these genealogies cannot both be right. The church fathers from the fifth century on, however, have submitted the simple solution that Matthew gives the descent from Joseph while Luke cites His lineage through Mary. The fact that sons-in-law are listed as sons is seen where Shealtiel is said to be the son of Jeconiah in Matthew (which he was by birth) and Neri in Luke (which we presume he was by marriage). Joseph would likewise be listed as a son to Mary's father. This distinction of bloodlines is in keeping with the respective themes of the books: Matthew presenting Christ the King, who continued the royal line through Joseph, His legal father; and Luke presenting the Son of man, who became flesh through Mary, who actually bore Him. (Jewish law stated that any child born to a man's fiancée was his legal child. Joseph and Mary were engaged at the time of the virgin conception [Matt. 1:18]). This seems to be an adequate explanation.

ETHICAL PROBLEMS

Slaughter of the Amalekites

First Samuel 15:2-3 says, "Thus says the Lord of hosts, 'I will punish Amalek for what he did to Israel . . . while he was coming

TWO GENEALOGIES OF JESUS

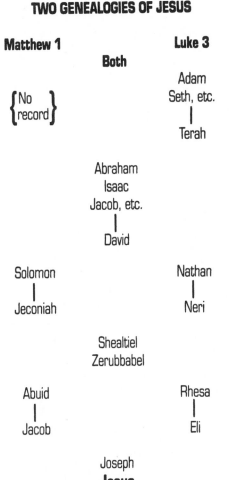

Matthew 1	Both	Luke 3
		Adam
{ No record }		Seth, etc.
		Terah
	Abraham	
	Isaac	
	Jacob, etc.	
	David	
Solomon		Nathan
Jeconiah		Neri
	Shealtiel	
	Zerubbabel	
Abuid		Rhesa
Jacob		Eli
	Joseph	
	Jesus	

up from Egypt. Now go and strike Amalek and utterly destroy all that he has, and do not spare him; but put to death both man and woman, child and infant, ox and sheep, camel and donkey.'" Similar passages refer to the slaughter of the Canaanites as Israel entered the land (Deut. 7:2; Josh. 6:15-21; 8:26-27; 10:40; 11:12, 20). One critic says of this,

I speak for no one except myself, but I believe that killing innocent people is morally wrong. And killing Canaanite civilians is to be sharply distinguished from killing soldiers in the battles that were necessary for the Israelites to conquer the land that God had promised them. I frankly find it difficult to believe that it was God's will that every Canaanite—man, woman, and child—be slaughtered. Since the Bible clearly says that this was God's will, I must conclude that the biblical writers in this case were mistaken. The error of confusing patriotic sentiment with God's will is a common one in human history, but it is an error nonetheless.[1]

Were the human authors of Scripture speaking for themselves and not for God? Is it possible that God could have commanded these massacres? First, we must recognize that the reason for asserting that there is an error here is a subjective one—personal moral sentiment. This is the authority that judges what can or cannot be called the Word of God. Second, it is misplaced sentiment. True, it is wrong for man to kill innocent people, but it is not necessarily wrong for God. As the Giver of life, He has the right to take it as He wills (Job 1:21; Deut. 32:39). If the above critic's thinking were carried out consistently, wouldn't one have to repudiate the destruction of Sodom and Gomorrah and the flood in Noah's time too? Third, it is false to assume that these people were "innocent." In fact, the Bible tells us that the Canaanites were so guilty that the land "vomited" them out (Lev. 18:25, NIV). Even children are conceived in sin (Ps. 51:5). Finally, it is presumptuous to think that our own moral standards should judge God and tell Him what is right and wrong. God's unchangeably just nature is the standard for justice.

David's census

What motivated David to take the census that brought a pestilence on Israel and death to 70,000 men? Second Samuel 24:1 says that God prompted David to do it in His anger, but 1 Chronicles 21:1 ascribes the deed to Satan. How can this be?

As the story unfolds, we see that David had become overly concerned with the material abundance and physical military power that the nation had amassed, and probably the whole country was beginning to feel proud and self-sufficient. God evidently

Satan and Believers

The same dynamics are seen for believers in 1 Peter 4:19 and 5:8. God's purpose in our sufferings is that we might better understand the life we have in Christ, but Satan seeks only to devour us. God uses Satan's destructive tendencies to further His program for us. Sometimes we have to learn lessons the hard way, and Hebrews 12:6 reminds us that "He scourges every son whom He receives." As that author concludes, "All discipline for the moment seems not to be joyful, but sorrowful; yet to those who have been trained by it, afterwards it yields the peaceful fruit of righteousness."

wanted to correct this trend. In the first chapter of Job, we read that Satan challenged God to let him afflict Job and test him. God allowed this in order to perfect Job's faith. We see much the same thing happening here. God was angry at Israel and David for their lack of faith in His power, and Satan was willing to destroy whatever he could; so God allowed Satan to incite David to take the census.

Both God and Satan were at work in motivating David. Satan did so actively, and God did so permissively in accordance with His plan. The final result of this event was that David purchased the site which would become the location of the temple.

HISTORICAL PROBLEMS

Dating the Exodus

Many archeologists and scholars date Israel's Exodus from Egypt about 1290 B.C. This is based primarily on the reference in Exodus 1:11 to the city of Raamses as the site where the Israelite slaves worked. The assumption is that, if the city was named after Ramses the Great, then the Exodus must have taken place after 1300. However, 1 Kings 6:1 says that it was 480 years from the date of the Exodus to the commencement of Solomon's temple in 966 B.C., dating the Exodus around 1446 B.C.—150 years earlier than supposed. Who is right? The Bible or these scholars?

It should first be pointed out that the Bible is consistent on this point. Around 1100 B.C. Jephthah said that Israel had occupied its territory for 300 years, meaning that the Conquest was around 1400 (Jud. 11:26). When the 40 years of wandering is added to this, the date of the Exodus comes out near 1440 again. Likewise, Acts 13:19-20 states that 450 years had elapsed from the Exodus to the end of Samuel's days as a prophet. Samuel died near the beginning of David's reign about 1000 B.C., putting the flight from Egypt very near 1446. So if the author of Kings (probably Jeremiah) was wrong, then so was the author of Judges (Samuel?) and so was Paul! So to doubt the early date (ca. 1400) for the Exodus would be to doubt the reliability of major parts of both Testaments (Judges, 1 & 2 Samuel, 1 & 2 Kings, Jeremiah, Lamentations, Acts, and thirteen letters of Paul).

But what about the archeological evidence and the name Ramses? Well, the evidence never has fit very well with the later date. In fact, six of the cities that Joshua is said to have conquered did not have anyone living there in the early 1200s. The evidence that originally led archeologists to think that the Israelites would not have found Moabites and Edomites in Palestine before 1300 has been shown to be wrong as excavations have continued. Also, it has been found that there was considerable building going on in the region where Ramses the Great built his city both when the Israelites first became slaves and in the 1400s. The reference in Exodus could refer to either of these periods. The one time it cannot refer to is 1290, for this is said to be where the slaves worked before Moses was born. He was eighty years old when he told Pharaoh to let the people go, so that would mean that work was begun on Ramses' city well before Ramses was born! On the other hand, there was a nobleman named Ramose in the reign of Thutmose III (1482–1447 B.C.) and evidence traces the name to before the time of Moses' birth. After all, Ramses the Great was Ramses II; Ramses I came several centuries earlier. A new theory for redating some of the archeological evidence and reconstructing the history of the period has been proposed which would yield "a remarkable correlation between biblical tradition and archeological evidence."[2] Another theory shows that there is a duplication in the record of Egyptian kings which has disrupted the harmonization of Egyptian and Israelite history. In this theory, Ramses I had finished the building of those cities. The point stands, though, that there is no reason to suppose that the Exodus must be later than 1300. Much of the evidence supports the date given by the biblical authors, and no hard evidence contradicts it. (See chap. 9 for further discussion.)

Numerical discrepancies

In the Old Testament historical books, there are occasional disagreements between the numbers given in Samuel and Kings and those listed in Chronicles (written after the exile to Babylon). One such case is that 2 Samuel 10:18 records the number of charioteers killed by David as 700, while 1 Chronicles 19:18 lists 7,000 men killed in that incident. These are the numbers used in the accepted Hebrew text, but there is nothing to prove that the discrepancy existed in the original manuscripts (and inerrancy only refers to these). The error amounts to adding or subtracting a zero while copying. Because of the extreme care taken to make the copies uniform, once an error like this entered the text it would remain there and be faithfully reproduced.

The same kind of thing occurs in 2 Chronicles 36:9 where Jehoiachin is listed as eight years old when he becomes king rather than eighteen (2 Kings 24:8), and in 1 Kings 4:26 which multiplies the number of Solomon's stalls by ten (40,000 instead of 4,000 in 2 Chron. 9:25). Some have charged that Ezra inflated his figures when writing Chronicles to enhance the glory of Israel; however, of the eighteen discrepancies between historical books, Chronicles has the higher number only seven times. We must refer the reader elsewhere to deal with the other problems. Suffice it to say that transmissional errors seem to be the cause of these problems.

Parallel accounts in the Gospels

Many critics have blasted the Gospels because of variations in their records of the same events. Some even insist that it is impossible to harmonize all of the accounts into a cohesive whole. The existence of such harmonies as A.T. Robertson's should suffice to quiet these complaints, but some still persist. A common objection is found in Peter's denials. All accounts agree that Christ told Peter he would deny Him three times, but there appear to be more than three denials recorded. Also, Mark 14:30 says that the cock will crow twice and proceeds to mention two crows (vv. 68,

72), but there is only one crow spoken of in the other Gospels. There are, however, possible solutions which account for all the evidence without contradiction.

First, as to the number of cock crows, there is no real problem if we understand that Mark simply included a detail that the others omitted. Since Peter himself was probably the source of Mark's information (they are related in 1 Peter 5:13), there is no reason to doubt his word. It is reasonable to think that Peter might have noticed a cock crowing after the first denial and that he would include such details that the other disciples ignored because it had more personal relevance to him.

The number of denials can be harmonized as follows:

First Denial	Second Denial	Third Denial
Matt. 26:69-70; Mark 14:66-68; Luke 22:55-57; John 18:17-18 Peter is warming himself by a fire in the court and a servant of the high priest brings the accusation, knowing that he entered with John. John's description of the scene follows his account of the denial. A cock crows, noted by Mark.	Matt. 26:71-72; Mark 14:69-70a; Luke 22:58; John 18:25 Peter has moved to a different fire on the porch when a second servant brings the same accusation.	Matt. 26:73-74; Mark 14:70b-72; Luke 22:59-60; John 18:26-27 A relative of Malchus first recognizes Peter, then others note that his accent is Galilean. A second cock crows, noted by all.

Second, it is possible that there is a copyist's mistake in Mark 14:68, 72. The statement "and a cock crowed" may have been inadvertently written into verse 68 when it was originally only in verse 72. The word "second" would have been inserted later by someone seeking to clarify it. One of the very best Greek manuscripts supports this and a few other copies agree.

As long as it is possible to reconcile alleged contradictions in one of these ways, there is no real contradiction. Since there are possible solutions, the Bible should be given the benefit of the doubt.

Gospel Harmonization

There are two big problems that face anyone trying to put the Gospels together into a single story: the similarities in Matthew, Mark, and Luke, and the differences in John. Some early critics thought that John was making up his own life of Christ, but careful study has shown that the different events mentioned in John really hold the keys to the chronological order of the other Gospels. Also, John sometimes adds details that make sense of puzzling things. The other three Gospels, because of their similarities, are called the Synoptics (which means "seeing together"). While these Gospels often record the same events, they do it in a different order and often with some real differences. In some cases, we find that Jesus used the same phrase or parable on more than one occasion and this has caused confusion. Luke tends to organize events by subject while Mark puts all the parables in one place, then all the miracles, etc.

QUOTATION PROBLEMS

Citing Old Testament authors

The New Testament quotes the Old numerous times, but sometimes it does not appear to refer to the right source. Matthew 27:9 attributes to Jeremiah a sentence found in Zechariah 11:13. The solution to this may be found in the frequent practice that, whenever referring to more than one prophet, the more famous of the two is named. In this case, Zechariah's verse tells us that the thirty pieces of silver paid to Judas was given to the potter, but the context makes it clear that the point of the quotation is in the second sentence which is added on to the first and comes from Jeremiah (19:2, 11). Zechariah does not mention the field, but Jeremiah does. So Matthew simply follows the practice of citing the more important author. The same thing occurs in Mark 1:2-3, where both Malachi and Isaiah are quoted, but only Isaiah is mentioned in the reference.

Extrabiblical sources

Especially in the Book of Jude, there has been a great deal of discussion about the use of questionable sources. Jude seems to quote from the Book of Enoch, a forgery of the period between

Old Testament in the New

Any serious student of Scripture has run across an occasion where a New Testament author has changed the words of an Old Testament passage or applied it in a way that does not seem to fit its original meaning. We expect that they should recite verses in the same way we do our memory verses; however, the apostles tended to use either free renditions or a Greek translation when quoting the Old Testament. There were no standardized translations at that time, and some Greek translations were either not accurate or not specific enough for the biblical writer. The real question is, "Is the meaning that the apostle uses found in the original text?" In some cases, it takes a lot of research, but the New Testament has proven to be the best interpreter of the Old.

the Old and New Testaments, as if the patriarch Enoch, "the seventh from Adam," had really said it (v. 14). He also alludes to the dispute over Moses' body—an event that is recorded in the Assumption of Moses, a book of similar character (v. 9). Did Jude really think that these sources were reliable, and perhaps even inspired?

The critical premise for this objection is that Jude could have only known what he read and accepted this uncritically. However, this ignores the work of the Holy Spirit in Jude's writing. First of all, the text does not say that he quoted from any book. It is at least possible that God gave Jude information about these events that we have only in Jude's record itself. Second, it is also possible that both Jude and these other sources are referring to true oral traditions which are not recorded anywhere in Scriptures, but relate facts from the historical events. Such an oral tradition may have been the basis of Moses' information about the times from Adam to Joseph. Finally, even if Jude is quoting from these books, there is no reason to suppose that his confirmation of these details requires that either he or we should accept the whole of these works. Paul quotes from pagan poets (Acts 17:28; 1 Cor. 15:33; Titus 1:12), but does not suggest that their writings are inspired, only that what they say in one aspect is true. Paul even confirmed in Titus 1:12 that only the statement he referred to was trustworthy, because the quotation is from a Cretan saying, "All Cretans are liars." Anything else that poet said could be a lie, but we have Paul's assurance here.

SCIENTIFIC PROBLEMS

Joshua's extended day

Since chapter 10 will deal with the major issues of science, this section will just mention a scientific problem that isn't discussed there. Joshua records that God extended the daylight for a period of about a day so that Israel could defeat the Gibeonites (Josh. 10:12-14). This has raised the objection that, if the earth were to cease its rotation, the laws of physics would wreak havoc on everything on the planet's surface including the seas. There are two ways to respond to this, both having some merit. First, the text does not demand that the earth's rotation stop. Rather, it suggests that it slowed down as verse 13 says, the sun "did not hasten to go down for about a whole day." This indicates that the sun still moved across the sky, speaking in terms of appearance, but did so at a slower rate. It is still possible, though, that even this slowing would upset the gravitational balance, which leads to the second response. If God could make the sun shine for an extra twenty-four hours, couldn't He work out the details of how it was done too? This is a miracle, after all. Whatever supernatural causes God used to slow the earth, why couldn't He also use these causes to maintain order while He did it? Any God big enough to accomplish the first part of the miracle is big enough to do the whole thing. The only reason to raise such an objection is disbelief that a miracle could have happened at all. In that case, see chapter 5.

The critics can shout "Contradiction!" or "Error!" all day long, but they better do their homework first. Sometimes they have asked questions that really needed an answer, and this has initiated research which helped us to understand more about the Bible, but they haven't really shown that the Bible is wrong. The principles for solving the problems are reasonable and the answers often incorporate the best and latest scholarship available. But keep this chapter in perspective. As Kenneth Kantzer has said,

Evangelicals do not try to prove that the Bible has no mistakes so that they can be sure the Bible is the Word of God. One might prove that a newspaper article is free from all mistakes, but that would not prove that the newspaper article is the Word of God. Christians hold the Bible to be the Word of God (and inerrant) because they are convinced that Jesus, the Lord of the church, believed it and taught His disciples to believe it.[3]

NOTES

1. Stephen T. Davis, *The Debate about the Bible* (Philadelphia: Westminster Press, 1977), pp. 96–97.

2. John J. Bimson and David Livingston, "Redating the Exodus" in *Biblical Archeology Review*, 8:5 September–October 1987, pp. 40–53, 66–68.

3. Kenneth Kantzer, Foreword to Gleason L. Archer, *Encyclopedia of Bible Difficulties* (Grand Rapids: Zondervan, 1982), p. 7.

9

QUESTIONS ABOUT ARCHEOLOGY

Biblical archeology is a fascinating subject. Over the years it has shed so much light on the historicity and meaning of the biblical stories that archeology has a mutually beneficial relationship with biblical studies. Noted archeologist Nelson Glueck has boldly asserted,

> As a matter of fact, however, it may be clearly stated categorically that no archeological discovery has ever controverted a single biblical reference. Scores of archeological findings have been made which confirm in clear outline or exact detail historical statements in the Bible.[1]

Before we go on, let's talk a little bit about the nature of interpreting archeological evidence. It must first be remembered that there are no self-interpreting facts. There are no pieces of evidence that carry their own interpretation. Meaning can only be derived from context. Archeological evidence is dependent on the context of date, place, materials, and style. Most important, how it is understood depends on the interpreter's presuppositions and worldview. Therefore, not all interpretations of the evidence will be friendly to Christianity.

Also, archeology is a special kind of science. Physics and chemistry can do all kinds of experiments to re-create the processes they study and watch them over and over again. Archeologists cannot. They have only the evidence left from the one and only time that

that civilization lived. They study past singularities, not present regularities. And because they can't re-create the societies that they study, their conclusions can't be tested in the same way as other sciences. Archeology tries to find plausible and probable explanations for the evidence it finds. It cannot make laws like physics can. For this reason, all conclusions must be subject to revision. The best interpretation is that which explains the evidence in a consistent way.

There would not be room in several books this size to cover all of the information that archeology has contributed in helping us understand more about the times and peoples of the Scriptures. This chapter cannot answer all of the challenges to biblical authority. Our purpose here is to show that archeology does confirm the historicity of the Bible and that, in doing so, it often enhances our understanding of that text.

DOES ARCHEOLOGY CONFIRM
THE OLD TESTAMENT?

While there may still be some questions unanswered and others that may never be answered, the overall conclusion remains the same: Archeology has confirmed the history of the Old Testament, not only in its general outline, but in many details also. We will discuss several periods of history and show a few of the things which archeology has enlightened in each.

THE CREATION

Genesis 1–11 is typically thought of as a mythological explanation derived from the earlier versions of the story found in the ancient Near East. Could Moses really have had such intimate knowledge of things that happened thousands of years before he was born? (Adam's conversations in the Garden? the materials used in the Tower of Babel? the measurements of the ark?) Archeology has shown that the earlier attempts to discredit the Bible for these reasons were premature. Let's take it one question at a time.

Is the Creation account history or myth?

Some choose only to notice the similarities between Genesis and

Creative Apologetics?

There is no doubt that a man with Moses' fine education was familiar with the creation accounts of the Babylonians and Sumerians. They were as popular in their day as Homer was to the Greeks or Shakespeare to the English. The similarities between them and the Bible don't appear coincidental. So why would Moses make his story of Creation so much like the others? The answer probably lies in the differences. The other versions speak of Tiamat battling with Marduk; but Moses uses similar words to show that God created the sea without doing battle. Both accounts speak of a separation of heaven and earth, but in Genesis it is by divine command, not conflict. The sun, moon, and stars already existed in the Babylonian tale, but Moses said that God created these too. Man was created to relieve the workload of the pagan gods; however, the true God made man as the ruler over creation—the one who would receive His blessing, His fellowship, and His image. In short, Moses could have been making a direct comparison to show that God is superior to any other deity. In this way, Moses was doing basic apologetics by making these differences clear.

the creation stories in other ancient cultures; however, the differences are even more important. The similarities might lead one to think that Moses was copying ancient legends, but the likenesses are only skin-deep. The Babylonian and Sumerian accounts describe the creation as a conflict between several finite gods. When one god is defeated and split in half, the River Euphrates flows from one eye and the Tigris from the other. Man is eventually made of the blood of an evil god mixed with clay. These tales display the kind of perversion and embellishment that we expect to find when a historical account becomes mythologized. You know how a rumor always swells and grows until you can hardly recognize the facts that started it. That happens to all stories. It is becoming increasingly accepted that myths and legends are usually based on fact. In the case of the creation accounts, the polytheistic accounts, though earlier than the Hebrew version, seem to be embellishments of the facts found in Genesis.

The common assumption that the Hebrew account is simply a purged and simplified version of the Babylonian legend (applied also to the Flood stories) is fallacious on methodological grounds. In the ancient Near East, the rule is that simple accounts or traditions may give rise (by accretion and embellishment) to elaborate legends, but not vice versa. In the ancient Orient, legends were not simplified or turned into pseudo-history (historicized) as has been assumed for early Genesis.[2]

The recent discoveries of Creation accounts at Ebla confirm this. This library of more than 17,000 clay tablets predates the Babylonian account by about 600 years. The Creation tablet is strikingly close to Genesis, speaking of one being who created the heavens, moon, stars, and earth. People at Ebla even believed in Creation from nothing. This shows that it is the Bible that contains the ancient, less embellished version of the story and transmits the facts without the corruption of the mythological renderings.

WAS THE FLOOD A REAL EVENT?

As with the Creation accounts, the Flood narrative in Genesis can be shown to be more realistic and less mythological than the other ancient versions, indicating its authenticity. The superficial similarities point not toward plagiarism by Moses, but toward a historical core of events that gave rise to all. While the names may change (Noah is called Ziusudra by the Sumerians and Utnapishtim by the Babylonians), the basic story doesn't. A man is told to build a ship to specific dimensions because God(s) is going to flood the world. He does it, rides out the storm, and offers sacrifice on exiting the boat. The Deity(ies) responds with remorse over the destruction of life, and make a covenant with the man. These core events point to a historical basis. Similar accounts are found all over the world. The Flood is told of by the Greeks, the Hindus, the Chinese, the Mexicans, the Algonquins, and the Hawaiians. Also, one list of Sumerian kings treats the Flood as a real event. After naming eight kings who lived extraordinarily long lives (tens of thousands of years), this sentence interrupts the list: "[Then] the Flood swept over [the earth] and when kingship was lowered [again] from heaven, kingship was [first] in Kish."[3]

But is there good reason to believe that Moses has given us the most historically reliable record? A lot of things suggest that to be the case. The other versions contain elaborations that display corruption. Only in Genesis is the year of the Flood given, as well as dates for the whole chronology relative to Noah's life. In fact, Genesis reads almost like a diary or ship's log of the events. The cubical Babylonian ship could not have saved anyone from the Flood. The raging waters would be constantly turning it over on every side. However, the biblical ark is rectangular—long, wide, and low—so that it would ride the rough seas well. The length of the rainfall in the pagan accounts (seven days) is not enough time for the devastation they describe. The waters would have to rise at least above most mountains, to a height of above 17,000 feet, and it is more reasonable to assume a longer rainfall to do this. The idea that all of the floodwaters subsided in one day is equally absurd. There is also a striking note of realism because, in the other accounts, the hero is granted immortality and exalted, while in the Bible, we see that Noah sinned. Only a version that seeks to tell the truth would include this.

Some have suggested that this was a severe but local flood, not a worldwide flood. There is geological evidence to support a worldwide Flood. Partial skeletons of recent animals are found in

---

Wait a Minute

It would seem like the most natural thing in the world to argue that if there are flood stories in the Middle East, Asia, Hawaii, North America, and Mexico, then the Flood must have happened in all those places. But wait a minute, if there was a Flood, and Noah's kin were the only survivors, then there wasn't anyone left in all those other places to tell the story. Doesn't that prove that it is all just a popular legend? We have to admit that these worldwide stories don't prove that the Flood occurred in all these places. Rather, it shows that all of these stories had a common origin. If Noah and his family were indeed the only survivors, and these survivors spread all over the earth, then they took with them the tale of the Flood as a part of the folklore to explain why they were going to new lands. These stories don't necessarily prove the worldwide nature of the deluge, but they do indicate a reliable tradition that it really happened.

deep fissures in several parts of the world, and the Flood seems to be the best explanation for these skeletons.

Rehwinkel (*The Flood*) indicates that these fissures occur even in hills of considerable height, and they extend from 140 feet to 300 feet. Since no skeleton is complete, it is safe to conclude that none of these animals (mammoths, bears, wolves, oxen, hyenas, rhinoceros, aurochs, deer and many smaller mammals) fell into these fissures alive, nor were they rolled there by streams. Yet because of the calcite cementing of these heterogeneous bones together, they must necessarily have been deposited underwater. Such fissures have been discovered in Odessa by the Black Sea, in the island of Kythera off the Peloponnesus, in the island of Malta, in the Rock of Gibraltar, and even at Agate Springs, Nebraska. . . . This is exactly the kind of evidence that a brief but violent episode of this sort would be expected to show within the short span of one year.[4]

The widespread findings of these skeletons make a worldwide Flood likely (cf. Gen. 6–9; 2 Peter 3:5-7).

WAS THERE REALLY A TOWER OF BABEL?

There is considerable evidence now that the world did indeed have a single language at one time. The Sumerian literature alludes to this several times. Linguists also find this theory helpful in categorizing languages. But what of the tower and the confusion of tongues?

It is interesting to note that Ur Nammu, King of Ur from about 2044 to 2007 B.C., supposedly received orders to build a great ziggurat (temple tower) as an act of worship to the moon god Nannat. A stele (monument) about five feet across and ten feet high shows Ur Nammu's various activities, and one panel has him setting out with a mortar basket to begin construction of the great tower. In this way he was showing his allegiance to the gods by taking his place as a humble workman. A clay tablet has been unearthed that states that the erection of the tower offended the gods, so they threw down what the men had built,

Trivial Genealogies

Most people wonder sometimes why God took the trouble to write down the names of all those folks in a list like the one in Genesis 10. The only benefit some can see is that it lets them practice their speed reading during their quiet time. These lists were not trivial to the people who wrote them though. They were the family tree. And you can never tell when something might come to light that makes one of those names really meaningful. For example, one of the names found in the Ebla tablets is Ibrium. There has been some talk about this being Eber, a forefather of Abraham. The names Abraham and Hebrew are derived from this name. It turns out that he was a king of Ebla. That makes him pretty important, and it tells us something of Abraham's social standing. Can't we derive some benefit from knowing that God can move so mightily in the life of a wealthy man of royal lineage who was in the public eye like Abraham? What a dramatic decision it must have been for him to leave the land where his roots were so deep.

scattered them abroad, and made their speech strange. This, of course, bears an interesting similarity to the record in the Bible[5] (Gen. 11).

HOW COULD MOSES HAVE KNOWN ABOUT ALL THESE THINGS?

The simple answer to this is that God revealed them to him, but that answer requires a belief that God could and would do so, which is exactly what the skeptic doubts. However, there may be an explanation which, while it doesn't rule out divine guidance, can explain how ancient traditions can be passed on without corruption. P.J. Wiseman has argued that the history of Genesis was originally written on clay tablets and passed on from one generation to the next with each "clan leader" being responsible for keeping them edited and up-to-date. The main clue that Wiseman found for this in the Bible is the periodic repetition of words and phrases. Tablets are kept in order by making the first words of a new tablet a repetition of the last words of the previous stone. The author would then put his name at the end of what he had written with the phrase, "These are the generations of" (Gen. 2:4; 5:1; 6:9; 10:1; 11:10, 27; 25:12, 19; 36:1, 9; 37:2). It's not as efficient as page numbers, but certainly effective. He shows quite convincingly that this was an established pattern in the ancient Orient. This literary evaluation of the book indicates that "every part of the Book of Genesis furnishes evidence that it was compiled in the present form by Moses and that the documents from which it was compiled were written much earlier, certainly not later than the time of Moses."* It is quite possible that Genesis is a family history recorded by the patriarchs themselves and passed on to Moses.

THE PATRIARCHS

While the narratives of the lives of Abraham, Isaac, and Jacob do not present the same kinds of difficulties as the earlier chapters of Genesis, they were long considered legendary because they did not seem to fit into the known evidence of that period. As more has become known, however, these stories become increasingly enlightened and verified. Law codes have now been found from the

---

Legal Jargon

One of the things that we have learned about ancient times is that there were specialized legal patterns when making covenants. It just so happens that Deuteronomy follows one of those patterns. It is the kind of contract that is drawn up between a ruler and his servants, called a suzerainty covenant. The Hittites of Moses' time used this form frequently. It consists of six parts:

1. The author is named in the preamble.
2. There is a brief history of the relationship between the two parties emphasizing why the servant should be grateful for past blessings.
3. The stipulations or responsibilities of the vassal are laid out by the sovereign.
4. A copy of the covenant is to be deposited in the worship place of the people. This copy is to be read periodically.
5. Several gods are cited as witnesses to the agreement.
6. A set of blessings and cursings is laid out to show how the Lord will respond if His servants do or do not keep their part of the covenant.

The Book of Deuteronomy follows this pattern. It is really a legal document—a contract between God and Israel.

time of Abraham that show why the patriarch would have been hesitant to throw Hagar out of his camp, for he was legally bound to support her. Only when a higher law came from God was Abraham willing to put her out. The discovery of the Mari letters reveals such names as Abam-ram (Abraham), Jacob-el, and Benjamites. Though these do not refer to the biblical people, they at least show that the names were in use. These letters also support the record of a war in Genesis 14 where five kings fought against four kings. The names of these kings are now seen to fit with the prominent nations of the day. For example, Genesis 14:1 mentions an Amorite king, Arioch; the Mari documents render the king's name Ariwwuk. All of this evidence leads to the conclusion that the source material of Genesis may have come from firsthand accounts of someone who lived during Abraham's time.

The destruction of Sodom and Gomorrah was thought to be spurious until evidence began pouring in to show that all five of the cities mentioned in Genesis 14 were in fact marketing centers in the area and are geographically situated as the Scriptures say. The biblical description of their demise seems to be no less accurate.

> The reconstruction of this incident points to earthquake activity, and the evidence is strong that the various layers of the earth were disrupted and hurled high into the air. Bitumen is plentiful there, and a good pictorial description would be to say that brimstone (bituminous pitch) was hurled down on those cities that had rejected God. There is evidence that the layers of sedimentary rock have been molded together by intense heat. Evidence of such burning have been found on the top of Jebel Usdum (Mount Sodom). This is permanent evidence of the great conflagration that took place in the long distant past, possibly when an oil basin beneath the Dead Sea ignited and erupted.[7]

Such an explanation in no way subtracts from the miraculous quality of the event, for God is certainly in control of natural causes too. The timing of the event, in the context of warnings and visitation by angels, is indicative of divine involvement.

THE DATING OF THE EXODUS

While scholars do not doubt that the nation Israel came out of Egypt and came into Palestine, they do not agree with the biblical statements as to when this happened. The Generally Accepted Date (GAD) for the entrance into Canaan is about 1230–1220 B.C. The Scriptures, on the other hand, teach in three different places (1 Kings 6:1; Jud. 11:26; Acts 13:19-20) that the Exodus occurred in the 1400s B.C. and the entrance into Canaan forty years later. There are several ways that this problem can be handled, and the verdict is not yet in as to which is the best. At least we can say that (1) there is no longer any reason to accept the GAD and (2) that some resolution is possible.

The GAD was based on three faulty assumptions: that "Raamses" in Exodus 1:11 was named after Ramses the Great, that there were no building projects in the Nile Delta before 1300, and that there were no great civilizations in Canaan from the nineteenth century to the thirteenth. All of these, if true, would make the conditions described in Exodus impossible before 1300 B.C. However, the name Raamses is not an uncommon name in Egyptian history and may have honored an earlier nobleman by that name. Since Ramses the Great is Ramses II, there must have been a Ramses I. Also, in Genesis 47:11, the name Raamses is used to describe the area of the Nile Delta where Jacob and his sons settled. This may be the name that Moses normally used to refer to the area. Second, there have been building projects now found in the area that date from the nineteenth–seventeenth centuries, the time of the Israelites' arrival, at Pi Ramesse (Raamses) and at both possible sites for Pithom. These also show strong Palestinian influence. Digging done in 1987 shows that there was building at Pi Ramesse and one of the Pithom sites in the 1400s. So whether Exodus 1:11 refers to the building projects that were going on at the time the Israelites became slaves, or what they were working on at the time of the Exodus, there is evidence that building was being done at both times. Finally, surface surveys have yielded no signs of civilizations like the Moabites and the Edomites prior to Israel's entrance to the land, but digging deeper has found many sites that fit into the period. Even the man who did the initial research changed his position later. So all three of the arguments for dating the Exodus after 1300 have been proven false by further research. Now if these three assumptions are wrong, then there is no reason to suppose a late date for the Exodus, and we can look for evidence to support the Bible's date of about 1446 B.C.

There are at least two ways to reconcile the data with the date suggested by the Bible. Both agree that the chronology of ancient history must be adjusted to make their theories work. The first offers a basis for adjusting the archeological periods, and the second reinterprets the chronology of Egyptian rulers. Because these changes would shake up a lot of widely held opinions about ancient history, they have faced much opposition, but the evidence for both theories has some merit.

Bimson-Livingston revision

The first theory, introduced by John Bimson and David Livingston in 1987, is that the date of the shift from the Middle Bronze to Late Bronze Ages be moved. They first show that the late date is unacceptable, as we have. But the problem does not end there because the destroyed cities in Caanan are dated about 1550 B.C.—150 years too early. This date is assigned to them because it is supposed that they were destroyed when the Egyptians drove out the Hyksos, a hostile nation that dominated Egypt for several centuries. Bimson suggests that moving the end of the Middle Bronze Age which would show that this destruction was done by the Israelites, not the Egyptians.

Can such a change be justified? The Middle Bronze (MB) was characterized by fortified cities; the Late Bronze (LB) had mostly smaller, unwalled settlements. So whatever caused the destruction of these cities gives us our date for the period division. The traditional date has come under fire lately because the evidence is sparse and unclear. Also, there is doubt that the Egyptians, just establishing a new government and armies, were in any position to be carrying out long sieges throughout Canaan. Positive evidence has come from recent digs which has shown that the last phase of the Middle Bronze Period needs more time than originally thought, so that its end is closer to 1420 B.C.

Now how does the evidence stack up? We find that the cities in Caanan are "large and fortified to heaven" (Deut. 1:28) just as

DATING THE CONQUEST OF CANAAN

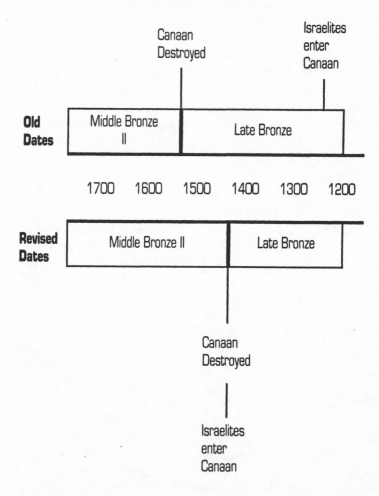

Moses said. Also, the extent of destruction, with only a few exceptions, matches the biblical description. "Indeed, generally speaking, the area in which destruction occurred at the end of [the Middle Bronze Period] corresponds with the area of Israelite settlement, while cities that survived lay outside that area."[8]

Now some archeologists ask, "Where is the evidence of Israelite dominance of the culture in the Late Bronze? We have always held them responsible for the shift from the Bronze Age to the Iron Age in 1200." The problem with that view is that those changes are the same all over the Mediterranean, not just in Palestine. The Hebrews could not be responsible for such widespread change. As nomads, they probably brought nothing with them, lived in tents for some time, and bought their pottery at the Canaanite markets. Besides, have you ever read the Book of Judges? When they entered the land, they didn't dominate ANYBODY for several hundred years. They were constantly dominated by everyone around them.

Bimson summarizes his proposal in this way:

> We have proposed: (1) a return to the biblical date for the conquest of Canaan (i.e., shortly before 1400 B.C.), and (2) a lowering of the date for the end of the Middle Bronze Age, from 1550 B.C. to shortly before 1400 B.C. The result is that two events previously separated by centuries are brought together: the fall of Canaan's MB II cities becomes the archeological evidence for the Conquest. These twin proposals create an almost perfect match between the archeological evidence and the biblical account.[9]

Velikovsky-Courville revision

A second possible solution sees a problem in the traditional

The Greek Problem

Following Egyptian history not only causes problems in the history of Israel, but also in the history of Greece. Historians have long been puzzled by the 300-year gap in Greek history between the Dorian invasion and the beginning of the Spartan kings. It is as if Greek civilization ceased to exist for some time. The latter date is set by reckoning backward from known dates in Greek history, but the former date is established by references in Egyptian history. Courville shows that this problem can be solved in the same way as the problem of the Exodus, by reconstructing the chronology of Egypt. That very 300-year period can be eliminated by seeing that there is a dynasty of lesser rulers inserted in the traditional chronology. This revision sets these two events only fifty years apart. The revision also helps synchronize the histories of Greece and Rome.

view of Egyptian history. The chronology of the whole ancient world is based on the order and dates of the Egyptian kings. Mostly, we know this order from an ancient historian named Manetho, who is quoted by three other historians. There are also monuments that give partial lists. This order has been thought of as rigid and sure; however, the only absolutely fixed date in it is its end, when Alexander the Great conquered Egypt. Velikovsky and Courville assert that there are 600 extra years in that chronology which throw off the dates for events all around the Near East.

What evidence can establish this? If we set aside the idea of Egyptian history as fixed, we find three pieces of evidence where the history of Israel matches up with the history of Egypt. When we find this kind of match, where the same event is recorded in both countries, we call it a synchronism. The three places we find synchronisms are the plagues of Moses, the defeat of the Amalekites, and reign of Ahab.

A very old papyrus written by an Egyptian priest named Ipuwer, though various interpretations have been given to it, tells of two unique events: a series of plagues and the invasion of a foreign power. The plagues match very well with the record of Moses' plagues in Exodus 7–12. It speaks of the river turning to blood (cf. 7:20), crops consumed (9:25), fire (vv. 23-24), and darkness (10:22). The final plague, which killed Pharaoh's son, is referred to also: "Forsooth, the children of princes are dashed against the walls. . . . The prison is ruined. . . . He who places his brother in the ground is everywhere. . . . It is groaning that is throughout the land, mingled with lamentations" (Papyrus 4:3; 6:13; 2:13; 3:14). This parallels the biblical account which says, "the Lord struck all the firstborn in the land of Egypt, from the firstborn of the Pharaoh who sat on his throne to the firstborn of the captive who was in the dungeon. . . . and there was a great cry in Egypt, for there was no home where there was not someone dead" (Ex. 12:29-30). Following these disasters, there was an invasion of "a foreign tribe" which came out of the desert (Papyrus 3:1). This invasion must have been the Hyksos, who dominated Egypt between the Middle Kingdom and the New Kingdom.

The monolith of el-Arish tells a similar story of darkness and suffering in the land in the days of King Thom. It also relates how the Pharaoh "went out to battle against the friends of Apopi (the god of darkness)," though the army never returned: "His majesty leapt into the so-called Place of the Whirlpool." The place of the incident is Pi-Kharoti, which may be equivalent to Pi-hahiroth, where the Israelites camped by the sea (Ex. 14:9). This is very interesting to us because the name of the city built by the Israelites is Pi-Thom, "the abode of Thom." And the king who reigned just before the Hyksos invasion was (in Greek) Timaios. But the Egyptian date for King Thom is about 600 years too early, around 2000 B.C. Either the Egyptian chronology is wrong or history repeated itself in very unusual ways.

According to Velikovsky, the Hyksos should be identified as the Amalekites, whom the Israelites met before they even reached Sinai (17:8-16). They might have reached Egypt within days after the Israelites left. The Egyptians referred to them as Amu and Arabian historians mention some Amalekite pharaohs. But the scriptural parallels are quite interesting. As the false prophet Baalam faced Israel, he blessed them despite his instructions, but when he turned, facing Egypt, "He looked at Amalek . . . and said, 'Amalek was the first of the nations' " (Num. 24:20). Why did he curse Amalek rather than Egypt, unless Egypt was under Amalekite domination? Also, the names of the first and last Amalekite kings in the Bible (Agag I and II, see v. 7 and 1 Sam. 15:8) correspond to the first and last Hyksos kings. This would indicate that the Hyksos entered Egypt just after the Exodus and remained in power there until Saul defeated them and released the Egyptians from bondage. This would explain the genial relations that Israel had with Egypt in David and Solomon's time. In fact, Velikovsky shows striking similarities between the Queen of Sheba and the Egyptian queen Hatshepsut. She is said to have journeyed to the Divine Land, and the gifts that she received there are much like those of Solomon to his visitor (see 1 Kings 10:10-22). She also built a temple in Egypt that is similar to the temple of Solomon. But according to Egyptian chronology, she lived before the Exodus. Only if this chronology is revised can this parallelism be explained. The invasion of Thutmose III into Palestine might also be equated with the attack of Shishak (2 Chron. 12:2-9).

The third synchronism is a series of letters (on clay tablets) called the el-Amarna letters. These are correspondence between the rulers in Palestine (Jerusalem, Syria, and Sumur) and the Pharaohs Amenhotep III and his son Akhnaton. The Palestinians were concerned about an army approaching from the south called the Habiru, who were causing great destruction. On the basis of such a description, it has traditionally been held that these letters speak of the Israelites entering Canaan. Velikovsky shows that a closer look at these tablets reveals another picture entirely. First, Sumur can be identified as the city of Samaria, which was not built until after Solomon (1 Kings 16:24). Second, the "king of Hatti" threatens to invade from the north, which seems to be a Hittite invasion. Third, none of the names in the letters match the names of rulers given in the Book of Joshua. In other words, the political situation is all wrong for these letters to have come from the time

THE VELIKOVSKY-COURVILLE REVISION

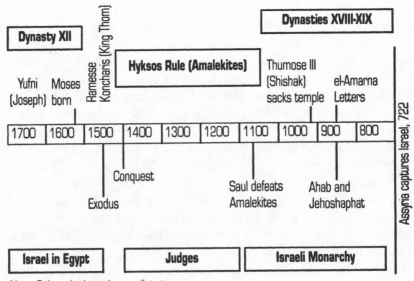

Note: Only main dynasties are listed.

of the Exodus. If we move their date to the time when Ahab ruled from Samaria and was threatened by both the Moabites and the Hittites, then all of the names, places, and events can be located in Kings and Chronicles, even to the names of the generals of armies. But this dates Amenhotep III 500 years later than the standard chronology! Either the chronology is wrong or one has to maintain that history repeated itself exactly half a millennium later.

The picture that emerges is a consistent one only if the Israelite history is used to date Egyptian events. Such an interpretation also requires a new chronology for Egyptian history. Velikovsky's handling of this chronology has been criticized, but Courville has shown that the lists of Egyptian kings should not be understood as completely consecutive. He shows that some of the "kings" listed were not Pharaohs, but local rulers or high officials. Among those mentioned are Joseph (Yufni) and Moses' adoptive father Chenephres, who was a prince only by marriage.

The recognition of the rulers of the XIIIth Dynasty as princes over local nomes, or at least as important officials or sub-rulers in the government worthy of the appellation "kings," provides

---

Ramifications of Velikovsky
1. The end of Dynasty XII explains the statement that no one sought Moses' life any longer (Ex. 4:19).
2. The cities that the Israelite slaves built may have been named for the last two Egyptian Pharaohs (Pi Ramesse and Pi Thom), since they took control at the end of Dynasty XII.
3. The new kingdom was exactly that: a rebuilding of Egyptian culture after four centuries of domination. Though most conservatives hold that the Exodus took place in the time of Thutmose III or Amenhotep II, these rulers should be dated after the time of Solomon.
4. Psalm 104 bears resemblance to a poem written by Akhnaton, not because the psalmist copied an ancient Egyptian song, as some have thought, but because Psalm 104 is a contemporary of it. Since Akhnaton was probably influenced toward his monotheism by Hatshepsut, it may be that the psalm was written first and adapted to fit the Egyptian scheme.

us with a deeper insight into what Manetho regarded as compromising a dynasty. It was evidently not outside his thinking to give the names of the main line of kings as composing one dynasty and then to return on the time scale to pick up a line of secondary rulers as a distinct dynasty. Not only so, he did not hesitate to label these secondary rulers as kings. . . . It would seem that herein lies a major factor in the acceptance of an erroneous and grossly expanded chronology of Egypt.[10]

Historians had assumed that each dynasty follows after the one before it when many dynasties list subrulers who lived at the same time as the preceding dynasty. Working out this new chronology places the Exodus about 1440 B.C. and makes the other periods of Israelite history fall in line with the Egyptian kings mentioned.

We are not sure which of these is the best solution to the problem and there is no consensus on the issue. The important point is that there is no longer any reason to accept the late date for the Exodus and that some resolution is possible to explain the biblical date in the 1400s B.C.

SAUL, DAVID, AND SOLOMON

Kingship came to Israel only because the people wanted "a king for us to judge us like all the nations" (1 Sam. 8:5), but it was not God's pleasure or time. The descriptions we now have show us that having a king would mean introducing high taxes, a draft, military appropriation of private property, and working for the government on demand without pay. Saul became the first king of Israel and his fortress at Gibeah has been excavated. One of the most noteworthy finds was that slingshots were one of the most important weapons of the day. This relates not only to David's victory over Goliath, but to the reference of Judges 20:16 that there were 700 expert slingers in Israel who "could sling a stone at a hair and not miss."

At Saul's death, Samuel tells us that his armor was put in the temple of Ashtaroth (a Canaanite fertility goddess) at Bethshan, while Chronicles says that his head was put in the temple of Dagon, the Philistine corn god. This was thought to be an error because it seemed unlikely that enemy peoples would have temples in the same place at the same time. However, excavations have found that there are two temples at this site that are separated by a hallway: one for Dagon, and the other for Ashtaroth. It appears that the Philistines had adopted the Canaanite goddess as their own.

One of the key accomplishments of David's reign was the capture of Jerusalem. This was problematic in that the Scriptures say that the Israelites entered the city by way of a tunnel that led to the Pool of Siloam; however, that pool was thought to be *outside* the city walls at that time. It was not until the 1960s that excavations finally determined that the wall did indeed extend well past the pool.

The psalms attributed to David are often said to have been written much later because their inscriptions suggest that there were musicians' guilds (e.g., the sons of Korah). Such an organization leads many to think that these hymns should be dated to about the time of the Maccabeans in the second century B.C. Following the excavations at Ras Shamra, and knowing now that there were such guilds in Syria and Palestine in David's time, it is

---

Solomon's Wall?

Most scholars would insist that there are no remains in Jerusalem from Solomon's time, but one man argues convincingly that a portion of the original eastern retaining wall still supports the temple mount. Ernest-Marie Laperrousaz notes that when walls were built to undergird the temple by Solomon and Herod, the construction took thirty to forty years; however, the Bible tells us that the foundation for the temple built after the Exile was completed within three months after their return and construction of the temple took only about five years. This means that they must have built over the existing structure. This retaining wall would not have been destroyed by the Babylonians because it faces a sharp drop to the Kidron Valley and it is a support, not a fortification. We also know that Herod did not rebuild this part of the wall because we can still see the straight joint where he added his extension to the existing support. All of this points to Solomon as the builder responsible for this foundation that remains until today. [See *Biblical Archeology Review*, 13:3 May–June 1987, pp. 34–44.]

unreasonable to attribute such psalms to the Maccabean period.[11]

The time of Solomon has no less corroboration from archeology. The site of Solomon's temple is near the Muslim holy place, the Dome of the Rock and is now being excavated. However, what is known about Philistine temples built in Solomon's time fits well with the design, decoration, and materials designated in the Bible. The only piece of evidence from the temple itself is a small ornament, a pomegranate, that sat on the end of a rod and bears the inscription, "Belonging to the Temple of Yahweh." It was first seen in a shop in Jerusalem in 1979, verified in 1984, and was acquired by the Israel Museum in 1988.

The excavation of Gezer in 1969 ran across a massive layer of ash that covered most of the mound. Sifting through the ash yielded pieces of Hebrew, Egyptian, and Philistine artifacts. Apparently all three cultures had been there at the same time. This puzzled researchers greatly until they realized that the Bible told them exactly what they had found. "For Pharaoh king of Egypt had gone up and captured Gezer, and burned it with fire, and killed the Canaanites who lived in the city, and had given it as a dowry to his daughter, Solomon's wife" (1 Kings 9:16).

THE ASSYRIAN INVASION

We have learned a great deal about the Assyrians, mostly because of 26,000 tablets found in the palace of Ashurbanipal, the son of

---

The Destruction of Tyre

It does not usually surprise us to learn that prophecies have been fulfilled, but sometimes the way in which they are fulfilled is incredible. For example, Ezekiel had said that Tyre would be destroyed and that the ruins would be cast into the sea (26:12). This provoked scoffing because, when Nebuchadnezzar destroyed Tyre, he left the ruins right where they fell—on the land. But 200 years later, Alexander the Great attacked Tyre and the inhabitants withdrew to an island just off the coast for safety. In order to reach them, Alexander threw all of the debris, stones, timbers, dust, and everything else, into the sea to build a causeway that would reach the island. Just as Ezekiel said, "You will be a place for the spreading of nets" (v. 14).

Esarhaddon who had taken the Northern Kingdom into captivity in 722 B.C. These tell of the many conquests of the Assyrian Empire and record with honor the cruel and violent punishments that fell to those who opposed them.

Several of these records confirm the Bible's accuracy. Every reference in the Old Testament to an Assyrian king has proven correct. Even though Sargon was unknown for some time, when his palace was found and excavated, there was a wall painting of the battle mentioned in Isaiah 20. The Black Obelisk of Shalmaneser adds to our knowledge of biblical figures by showing Jehu (or his emissary) bowing down to the king of Assyria.

Among the most interesting finds is Sennacherib's record of the siege of Jerusalem. Thousands of his men died and the rest scattered when he attempted to take the city and, as Isaiah had foretold, he was unable to conquer it. Since he could not boast about his great victory here, Sennacherib found a way to make himself sound good without admitting defeat:

> As to Hezekiah, the Jew, he did not submit to my yoke, I laid siege to 46 of his strong cities, walled forts, and to the countless small villages in their vicinity . . . I drove out of them 200,150 people, young and old, male and female, horses, mules, donkeys, camels, big and small cattle beyond counting and considered (them) booty. Himself I made a prisoner in Jerusalem, his royal residence, like a bird in a cage.[12]

THE CAPTIVITY

Various facets of the Old Testament history regarding the Captivity have been confirmed. Records found in Babylon's famous Hanging Gardens have shown that Jehoiachin and his five sons were being given a monthly ration and place to live and were treated well (2 Kings 25:27-30). The name of Belshazzar had caused problems because there was not only no mention of him, but no room for him in the list of Babylonian kings; however, Nabodonius left a record that he appointed his son, Belshazzar, to reign for a few years in his absence. Hence, Nabodonius was still king, but Belshazzar ruled in the capital. Also, the edict of Cyrus as recorded by Ezra seemed to fit the picture of Isaiah's prophecies too well to be real. But a cylinder was found that confirmed the decree in all the important details.

In every period of Old Testament history, we find that there is good evidence from archeology that the Scriptures are accurate. In many instances, the Scriptures even reflect firsthand knowledge of the times and customs it describes. While many have doubted the accuracy of the Bible, time and continued reasearch have consistently demonstrated that the Word of God is better informed than its critics.

DOES ARCHEOLOGY CONFIRM THE NEW TESTAMENT?

After the period of the Judges, the archeological evidence becomes increasingly clear that the biblical authors knew what they were talking about. By the time we reach the New Testament period, the evidence for its historical reliability becomes overwhelming. This evidence will be summarized in three parts: historical accuracy of Luke, the testimony of secular historians, and the physical evidence relating to Christ's crucifixion. The evidence for the Resurrection was given in chapter 6.

THE HISTORICAL ACCURACY OF LUKE

It was once thought that Luke had concocted his narrative from the ramblings of his imagination, because he ascribed odd titles to authorities and mentioned governors that no one knew. The evidence now points in exactly the opposite direction.

The census in Luke 2:1-5

Several problems are involved in the statement that Augustus conducted a census of the empire during the reigns of Quirinius and Herod. There is no record of such a census, but we now know that regular censuses were taken in Egypt, Gaul, and Cyrene. It is quite likely that Luke's meaning is that censuses were taken throughout the empire at different times and Augustus started this process. The present tense that Luke uses points strongly toward understanding this as a repeated event. Now Quirinius did take a census, but that was in A.D. 6, too late for Jesus' birth, and Herod died before Quirinius became governor. Was Luke confused? No; in fact, he mentions Quirinius' later census in Acts 5:37. It is most likely that Luke is distinguishing this census in Herod's time from the more well-known census of Quirinius. There are several New Testament parallels for this translation.[13]

Gallio, proconsul of Achaea

This designation in Acts 18:12-17 was thought to be impossible. But an inscription at Delphi notes this exact title for the man, and it dates him to the time Paul was in Corinth (A.D. 51).[14]

Lysanias, tetrarch of Abilene

This man was unknown to modern historians until an inscription was found recording a temple dedication which mentions the name, the title, and is in the right place. The inscription is dated between A.D. 14 and 29, compatible with the beginnings of John's ministry, which Luke dates by Lysanias' reign (Luke 3:1).

Erastus

In Acts 19:22, Erastus is named as a Corinthian who becomes a coworker of Paul. If Luke were going to make up any names, this would seem to be the best place to do it. How would anyone know? Well, in excavating Corinth, an inscription was found near the theater which reads, "Erastus in return for his aedileship laid the pavement at his own expense." If these are the same man, then it explains why Luke would have included the detail that a prominent and wealthy citizen of Corinth had converted and given his life to the ministry.

In addition to these, Luke gives correct titles for the following officials: Thessalonica—"politarchs," Ephesus—"temple wardens," Cyprus—"proconsul," Malta—"the first man of the island." Each of these have been confirmed by Roman usage. All in all, Luke names thirty-two countries, fifty-four cities, and nine islands without making a single error. This led the prominent historian Sir William Ramsay to recant his critical views:

I began with a mind unfavorable to it [Acts], for the ingenuity and apparent completeness of the Tubingen theory had at one time quite convinced me. It did not lie then in my line of life to investigate the subject minutely; but more recently I found myself often brought into contact with the Book of Acts as an authority for the topography, antiquities, and society of Asia Minor. It was gradually borne in upon me that in various details the narrative showed marvelous truth.[15]

In full agreement, A.N. Sherwin-White says, "For Acts the confirmation of historicity is overwhelming. . . . Any attempt to reject its basic historicity must now appear absurd. Roman historians have long taken it for granted."[16] As for the critical theories which were spawned in the early 1800s but still persist today, they are left without substantiation. The great archeologist William F. Albright says, "All radical schools in New Testament criticism which have existed in the past or which exist today are pre-archeological, and are therefore, since they were built in der Luft [in the air], quite antiquated today."[17]

CONFIRMATION BY SECULAR HISTORIANS
One of the popular misconceptions about Jesus is that there is no mention of Him in any ancient sources outside of the Bible. On the contrary, there are numerous references to Him as a historical figure who died at the hand of Pontius Pilate. Some even noted that He was reported to have risen from the dead, and was worshiped as a god by all who followed Him. Gary Habermas, in his book *Ancient Evidences for the Life of Jesus* (Nashville: Thomas Nelson, 1984), discusses all of these. Here are some of these references

Tacitus
A Roman historian who lived from A.D. 55–120, Tacitus made at least three references to Christ. In the first, he explains how Nero blamed the Christians for the fire that burned Rome.

Consequently, to get rid of the report, Nero fastened the guilt and inflicted the most exquisite tortures on a class hated for their abominations, called Christians by the populace. Christus, from whom the name had its origin, suffered the extreme penal-

One interesting mention of Christ in history comes from a Roman satirist named Lucian. His words ring with the sarcasm of Mark Russell or Johnny Carson.

"The Christians, you know, worship a man to this day—the distinguished personage who introduced their novel rites, and was crucified on that account. . . . You see, these misguided creatures start with the general conviction that they are immortal for all time, which explains the contempt of death and voluntary self-devotion which are so common among them; and then it was impressed on them by their original lawgiver that they are all brothers, from the moment they are converted, and deny the gods of Greece, and worship the crucified sage, and live after his laws. All this they take quite on faith, with the result that they despise all worldly goods alike, regarding them as common property." [*The Death of Peregrine,* 11–13, in *The Works of Lucian of Samasota,* trans. by H.W. Fowler and F.G. Fowler, 4 vols. (Oxford: Clarendon Press, 1949).]

ty during the reign of Tiberius at the hands of one of our procurators, Pontius Pilate, and a most mischievous superstition, thus checked for the moment, again broke out not only in Judea, the first source of the evil, but even in Rome, where all things hideous and shameful from every part of the world find their center and become popular. Accordingly, an arrest was first made of all who pleaded guilty; then, upon their information, an immense multitude was convicted, not so much of the crime of firing the city, as of hatred against mankind. Mockery of every sort was added to their deaths. Covered with the skins of beasts, they were doomed to the flames and burnt, to serve as a nightly illumination, when daylight had expired.[18]

Notice that the basic details of Christ's death are borne out. The "mischievous superstition" that he refers to was probably that Jesus would rise from the dead.

Suetonius

The chief secretary to Emperor Hadrian (A.D. 117–138) likewise says, "After the great fire at Rome . . . less punishments were also inflicted on the Christians, a sect professing a new and mischievous religious belief."[19] He also notes that Claudius expelled the Jews from Rome in A.D. 49 because of rioting "at the instigation of Chrestus."[20] This explains why Aquila and Priscilla, whom Paul met in Corinth (Acts 18:2), had to leave their home in Italy.

Josephus
This was a Jewish historian working for the Romans in the first century. In a disputed passage, he gives a description of Jesus.

> At this time there was a wise man who was called Jesus. And his conduct was good and [he] was known to be virtuous. And many people from among the Jews and other nations became his disciples. Pilate condemned him to be crucified and to die. And those who had become his disciples did not abandon his discipleship. They reported that he had appeared to them three days after his crucifixion and that he was alive; accordingly, he was perhaps the messiah concerning whom the prophets have recounted wonders.[21]

This should not be taken to indicate that Josephus believed this, but the fact that *neither he nor any other contemporary of the apostles* make any attempt to refute the Resurrection is significant. If the tomb was still sealed or the body had been found, it seems that they would have mentioned it. Instead they present it is as the belief of Christians without comment.

The Talmud
The rabbinical commentary on the Torah makes an interesting note about Jesus:

> On the eve of Passover Yeshua was hanged. For forty days before the execution took place, a herald went forth and cried, "he is going forth to be stoned because he has practiced sorcery and enticed Israel to apostasy. Anyone who can say anything in his favour, let him come forward and plead on his behalf." But since nothing was brought forward in his favour he was hanged on the eve of the Passover.[22]

Some of this information may surprise us. The sending forth of a herald is not mentioned in the New Testament, but it is not

Support from Heretics

The Gnostic gospels may not be a good source of information about Jesus' life or theology, but they do contribute something to our understanding of history. They show that there was a certain core of information about Jesus' life and death that was so widely accepted, that they could not alter it—they had to build on top of it. These books, written mostly by men pretending to be biblical apostles, are the legendary developments and myths that arose from the historical facts of Christianity's origin. Their agreement in the essentials that (1) Jesus was God in human form, (2) that He was persecuted and crucified, (3) that He was believed to have risen from the dead, and (4) that this had significance for His followers is confirmation that these facts were known well and unalterable by the second century.

surprising in light of the threats made on Jesus' life. Also, there may be an indirect reference to it in John 11:8 and 16, as an explanation of why Thomas was so sure that going to Bethany (just outside Jerusalem) would mean certain death. Notice that the passage says that He was to be stoned, which is the prescribed punishment for sorcerers and false prophets, yet it admits that he was crucified ("hanged" is synonymous with crucifixion in Luke 23:39 and Gal. 3:13). Since the Jews were prohibited from using capital punishment, His death would have to be at the hands of the Romans, and their mode of punishment was the cross. But why was Jesus allowed freedom in Jerusalem for a week prior to His arrest? Perhaps this was so because the forty days of the decree had not been completed, but equally likely is that they hesitated because of His popularity (remember how He was greeted when He entered the city on Palm Sunday?). These differences only serve to highlight the truth of Gospel accounts.

This sampling of the historical sources shows widespread agreement about the basic details of Jesus' life, especially His death and its causes, with some consideration given to the belief that He rose from the dead.

EVIDENCE RELATING TO JESUS' DEATH

There are two fascinating discoveries which illuminate for us the death of Christ and, to some degree, His resurrection. The first is an unusual decree; the second is the body of another crucifixion victim.

The Nazareth decree

This slab of stone was found in Nazareth in 1878. It is a decree issued by the Emperor Claudius (A.D. 41–54) that no graves should be disturbed or bodies extracted or moved. This type of decree is not uncommon, but the startling fact is that here "the offender [shall] be sentenced to capital punishment on the charge of violation of a sepulcher." Other notices warned of a fine, but death for disturbing graves? A likely explanation is that Claudius, having heard of the Christian doctrine of Resurrection while investigating the riots of A.D. 49, decided not to let any such report surface again. This certainly makes sense in light of the Jewish argument that the body had been stolen (Matt. 28:11-13). This is early testimony to the strong and persistent belief that Jesus rose from the dead.

Instruments of Crucifixion

Archeology has told us much about the tools used in crucifixion.

The Cross: Several types of crosses were used by the Romans, varying in height and shape, but the one most common in Jesus' time looked like our capital "T." The top of it was only about six–eight feet off the ground and it is found both with and without a seat. The condemned would customarily carry the crossbar, not the upright part, to the crucifixion site. This piece weighed between 75 and 125 pounds. A titulus, with the name and crime of the victim, could be nailed to the top of the crossbeam.

The Nails: Square nails five to seven inches long and three eighths inch wide were standard, though some victims were simply tied to the crossbeam with ropes. The nails could be driven between the bones of the forearms and feet.

The Crucifragium: Looking something like a modern meat mallet, though larger and heavier, this hammer was designed specifically for the purpose of breaking a man's legs with a single blow. Doing this prevented him from using his legs to lift himself, hastening death as the chest cavity constricted.

The Scourging

Roman historians and archeology have revealed much about the practice of scourging. The instrument used was a Roman flagrum —a three-lash whip with pieces of bone or lead at the tips. As this lash was used, it would tear through anything: skin, muscle, nerves, even chipping bones. The victim was either tied to an upright stake or bent over a thrashing post. There were sometimes two scourgers standing on either side who would alternate blows, not only on the back, but swinging up into the chest and around the legs in both directions. It is not known if the Romans accommodated to the Jewish limit of thirty-nine lashes. Roman soldiers would often taunt their victims after whippings, so one would expect the victim to have facial bruises, swelling, a broken nose, and portions of the beard plucked out.

Yohanan—a crucifixion victim

In 1968, an ancient burial site was uncovered in Jerusalem containing about thirty-five bodies. It was determined that most of these had suffered violent deaths in the Jewish uprising against Rome in A.D. 70. One of these was a man named Yohanan Ben Ha'galgol. He was about twenty-seven to twenty-eight years old, had a cleft palate, and a seven-inch nail was still driven between his feet. The feet had been turned outward so that the square nail could be hammered through both feet sideways at the heel (just inside the Achilles tendon). This would have bowed the legs outward as well so that they could not be used for support on the cross. The nail had gone through a wedge of acacia wood, then through the heels, then into an olive wood beam. There was also evidence that similar spikes had been put between the two bones of each lower arm. These had caused the upper bones to be worn smooth as the victim repeatedly raised and lowered himself to breathe (breathing is restricted with the arms raised). Crucifixion victims had to lift themselves to free the chest muscles, and when they grew too weak to do so, died by suffocation. Yohanan's legs were crushed by a blow, consistent with the common use of the Roman *crucifragium* (John 19:31-32). Each of these details confirms the New Testament description of crucifixion.

This chapter has summarized some of the ways that, even in the face of challenges, archeology has confirmed the truth of the

Scriptures. The evidence is substantial, and the rewards in under-standing and confidence that it brings are well worth the trouble.

NOTES

1. Nelson Glueck, *Rivers in the Desert* (New York: Farrar, Strauss and Cudahy, 1959), p. 136.

2. K.A. Kitchen, *Ancient Orient and the Old Testament* (Chicago: InterVarsity Press, 1966), p. 89.

3. Translation by A. Leo Oppenheim in *Ancient Near East Texts,* ed. by James B. Pritchard (Princeton: The Princeton Press, 1950), p. 265.

4. Gleason L. Archer, *Encyclopedia of Bible Difficulties* (Grand Rapids: Zondervan, 1982), pp. 82–83.

5. Clifford A. Wilson, *Rocks, Relics and Biblical Reliability* (Grand Rapids: Zondervan, 1977), p. 29.

6. P.J. Wiseman, *Ancient Records and the Structure of Genesis* (Nashville: Thomas Nelson, 1985), p. 74.

7. Wilson, *op. cit.*, p. 42.

8. John J. Bimson and David Livingston, "Redating the Exodus" in *Biblical Archeology Review,* 8:5, September–October 1987, p. 46.

9. Ibid., p. 51.

10. Donovan A. Courville, *The Exodus Problem and Its Ramifica-tions* (Loma Linda, Calif.: Challenge Books, 1971), pp. 158–59.

11. W.F. Albright, *History, Archaeology, and Christian Humanism* (New York: MacGraw-Hill, 1964), pp. 34–35.

12. Pritchard, *op. cit.,* p. 288.

13. See Harold W. Hoehner, *Chronological Aspects of the Life of Christ* (Grand Rapids: Zondervan, 1977), pp. 13–23 for a full argument.

14. F.F. Bruce, *New Testament History* (Garden City, N.Y.: Doubleday, 1980), pp. 298, 316.

15. William M. Ramsay, *St. Paul the Traveler and the Roman Citizen* (Grand Rapids: Baker, 1982), p. 8.

16. A.N. Sherwin-White, *Roman Society and Roman Law in the New Testament* (Oxford: Clarendon Press, 1963), p. 189.

17. William F. Albright, "Retrospect and Prospect in New Testament Archaeology," in *The Teacher's Yoke,* ed. by E. Jerry Vardaman (Waco, Texas: Baylor University, 1964), p. 288ff.

18. Tacitus, 15:44.

19. Suetonius, *Nero,* 16.

20. _____, *Claudius,* 25.

21. Josephus, *Antiquities,* 18:3 from the Arabic text as it appeared in "New Evidence on the Life of Jesus," *The New York Times,* February 12, 1972, pp. 1, 24.

22. *The Babylonian Talmud,* Sanhedrin, 43a.

10

QUESTIONS ABOUT SCIENCE AND EVOLUTION

Two men were walking through the forest and happened across a glass ball lying on the carpet of twigs and fir needles. There were hardly any sounds other than the pair's own footsteps and certainly no signs of other people. But the very obvious inference from the evidence of the ball was that someone had put it there. Now one of these men was a scientist, trained in the modern view of origins, and the other a layman. The layman said, "What if the ball were larger, say ten feet around, would you still say that someone put it there?" Naturally, the scientist agreed that a larger ball would not affect his judgment. "Well, what if the ball were huge—a mile in diameter?" probed the layman. His friend responded that not only would someone have put it there, but that there should be an investigation to find out what caused the ball to be there. The layman then pursued one more question, "What if the ball were as big as the whole universe? If little balls need causes, and bigger balls need causes, doesn't the biggest ball of all need a cause too?"

The Bible's views on the origins of the universe, first life, and new life forms, have caused many to falter in their acceptance of the Scriptures as truth. Modern science claims to have proven them wrong beyond a shadow of a doubt. The theory of evolution is now posited as fact. Who is right? The Bible or science?

This chapter will deal with this problem by stating a basic argument, then applying that argument to the three areas of origins: the universe, first life, and new life forms. But before we embark, let's be sure that we understand what evolution is and how modern evolutionists view origins.

Most of us think of evolution as an invention of Charles Darwin in 1859, but it is really a very old view that has naturalistic philosophical roots. In chapter 3, we mentioned that nontheists say the universe is uncaused—it just always was and will be. All matter (if it exists in any sense) carries in it the principles of life. The idea of life arising from nonliving things is not a problem with this starting point. Indeed, it would be inevitable. Equally certain would be the progress from less complex life forms to more complex ones, since all things would be ever striving toward perfection and the realization of higher states.

Modern evolution does not look very much like this picture. Since many scientists are materialistic, they hold to the basic design but without the spiritual connotations. However, without the spiritual aspects guiding the system, there is no mechanism to explain the progress of species. Enter Charles Darwin. He provided a mechanism to make evolution work beginning with matter alone. He called it natural selection. Much of what Darwin taught has been rejected and surpassed by modern evolutionists, but the doctrine of natural selection has been maintained.

As to the origin of the universe, classic evolutionists have said that the world was uncaused. Carl Sagan has expressed this in his

---

Modern Science and Creation
The ancient Greeks viewed science as a philosophical matter. Reason was the chief tool of science rather than experimentation. Much of this attitude came from their belief that the world was a corruption of perfection. The world was to them an uncreated, unknowable, yet necessary evil which God directed but did not really control. Only when the theistic view of Creation took over did science begin to study the world experimentally. It was the thought that God had created matter that made it a thing worth studying. In this view, matter was real, good, and knowable. By seeing God as the Creator in complete control, science could make the assumption that the universe made sense. Most of the scientists who formulated the studies of modern science were creationists. Without this basis, modern science would probably never have gotten started.

saying, "The Cosmos is all that is or ever was or ever will be."[1] This view is still being taught by those who have not kept up with new discoveries in cosmology (study of the universe). Evolutionists also teach that life first began as a result of chemical reactions in what Darwin called a "warm little pool." Research done in the last thirty years has shown that it is possible to generate some amino acids necessary for life using only a few basic gases, water, and an electrical charge. This has encouraged the view that life arose from nonliving matter. As to new life forms, these are said to have evolved through natural selection. As the conditions of the earth changed, animals adapted new characteristics to meet the new challenges. Those who adapted survived and those that did not passed into extinction. The great variety of extinct animals found in fossils and their similarities to living species are used to confirm this thesis. If virtually all scientists agree on these principles and have the evidence to prove it, can we still believe the Bible?

THE BASIC ARGUMENT AGAINST EVOLUTION

Let it first be said that we need not argue on religious grounds. We do not need to simply stand firm crying, "The Bible said it; I believe it; that settles it!" That attitude can be good, but there are good scientific grounds to reject evolution and believe in Creation. In fact, it is all based on the whole idea of what science is.

Science is based on causality; every event has a cause. Things don't happen willy-nilly. Even if we can't know specifically what *particular* cause produced a certain event, we can say what *kind* of cause it must have been because of the kinds of effects we see today. The idea that whatever caused some effect in the past will cause the same effect in the present is called the principle of uniformity. All science is based on finding causes using these two principles: causality and uniformity.

When scientific principles were first being developed into the scientific method, scientists like Francis Bacon, Johannes Kepler, Issac Newton, and William Kelvin made a distinction between primary and secondary causes. A primary cause was a first cause that explained singularities—events that only happened once and had no natural explanation. Secondary causes were thought of as natural causes and laws that govern the way things normally operate. Unfortunately, some scientists began using supernatural causes to explain natural irregularities like earthquakes and meteors. When the truth was learned about these things, scientists eliminated primary causes from consideration altogether and sought to explain everything in terms of natural causes. But just as it was wrong for supernaturalists to explain ordinary events using primary causes, it is also wrong for the naturalist to explain all singularities by natural causes.

THE DIFFERENCE BETWEEN OPERATION AND ORIGIN SCIENCE

Operation science deals with the way things normally operate. It examines how the world normally works in the present. It studies things that happen over and over again in a regular and repeated way. Operation science seeks answers that are testable by repeating the experiment over and over, and falsifiable if the cause does not always yield the same effect. Its conclusions should allow one to project what will happen in future experiments. Operation science likes things to be very regular and predictable. No changes; no surprises. So the idea of a supernatural being coming around to

---

Creationists Who Founded Modern Science
Kepler—Astronomy
Pascal—Hydrostatics
Boyle—Chemistry
Newton—Physics
Steno—Stratigraphy
Faraday—Magnetic theory
Babbage—Computers
Agassiz—Ichthyology
Simpson—Gynecology
Mendel—Genetics
Pasteur—Bacteriology
Kelvin—Thermodynamics
Lister—Antiseptic surgery
Maxwell—Electrodynamics
Ramsay—Isotopic chemistry

ORIGIN SCIENCE	OPERATION SCIENCE
Studies past	Studies present
Studies singularities	Studies regularities
Studies unrepeatable	Studies repeatable
Re-creation not possible	Re-creation possible
How things began	How things work
May find primary cause	Finds secondary causes
Conclusions not falsifiable	Conclusions falsifiable

stir things up occasionally is strongly resisted. Because of this, it usually seeks out natural (secondary) causes for the events it studies.

Origin science is not just another name for giving evidence to support creationism. It is a different kind of science. Origin science studies *past singularities*, rather than present normalities. It looks at how things *began*, not how they work. It studies things that only happened once and, by their nature, don't happen again. It is a different type of study that requires a different approach. Rather than being an *empirical* science like physics or biology, it is more like a *forensic* science. Remember the TV show about a medical examiner named Quincy? Each week he tried to find out what and/or who caused a past singularity (a person's death) by examining the effect and deciding what kind of thing could have caused that event. That is what origin science seeks to do.

Now origin science works on different principles than operation science does. Since the past events that it studies cannot be repeated today, it uses analogies between the kinds of cause/effect relationships that we see today and the kind of effect that is being studied. Also, origin science does not claim to give definitive answers, but only plausible ones. We did not observe the events of origins, and we cannot repeat them (just as Quincy could not ask the murderer to kill the victim again). So the remaining evidence must be studied and interpretations of it measured by what seems most likely to explain the evidence. And just as operation science recognizes that some events demand an intelligent cause, origin science also admits an intelligent cause when the evidence calls for it.

The first step in the basic argument against evolution is that it has taken the wrong approach. It has applied the principles of operation science to the study of origins. It is seeking regular and repeated causes for events that occurred only once. It has forced the operations that are presently working in the world to explain how the world got here in the first place. Using this method, it is a foregone conclusion that it originated by a process; processes are what operation science studies. But it is confusion to assume that unique and singular events, such as the beginning of the universe or first life, should be studied in terms of a regular and repeated process. To understand origins, we must use origin science, not operation science.

EVIDENCE FOR INTELLIGENT PRIMARY CAUSES

But there is a second part to this argument. Because origin science is not restricted to secondary causes (the natural causes that operate the universe), it sometimes finds evidence to suggest an intelligent primary cause. On the TV show, Quincy had to determine whether he was looking for a natural cause of death or a murderer—an intelligent cause. What kind of evidence would show that an intelligent being has intervened? Carl Sagan has said that a single message from outer space would confirm his belief that

THREE TYPES OF ORDER

1. Orderly (repetitive) and specified
GIFT GIFT GIFT GIFT
Example: crystal, nylon

2. Complex (unrepeating) and unspecified
TGELDHT TBWMHQC PUQXHBT
Example: random polymers

3. Complex (unrepeating) and specified
A MESSAGE IS RIDING ON THIS SEQUENCE
Example: DNA

there is extraterrestrial life. In other words, some normal events, such as communication, require an intelligent cause. This is a type of order known as *specified complexity*.

This is more than simply design or order. It is order of a complex nature that has a clear and specific function. A chunk of quartz has order in its crystals, but it is repetitive, like the message: FACE, FACE, FACE, FACE. A chain of random polymers (called a polypeptide) is complex, but it does not give any specific function or message. It looks like this: DLAKI CHNAOR NVKOEN. But specified complexity has order that is not repetitious and communicates a message or a clear function, such as: THIS SENTENCE CARRIES A MESSAGE.

Now one of these types of design is the work of intelligent intervention, and I think you know which one it is. It is obvious that wherever we see a clear and distinct message—a complex design with a specified function—it was caused by some form of intelligent intervention imposing limits on the natural matter that it would not take by itself. There are natural phenomena that are orderly and awe-inspiring, but clearly caused by natural forces. We can see that the Grand Canyon and Niagara Falls did not require intelligence but only the forces of wind and water to shape them. However, the same cannot be said for the faces on Mount Rushmore or a hydroelectric plant. In these there is clearly a specified message or function. For these we know there must have been intelligent intervention. Whether it be a sculpture, a name written in the sand, or a smoke signal we instantly recognize that it took some smarts to do that—it just didn't happen by itself. And all of our present experience confirms this to us. It is universally true of things that we find in the world today, so it is reasonable to assume that it has always been that way.

BASIC ARGUMENT STATED

Our basic argument has now made two points. First, it is valid science to look for intelligent primary causes to events that show signs of intelligence. Archeologists do it all the time. When they find pottery or arrowheads, they rightly conclude that some intelligent being produced it. Operation science is only concerned with secondary natural causes, but origin science is not so restricted and

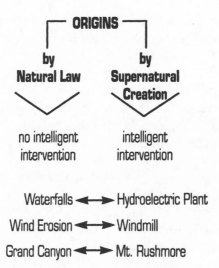

is the proper method for studying unique, past events. Second, present experience tells us that an intelligent cause should be sought wherever we find specified complexity. This gives us a criteria to show when an intelligent cause is operating and when it is not. So if it is valid for science to look for primary causes and we have some way of identifying them, the basic argument for Creation goes like this:

I. Origin science should be used to study origins.
    A. There are two kinds of science: operation science and origin science; and we must use one or the other to study origins.
    B. Operation science should not be used to study unique, unrepeatable past events because it is devoted to studying the normal operations of the present.
    C. So, origin science is the proper method for studying origins because it studies unique, unrepeated events, which origins are by definition.
II. Origin science admits the possibility of primary intelligent causes.
III. Primary intelligent causes can be identified when there is evidence of specified complexity.

IV. Therefore, wherever there is evidence of specified complexity, origin science should posit a primary intelligent cause.

We may now apply this type of argument to the three areas of origins: the origin of the universe, the origin of first life, and the origin of new life forms.

THE ORIGIN OF THE UNIVERSE

There are two views of origins. One says that everything came about by natural causes; the other looks to a supernatural cause. In the case of the origin of the universe, either the universe had a beginning or it did not. If it did have a beginning, then it was either caused or uncaused. If it was caused, then what kind of cause could be responsible for bringing all things into being?

Evolutionary scientists have told us that the universe either came from nothing by nothing or that it was always here. One such theory is called the steady state theory and also calls for the universe to be constantly generating hydrogen atoms from nothing. In either case, holding to such beliefs has a high cost for the scientist, for both of these violate a fundamental law of science: the law of causality. Both views require that the scientist believe in events happening without a cause. Even the great skeptic David Hume said, "I never asserted so absurd a proposition as that anything might arise without a cause."[2] Yet this absurd proposition is accepted by men who make their living by the law of causality. If

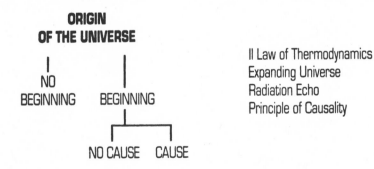

the whole universe is uncaused, why should we believe that the parts are caused? If the parts are all caused, then what evidence could suggest that the whole is uncaused? Nothing in the principle of causality supports this conclusion. The evidence is just not there.

Rather, a great deal of evidence now supports the option that the universe had a beginning. Robert Jastrow, founder and former director of NASA's Goddard Institute for Space Studies, has summarized the evidence in his book *God and the Astronomers,* saying, "Now three lines of evidence—the motions of the galaxies, the laws of thermodynamics, and the life story of the stars—pointed to one conclusion: all indicated that the Universe had a beginning."[3] Now if we are speaking of a beginning of the universe—a movement from no matter to matter—then we are clearly in the realm of unrepeatable events covered by origin science.

THE LAWS OF THERMODYNAMICS

The first law of thermodynamics says that the actual amount of energy in the universe remains constant—it doesn't change. The second law of thermodynamics says that the amount of usable energy in any closed system (which the whole universe is) is decreasing. Everything is tending toward disorder and the universe is running down. Now if the overall amount of energy stays the same, but we are running out of usable energy, then what we started with was not an infinite amount. You can't run out of an infinite amount. This means that the universe is and always has been finite. It could not have existed forever in the past and will not exist forever into the future. So it must have had a beginning.

THE MOTION OF THE GALAXIES

Scientists argue that the universe is not simply in a holding pattern, maintaining its movement from everlasting to everlasting. It is expanding. It now appears that all of the galaxies are moving outward as if from a central point of origin, and that all things were expanding faster in the past than they are now. Remember that as we look out into space, we are also looking back in time, for we are seeing things not as they are now, but as they were when the light was given off many years ago. So the light from a star 7 million light-years away tells us what it was like and where it was 7 million years ago.

> The most complete study made thus far has been carried out on the 200-inch telescope by Allan Sandage. He compiled information on 42 galaxies, ranging out in space as far as 6 billion light years from us. His measurements indicate that the Universe was expanding more rapidly in the past than it is today. This result lends further support to the belief that the Universe exploded into being.[4]

This explosion, sometimes called the Big Bang, was a beginning point from which the entire universe has come. Putting an expanding universe in reverse leads us back to the point where the universe gets smaller and smaller until it vanishes into nothing. So the universe, at some point in the distant past, came into being out of nothing.

THE RADIATION ECHO

A third line of evidence that the universe began is the radiation "echo" which seems to come from everything. It was first thought to be a malfunction or static on the instruments. But research has discovered that the static was coming from everywhere—the universe itself has low-level radiation from some past catastrophe that looks like a giant fireball.

> No explanation other than the big bang has been found for the fireball radiation. The clincher, which has convinced almost the last doubting Thomas, is that the radiation discovered by Penzias and Wilson has exactly the pattern of wavelengths expected for the light and heat produced in a great explosion. Supporters of the Steady State theory have tried desperately to find an alternative explanation, but they have failed.[5]

Again, this evidence must lead one to conclude that there was a beginning of the universe.

The law of causality tells us that whatever happens is caused, so what caused the universe to begin? It is possible that this big bang is simply the latest in a series of explosions that destroy all evidence of what came before. But that only backs the question up a few steps to "What caused the first explosion?" It is also possible that the steady state theory is right, that the universe had no beginning and is creating hydrogen from nothing to maintain energy without running down. But this explanation is contrary to the evidence and the law of causality. Both of these answers are possible; neither is plausible.

Logically, if we are looking for a cause which existed before the entirety of nature (the universe) existed, we are looking for a supernatural cause. Even Jastrow, a confirmed agnostic, has said as much: "That there are what I or anyone would call supernatural forces at work is now, I think, a scientifically proven fact."[6] Since he is speaking from the viewpoint of operation science, he probably means that there is no secondary cause which can explain the origin of the universe. But with the recognition of origin science, we can posit a supernatural primary cause that seems to be the most plausible answer to the question. Jastrow closes his book *God and the Astronomers* with these words:

> For the scientist who has lived by his faith in the power of reason, the story ends like a bad dream. He has scaled the mountains of ignorance; he is about to conquer the highest peak; as he pulls himself over the final rock, he is greeted by a band of theologians who have been sitting there for centuries.[7]

THE ORIGIN OF FIRST LIFE

There are two views of origins. One says that everything came about by natural causes; the other looks to a supernatural cause. In the case of the origin of first life, either it came about by spontaneous chemical generation without intelligent intervention, or by the intervention of an intelligent being through special Creation.

Evolutionists believe that life began in a spontaneous way from nonliving chemicals by purely natural processes. Shortly after the earth was cooled enough to allow it, they tell us, the combination of simple gases like hydrogen, nitrogen, ammonia, and carbon dioxide reacted to form elementary amino acids, which in time

**ORIGIN
OF FIRST LIFE**

SPONTANEOUS
GENERATION
(no intelligent
intervention)

SPECIAL
CREATION
(intelligent
intervention)

DNA Code
Uniformity

developed into DNA chains and finally cells. Of course, this is said to have taken several billion years and the extra energy of the sun, volcanic activity, lightning, and cosmic rays were needed to keep the process going. Experimentation begun by Stanley Miller and Harold Urey has attempted to reconstruct these conditions and has had success in producing various amino acids needed for life. From this, much of the scientific community has concluded that the spontaneous chemical generation of life from a prebiotic soup is the way life began.

There are, however, some very good reasons to reject this view. First, the early earth conditions necessary to produce life are just as likely to destroy it. The experimental work has shown that no oxygen can be present for the reaction to work. Also, the energy needed from the sun and cosmic radiation are damaging to the very substances produced. Under the conditions required for life to have arisen spontaneously, it is more likely that the elements would be destroyed faster than they could be produced. Even if the right chemicals could be produced, no satisfactory answer has been given for how they could have been arranged properly and been enclosed in a cell wall. This would require another set of conditions altogether.

Second, the geological record does not support this view. Evolutionists date this origin at about 3.5 billion years ago; however, cells capable of photosynthesis have been found in rock from South Africa dated more than 3.1 billion years old, and in Australian rock dated 3.5 billion years old five different kinds of cells have been identified. There also appears to be evidences of living cells in rock from Greenland dated 3.8 billion years ago. There are no signs in the geologic record of precellular life. But if the age of the earth is about 4.6 billion years and life seems to be abundant, complex, and diverse by 3.5 billion years, that allows only 170 million years after the earth cooled (3.98 billion years ago) for evolution to take place. This is considerably less than the 2 billion years originally estimated. Just to complicate matters further, there is growing evidence that the early earth was rich in oxygen but low in nitrogen—just the opposite of what evolution needs.

Third, the experiments which support the generation of living matter from nonliving chemicals are flawed by the very interference of the intelligent scientist performing the experiment. These experiments do not really reproduce the conditions of early earth. There were no traps to collect only the amino acids produced. The chemicals used were not nearly as concentrated and not hand-picked to form a better reaction. There were many sources of energy acting simultaneously on the chemicals, and not always in harmony. And the levels of energy and wavelengths of light were not controlled. In other words, the experimenters are only fooling themselves to think that they are observing a natural process. They have manipulated the process by their own intervention.

Finally, evolutionists have never shown any mechanism that can harness the energy to do the work of selecting amino acids and sorting which will build each gene to develop a living organism. It doesn't do any good to have a drawer full of batteries if we don't have a flashlight (a mechanism for harnessing energy) to put them in. The DNA molecule is very complex. In fact, it has the specified complexity that we spoke of earlier. The English alphabet has twenty-six letters; the Greek alphabet has twenty-four and the genetic alphabet has only four, but the method of communicating by the sequence of letters is the same. Information scientist Hubert P. Yockey insists, "It is important to understand that we are not reasoning by analogy. The sequence hypothesis applies directly to the protein and the genetic text as well as to written language and therefore the treatment is mathematically identical."[8] It turns out that a single strand of DNA carries the same amount of information as a volume of an encyclopedia. Granting that there may have been enough energy available to do the work, the only systems we know which can harness the energy to do this kind of work are either living (but these were not around before life began) or intelligent. It is easy to pump a lot of energy into a system at random if all you want to do is make it hot, but if you want to organize it—that is, put it in order and create information—that requires intelligence.

What could explain the sudden appearance of life and also provide for the informational organization of living matter? If we apply the principle of uniformity (analogy) to the question, the only cause that we know routinely does this kind of work in the present is intelligence. The reasonable assumption is that it also required intelligence to do it in the past. Uniform experience proves this to us and, as Hume said, "As a uniform experience amounts to a proof, there is here a direct and full *proof,* from the nature of the fact" that the information inherent in living things required an intelligent cause. Since it is not possible that we are speaking of human intelligence, or even living beings in the natural sense, it had to be a supernatural intelligence. This does create a disjunction in the course of nature, which irritates most scientists; however, once it is admitted that there is a radical disjunction from nothing to something at the beginning of the universe, there can be little objection to the idea of another intervention when the evidence clearly points to it.

Other theories have been advanced to explain the origins of first life on earth. One is that new natural laws need to be discovered, but scientists can only point out the need and cannot explain how the organizing work can be done. Others suggest that life may have come to earth from somewhere else in the universe, either on a meteorite or on an ancient spaceship, but both of these solutions just push the question back one step: Where did that life come from? Still others borrow from pantheism and hold that some mind within the universe can account for the origin of life. Thermal vents in the sea floor and clay deposits are being studied as possible breeding grounds for life's beginnings, but none of these views really accounts for a way to harness the energy to make specified complexity possible. The most probable cause is a supernatural intelligence.

ORIGIN
OF NEW LIFE FORMS

|
EVOLUTION
(no intelligent
intervention)

|
CREATION
(intelligent
intervention)

Lack of Transitional Fossils
DNA Information
Principle of Uniformity

THE ORIGIN OF NEW LIFE FORMS

There are two views of origins. One says that everything came about by natural causes; the other looks to a supernatural cause. In the case of the origin of new life forms, they appeared either by an evolutionary process of natural selection without any intelligent intervention or by special Creation through the work of an intelligent designer.

Darwin made one of his greatest contributions to the theory of evolution with his analogy of selection by breeders to selection in nature. This principle of natural selection became the hallmark of evolution because it provided a system by which new developments of life forms could be explained without recourse to a supernatural cause. The main evidence that he put forward to support this analogy was the fossil record. Introductory biology books ever since have pictured this gradual transition of life forms from simple to complex in acceptance of this view.

Darwin himself was aware that there were serious problems with the analogy between breeders and nature, but he hoped that what humans could do in a few generations could be done by nature in several hundred generations. However, time is not the only factor which weakens the analogy. E.S. Russell wrote:

It is unfortunate that Darwin ever introduced the term "natural selection," for it has given rise to much confusion of thought.

NATURAL SELECTION AND INTELLIGENT SELECTION

	Artificial Selection	Natural Selection
Goal	Aim (end) in view	No aim (end) in view
Process	Intelligently guided process	Blind process
Choices	Intelligent choice of breeds	No intelligent choice of breeds
Protection	Breeds guarded from destructive forces	Breeds not guarded from destructive processes
Freaks	Preserves desired freaks	Eliminates most freaks
Interruptions	Continued interruptions to reach desired goal	No continued interruptions to reach any goal
Survival	Preferential survival	Nonpreferential survival

Conclusion: Rather than being analogous, in the most crucial aspects, natural selection and artificial selection are exact opposites.

He did so, of course, because he arrived at his theory through studying the effects of selection as practiced by man in the breeding of domesticated animals and cultivated plants. Here the use of the word is entirely legitimate. *But the action of man in selective breeding is not analogous to the action of "natural selection," but almost its direct opposite.* . . . Man has an aim or an end in view; "natural selection" can have none. Man picks out the individuals he wishes to cross, choosing them by the characteristics he seeks to perpetuate or enhance. He protects them and their issue by all means in his power, guarding them thus from the operation of natural selection, which would speedily eliminate many freaks; he continues his active and purposeful selection from generation to generation until he reaches, if possible, his goal. Nothing of this kind happens, or can happen, through the blind process of differential elimination and differential survival which we miscall "natural selection."[9]

This objection is still a major problem for evolution. It amounts to the same problem that we saw in examining the origin of first life. The analogy used to prove that natural processes did it all contains a great deal of intelligent intervention that is overlooked in the theory. Breeders manipulate according to an intelligent plan to produce specific developments. Informationally speaking, this is going from a state of complexity in the DNA code to a higher, or at least more specific, state of complexity. It is like changing the sentence, "She had brown hair," to the more complex statement, "Her tresses were auburn and shown in the sun." This increase in information coded into the DNA requires intelligence just as surely as the original coding to produce life did. Indeed, if Darwin's analogy proves anything, it shows the need for intelligent intervention to produce new life forms. Again, the principle of uniformity leads us to this conclusion once it is realized that we are working within origin science, not operation science.

But what of the fossil evidence that has been so widely proclaimed? Darwin recognized this as a problem as well and wrote in *The Origin of Species,* "Why then is not every geological formation and every stratum full of such intermediate links? Geology assuredly does not reveal any such finely graduated organic chain, and this, perhaps, is the most obvious and gravest objection which can be urged against my theory."[10] In the 130 years since Darwin wrote, the situation has only become worse for his theory. Noted Harvard paleontologist Stephen Jay Gould has written, "The extreme rarity of transitional forms in the fossil record persists as the trade secret of paleontology. The evolutionary trees that adorn our textbooks have data only at the tips and nodes of their branches; the rest is inference, however reasonable, not the evidence of fossils."[11] Eldredge and Tattersall agree, saying:

Expectation colored perception to such an extent that the *most obvious single fact about biological evolution—non-change—*has seldom, if ever, been incorporated into anyone's scientific notions of how life actually evolves. If ever there was a myth, it is that evolution is a process of constant change.[12]

What does the fossil record suggest? Evolutionists like Gould now support what creationists like Agassiz, Gish, and others have said all along.

The history of most fossil species includes two features particularly inconsistent with gradualism:
1. *Stasis*. Most species exhibit no directional change during their tenure on earth. They appear in the fossil record looking much the same as when they disappear; morphological change is usually limited and directionless.
2. *Sudden appearance*. In any local area, a species does not arise gradually by the steady transformation of its ancestors: it appears all at once and "fully formed."[13]

The fossil evidence clearly gives a picture of mature, fully functional creatures suddenly appearing and staying very much the same. There is no real indication that one form of life transforms into a completely different form. While these two features seem to invalidate classical evolution, they are somewhat problematic to creationists also.

Some creationists say that the fossil record reflects the debris of the great Flood either because some animals were better able to escape the waters or by hydrodynamic sorting as the remains settled. These scientists are concerned with preserving a young earth on the grounds that they believe in a literal six-day, twenty-four-hour period Creation with no large gaps in the early genealogies of Genesis. Others, known as old earth creationists, hold that the earth need not be only thousands of years old. This group understands the fossil record to show that Creation was accomplished in a series of stages, each new appearance in the geological strata pointing to a new moment of direct creation. Invertebrates appeared first, followed by a long period of nature balancing itself before the next burst of creation. Fish appeared next and then amphibia and so on until man was created. The latter view does agree with the fossil record, but there is no consensus between creationists about the age of the earth. This is a hotly debated issue, but no matter which way it is resolved, they both agree that the existing fossil evidence supports Creation better than evolution.

Some evolutionists have attempted to deal with the fossil evidence by introducing the idea of punctuated equilibrium. These scientists say that the jumps in the fossil record reflect evolutionary jumps which brought on major changes in shorter times. Hence, evolution is not gradual, but punctuated by sudden leaps from one stage to the next. The theory has been criticized because they

---

When Did It All Begin?

Whether one follows a young earth or an old earth model will determine how you interpret much of the evidence, especially the fossils. The central motivation behind the young earth view is that this is thought to be what the Bible teaches. If the first chapter of Genesis refers to literal twenty-four-hour days, and if the genealogies in chapters 5 and 10 are understood to be closed, then Creation comes out to be around 4000 B.C. Really, only a few young earth advocates care to fix a date like that. They do desire to show that the long spans of time that evolution calls for are neither helpful to evolution nor without presupposition.

Of course, there are many Creationists who argue for an old earth. Biblically, this position that the word for *day* is used for more than twenty-four hours even in Genesis 2:4, the events of the sixth day surely took more than twenty-four hours, and Hebrews 4:4-5 implies that God is still in His seventh-day rest. If the seventh day can be long, then the others could too. Scientifically, this view does not require any novel theories to explain the evidence. One of the biggest problems for the young earth view is in astronomy. We can see light from stars that took 15 billion years to get here. To say that God created them with the appearance of age does not satisfy the question of how their light reached us. We have watched star explosions that happened billions of years ago, but if the universe is not billions of years old, then we are seeing light from stars that never existed—because they would have died before Creation. Why would God deceive us with the evidence? The old earth view seems to fit the evidence better and causes no problem with the Bible.

---

cannot produce any evidence for a mechanism of secondary causes which makes these sudden advances possible. Their theory then appears to be based solely on the absence of transitional fossils. Darwin, after all, understood suddenness to be evidence of Creation. If this is true, then it supports what Creationists said all along—the sudden appearance of fully formed animals is evidence of Creation.

Creationists reason that there are real limitations to genetic changes and that this indicates a special creation of each major category of life forms. Each new life form came into being by an act of intelligent intervention specifying its genetic information for its peculiar function. Just as letter sequences make up different words, DNA codes vary and produce different species. If it requires intelligence to create *King Lear* from selecting and sorting the words in a dictionary, then it also requires intelligence to select and sort genetic information to produce a variety of species which work together as a system in nature. The sudden appearance of these life forms only strengthens our case that a supernatural intelligence was at work to accomplish this organization. By the principle of uniformity, this is the most plausible solution to the problem.

CONCLUSION

Now that we have new evidence about the nature of the universe, the information stored in DNA molecules, and further fossil confirmation, the words of Louis Agassiz resound even more loudly than they did when first written in 1860: "[Darwin] has lost sight of the most striking of the features, and the one which pervades the whole, namely, that there runs throughout Nature unmistakable evidence of thought, corresponding to the mental operations of our own mind, and therefore intelligible to us as thinking beings, and unaccountable on any other basis than that they owe their existence to the working of intelligence; and no theory that overlooks this element can be true to nature."[14]

There are two views of origins. One says that everything came about by natural causes; the other looks to a supernatural cause. The overwhelming evidence supports the Creationist view.

NOTES

1. Carl Sagan, *Cosmos* (New York: Random House, 1980), p. 4.

2. David Hume, *Letters,* ed. by J.Y.T. Greig (Oxford: Clarendon, 1932), vol. 1, p. 187.

3. Robert Jastrow, *God and the Astronomers* (New York: Warner Books, 1978), p. 111.

4. Ibid., p. 95.

5. Ibid., p. 5.

6. Ibid., pp. 15, 18.

7. Ibid., pp. 105–106.

8. Hubert P. Yockey, "Self-Organization, Origin of Life Scenarios, and Information Theory" in *Journal of Theoretical Biology,* 1981, p. 16.

9. E.S. Russell, *The Diversity of Animals* ([1915] 1962), p. 124. Cited in James R. Moore, *The Post-Darwinian Controversies* (New York: Oxford University Press, 1979).

10. Darwin, *On the Origin of Species* (London: John Murray, 1859), p. 280.

11. Stephen Jay Gould, "Evolution's Erratic Pace" in *Natural History,* May 1977, p. 14.

12. Niles Eldredge and Ian Tattersall, *The Myths of Human Evolution* (New York: Columbia University Press, 1982), p. 8.

13. Gould, *op. cit.* pp. 13–14.

14. Louis Agassiz, "Contribution to the Natural History of the United States" in *American Journal of Science,* 1860.

11

QUESTIONS ABOUT THE AFTERLIFE

"If at first you don't succeed, try, try again." Not bad advice for facing the challenges of this life, but does it still apply in the afterlife? Some people think so. They believe that once is not enough in terms of lifetimes needed to work out our salvation; so we try, try again until we get it right. This doctrine is called reincarnation, and it is quickly becoming a major threat to people's understanding of the Gospel.

WHAT IS REINCARNATION?
The word is self-explanatory, but only if you know Latin. Chili *con carne* means chili with meat, right? The same word is used to form incarnation, which basically means "in the flesh." We often speak of Christ's incarnation because He came in the flesh. Well, *reincarnation* just means that it happens over and over again. We keep coming back in the flesh—in different bodies—but the soul or spirit remains the same. That may seem pretty foreign to your way of thinking, so we'll explain more about how it works and why people would believe it a little later. For now, let's just get the definition. Reincarnation is the belief that, after death, the soul passes on to another body.

WHO BELIEVES IT?
According to a Gallup poll in 1982, 23 percent or almost one in four Americans believe in reincarnation. Among college-age peo-

ple (18–24), that increases to 30 percent. The scary part about that is that nine out of ten Americans claim Christianity. In fact, the figures don't change that much for professing Christians: 21 percent of the Protestants and 25 percent of the Catholics in this country go right along with it. Reincarnation is the "In" thing.

Along with these statistics of the general populace, there are several celebrities that have proclaimed their belief in reincarnation. The most vocal of these has been Shirley MacLaine. Her three books about the spiritual realm and her seminars are consistently successful in the marketplace. *Out on a Limb,* the first book of the trilogy, she describes as a "quest for self"—the self that has survived so many reincarnations. "'I know that I must have been many different people in many different times . . . a former prostitute, my own daughter's daughter, and a male court jester who was beheaded by Louis XV of France'—all in past incarnations that she believes she has rediscovered with the aid of mediums, meditation and, in at least one case, acupuncture."[1] The New Age movement, of which MacLaine is a part, teaches this doctrine as part of the road to godhood.

Reincarnation in the New Age

How does the New Age movement interpret Jesus' resurrection? Easy—He reached *moksha,* the escape from bodily existence. The *Aquarian Gospel,* written by Levi Dowling, says, "Jesus did not sleep within the tomb. The body is the manifest of the soul; but the soul is soul without its manifest." Hence, when Jesus greets the Occult Masters in his disembodied state, he announces: "My brothers of the Silent Brotherhood, peace, peace on earth; goodwill to men!

"The problem of the ages has been solved; a son of man has risen from the dead; has shown that human flesh can be transmuted into flesh divine.

"Before the eyes of men this flesh in which I came to you was changed with speed of light from human flesh. And so I am the message that I bring to you. To you I come, the first of all the race to be transmuted to the image of AM.

"What I have done, all men will do; and what I am, all men will be." [*The Aquarian Gospel of Jesus Christ* (Santa Monica: DeVorss & Co., 1907, 1964), 172:15; 176:26-30.]

Joining MacLaine are some equally famous, though less vocal celebrities like Glenn Ford, Anne Francis (*Honey West*), Sylvester Stallone (*Rocky, Rambo*), Audry Landers ("Dallas"), Paddy Chayevsky (author of *Marty, The Hospital, Altered States*), General George S. Patton, Henry Ford, Salvador Dali, and Mark Twain. In music, ex-Beatle George Harrison, Ravi Shankar, Mahavishnu John McLaughlin, and John Denver have all dedicated their endeavors to spreading the message of their spiritual beliefs in a second chance. Even some comic books are getting in on the act. *Camelot 3000, Ronin,* and *Dr. Strange* have all dealt with themes of reincarnation.

The original source of the doctrine is the Hindu Vedas (Scriptures). The Buddhist, Jainist, and Sikhist forms seem to have been derived from these, as have the teachings of Transcendental Meditation and the Hare Krishnas. In the West, some forms may have arisen without knowledge of the Hindu teaching, such as Plato's. Psychic Edgar Cayce and theosophy writers like Helena Blavatsky also teach multiple lives. Several Christian theologians have attempted to harmonize reincarnation with Christianity. Among these are Geddes MacGregor and John Hick.

HOW DOES REINCARNATION WORK?

Philosophically, reincarnation is wrapped up in Eastern religions such as Hinduism, Buddhism, and Taoism (not Islam; they believe in one God who judges). But reincarnation is not confined to the East. Some of the early Western philosophers also believed that the soul lives on in different forms. Pythagoras, Plato, and Plotinus all believed that the spirit or soul was eternal and could not be destroyed.

Plato taught very clearly that the immortal soul takes on a body only as punishment for some sin, for which he will suffer tenfold; hence, the soul is forced to leave the ideal realm and enter into the material world. In one passage he speaks of two doors in heaven: one for the souls entering and the other for those leaving.[2] Before embarking on a new life, each is made to pass over the River of Forgetfulness. "The soul, then, as being immortal, and having been born again many times, and having seen all things that exist, whether in this world or in the world below, has knowledge of them all . . . for all enquiry and learning is but recollection."[3] Plato also taught that men might return as animals.[4]

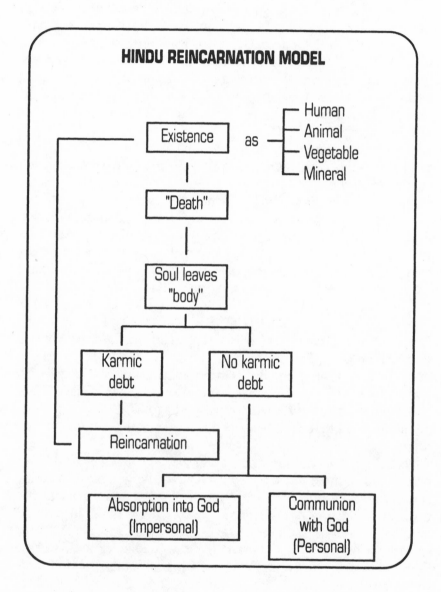

The similarities between Plato and the Hindu doctrine are striking, especially Ramanuja's "personal" system. This school developed from the earlier "impersonal" view, but the key ingredients are the same for both. The soul is called *jiva* or *jivatman* and it survives death as a mental entity called the subtle body. This entity will enter a new embryo and bring along with it the *karma* of all its past lives. Karma is both the actions or deeds done and the unalterable consequences attached to them. In a sense, it means "you reap what you sow." If you do good deeds, you are born into a "pleasant womb." If you do evil, your destiny will be proportionately less noble. You might even find yourself in a "foul and stinking womb," like that of an animal, vegetable, or mineral. The cycle of death and rebirth is often depicted as a wheel, with death as the gateway to new life. The goal, though, is to escape from this cycle.

This escape is called *moksha,* and it is here that the difference arises between the personal and impersonal forms of the doctrine. The impersonal version says that once all karmic debt is eliminated, the soul loses all identity and simply becomes one with the One; the self merges with Brahman (divine, impersonal Force). The personal view says that the soul is simply liberated to be itself, fully devoted to Bhagwan (the personal God).

Other forms of the doctrine of reincarnation differ on what happens at the point of death and the nature of the ultimate state of moksha, but the general pattern is retained. Buddhists say that the unconscious soul *(vinnana)* continues, but the self (its intellect, emotions, consciousness, etc.) is obliterated at death. Its *karma* remains in the cycle of rebirth called *samsara.* There are four interpretations of the final state *(nirvana)* in Buddhism, one of which is attained by the grace of Buddha. Jainism and Sikhism follow the same patterns as personal and impersonal Hinduism, respectively.

The "Christian" forms, likewise, do not differ in their basic concept, but other factors enter the situation. Most important, during the time of human existence, a decision is made about whether to accept or reject Christ. The simplest model here has those who accept Christ going to be with God while those who reject Him are reincarnated until they do recognize Christ. In this

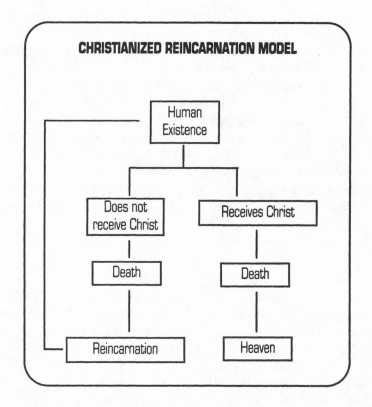

way, all will eventually be saved. There are only two examples (MacGregor and de Arteaga) of "Christian" reincarnation theories that provide ultimate punishment for those who are lost causes, and in one of those (MacGregor) the punishment is annihilation.

WHY DO PEOPLE BELIEVE IN REINCARNATION?

There are several rationales given for the belief in reincarnation. Three of the most basic reasons are the belief in an immortal soul, psychological evidence of past lives, and the justice of reincarnation as a system.

Immortality of the soul

Plato's main reason for believing in transmigration of souls (another name for souls going to different bodies) was that he considered the immaterial part of man to be uncreated and indestructible. It exists before we are born and it continues to exist after we die; and nothing, either good or evil, can corrupt it. If that is the case, then it is likely that it appears in the world in different bodies at various times. This is part of its perfecting process. In the same way, pantheistic philosophies assume that all is eternal and divine, so the soul is equally incorruptible.

Psychological evidence of past lives

Ian Stevenson, a parapsychologist and researcher of past-life recall, has said,

> The idea of reincarnation may contribute to an improved un-derstanding of such diverse matters as: phobias and philias of childhood; skills not learned in early life; abnormalities of child–parent relationships; vendettas and bellicose nationalism; childhood sexuality and gender identity confusion; birthmarks, congenital deformities and internal diseases; differences be-tween members of monozygotic twin pairs; and abnormal appe-tites during pregnancy.[5]

Past lives, recalled during hypnosis or other altered conscious-ness states, have been helpful to some in explaining feelings that the patient cannot account for or overcome. By finding some experience in a past life, many have been relieved of the feelings of fear, depression, or unwantedness. Though many psychologists and hypnotists who work with past-life recall do not really believe that the events recounted by their patients are real, they use it because it works. As one therapist said, "It doesn't matter if it is real or imagined if it helps someone [sic] make sense out of their lives. . . . If it works, who cares?"[6]

The justice of reincarnation

To many, the idea of having more than one chance at life seems to be the most equitable solution for several reasons. First, karma is just. If you do bad things, you pay the price; if you do good, you get a reward. Punishment is in proportion to how bad your karma is, not all or nothing. The idea of condemning someone to an infinite hell for a finite amount of sin sounds too harsh; but karma is just. Second, suffering in this life can be justified if it is really an outworking of our karma from past lives. This explanation eliminates the need to make God responsible for suffering in any way. All suffering can be explained as the just outworking of bad deeds done in former incarnations.

Third, as Quincy Howe has written, "One of the most attractive aspects of reincarnation is that it removes entirely the possibility of damnation."[7] The doctrine of eternal punishment for anyone seems totally incompatible with the love of God to many people. Reincarnation suggests a way in which God can punish sin (through the law of karma), demand faith in Christ (during at least one lifetime), and still save everyone ultimately. If someone rejects Christ, he gets a second chance, and a third, and so on, until he does believe. This even protects human freedom because God does not coerce anyone to believe; He merely gives them more time to exercise their freedom. Moral progress and spiritual growth can also occur during successive lifetimes, which will allow individuals to understand the love of God better. Indeed, some think that moral perfection cannot be attained without reincarnation.

Hell or Bust

Geddes MacGregor calls the doctrine of eternal punishment "barbarous" and cannot tolerate the idea "that even one sinner should be punished by everlasting torture." Instead, he thinks, "The notion that many people might be simply extinguished, fading gradually from existence, seems to me more intelligible. Such people do not want existence. Why, then, should the gift be thrust upon them?" So he teaches that "hell" is really a metaphor for annihilation— going bust into nonexistence. But how does he know what other people want? Atheist Friedrich Nietzsche said that he would rather choose eternally conscious suffering than nonexistence. Even a bad existence is better than no existence. And wouldn't a God who simply snuffs people out be just as cruel, if not more so, than one who allows men to freely choose their own destinies? Really, we can use the same argument: "Such people do not want [to live with God]. Why should the gift be thrust upon them?" [*Reincarnation as a Christian Hope* (Totowa, N.J.: Barnes and Noble Imports, 1982), p. 146.]

Finally, it is argued that reincarnation is just because it makes salvation a personal matter between the individual and God. Rather than dealing with problems of imputed guilt from Adam's sin or being reckoned righteous by faith, everyone is responsible for taking care of his own karma. Howe, arguing that the atonement by a substitute is no longer valid, says, "Man himself must make his peace with God."[8] MacGregor says clearly, "My karma is particular to me. It is my problem and the triumph over it is my triumph."[9] This eliminates the injustice of being punished, in any way, for Adam's sin and the injustice of Christ dying for sins that He did not commit. Instead, Jesus' death becomes our inspiration, "the perfect catalyst"[10] for working out our salvation and assuring us "that one stands in the unfailing light of God's love."[11] He died as our example, not as our substitute. In these ways, reincarnation satisfies justice.

WHAT IS WRONG WITH REINCARNATION?

There are two different ways to approach this question. We can say it is contrary to what the Bible teaches, but what good would that do for someone who does not believe that the Bible is the Word of God? Let's save those arguments for when we consider the biblical alternative, resurrection. Here, let's concentrate on the logical aspects of why reincarnation is wrong.

First, we have to admit that reincarnationists are at least stimulating discussion about the afterlife. In Christian circles, it is hard to find a really good book on the subject—one that deals with the issues seriously. Second, they try to defend the love, mercy, and justice of God in the face of the problem of evil. Third, they maintain the dignity of man by recognizing that he is a moral creature with free will. We must commend these concerns and the truths they reflect, but we don't have to buy the whole system.

Reincarnation does not solve the problem of evil

Rather than solving the problem of unjust suffering, reincarnation simply says that it is just. No one is really innocent because the karma of one's past lives is causing suffering in this life. Reincarnationists complain that when a Christian is faced with giving a reason to the grieving mother of a dying four-month-old, he can only say, "I don't know." But the law of karma can give her an answer: "Your sweet, innocent angel is dying because in an earlier incarnation she was a scumball." Would that make *you* feel any better? This is not a *solution* to the problem; it is merely a *subversion* of it. It doesn't *deal* with the difficulty; it *dismisses* it.

Is it really fair for God to punish children for the sins of adults? Especially when they don't remember those sins! It seems morally repugnant and terribly unjust to mete out judgment on someone who does not even know what his crime was. Besides this, by putting the guilt back one lifetime, one begins an infinite regress of explanations that never really pay off with an explanation. If the suffering of each life depends on the sins of a former life, then how did it all begin? If there was a first life, where did the karmic debt come from to explain the suffering in that life? Is evil an eternal principle, right alongside God? You can't keep "backpedaling" forever to solve the problem of evil. Even John Hick recognizes that the law of karma fails to resolve the conflict: "It only pushes the problem back into earlier lives without ever coming any nearer to a solution."[12]

Karma ≠ Law
One gets the impression, and some argue, that karma is the same as the Old Testament Law—a rigid, universal moral code.

Infinite Regress of Evil
Explaining suffering as results of karma from a past life never gets to a real explanation. For each previous life, there would have to be another life before that to account for its suffering. One could keep going on like that forever, but would never reach an explanation. He would just be putting it off indefinitely.

It would be like covering a hot check by depositing a check in one bank from an account in another bank, and covering that withdrawal by a check from another bank, and so on. Ultimately, some banker is going to ask you, "Where is the money?" And when he does, you had better have it in the account that the last check was written from. There has got to be a payoff somewhere. Reincarnation doesn't have a payoff when it tries to explain evil. It just keeps passing bad checks.

However, karma is not a moral prescription. It is a system of retribution only; it has no content that tells us what to do. It is enforcement, but not a moral law; it is a penal system without a legislature. It is impersonal, a moral law of act/consequence relations. Even comparisons with the act/consequence relationship in Proverbs fail to recognize that the Old Testament puts these forth as general principles, not absolute, unbreakable sanctions of retribution. For that matter, the Law was not as unalterable as karma—it could be transcended by a higher law of forgiveness in the sacrifices. The comparison just doesn't work.

So where do the moral standards that karma enforces come from? It turns out that **there are none!** In pantheism, there is no ultimate difference between good and evil, right and wrong, etc. Karma is not a moral law. As for morality, all is relative. Allan Watts, a spokesman for Zen Buddhism, has written:

Buddhism does not share the Western view that there is a moral law, enjoined by God or by nature, which it is man's duty to obey. The Buddha's precepts of conduct—abstinence from taking life, taking what is not given, exploitation of the passions, lying and intoxication—are voluntarily assumed rules of expediency.[13]

New Age Ethics

Mark Satin, in his book *New Age Politics*, includes a chapter on the values of the movement. "In a spiritual [i.e., mystical] state, morality is impossible. . . . If you wish something for yourself, even guidelines or principles, you've already separated yourself out from the One (and besides, everything is as it should be)" (p. 98). He goes on to propose four principles which suggest political and social values. Citing the abandonment of America's traditional values, he says, "This is where the trans-material worldview comes in. . . . It implies a whole new way of looking at people, and a whole new set of ethics, values, goals, and priorities." The first of these is the self-development ethic, which has some bearing on reincarnation. "Getting in touch with ourselves would appear to be, not just fun (though it can be that), and not self-indulgence at all, but an imperative for survival that's built into the structure of the universe. (Maybe even an evolutionary imperative)" (pp. 102–103).

Expediency is the watchword of situational ethics. If something works, do it. Any moral act, even murder and cruelty, might be justified as being expedient. This relativism poses real problems for reincarnation. Relativism is an impossible position to hold in ethics. You can't say, "All is relative," or even, "Relativism is better than absolutism," because both of these statements assume an absolute value that contradicts relativism. As C.S. Lewis explains:

> The moment you say that one set of moral ideas can be better than another, you are, in fact, measuring them both by a standard, saying that one of them conforms to that standard more nearly than the other. But the standard that measures the two things is something different from either. You are, in fact, comparing them both with some Real Morality, admitting that there is such a thing as real Right, independent of what people think, and that some people's ideas get nearer to that real Right than others.[14]

In other words, in order to say that relativism is right, you have to assume that some absolute right exists, which is impossible in relativism. Unless something is absolutely right, nothing can be actually right; and if nothing is right (or wrong), then karma has no business punishing anyone for it.

Reincarnation is ultimately antihumanitarian

Have you ever seen any pictures of India? Do you know what life is like there? Thousands of poor, crippled, maimed, homeless, and starving people are seen lining the streets and no one seems to even notice them. Why is that so? The law of karma has made it so. According to classic Hinduism, if someone were to help those people by easing their suffering, they would be working against the law of karma. People suffer to work off their karmic debt, and if you helped them, then they would have to come back again and suffer even more to work off that debt. Plus, you would be doing something cruel by not letting them suffer, and you would increase your own karma problems. Helping people is just out of the question in a society that believes in reincarnation.

Disinterestedness

When Gautama Buddha left the security of his secluded home and discovered the evil and suffering that exists in the world, he had to confront the moral conflict between allowing the Law of Karma to work or doing good deeds that interfere with it. His conclusion was that one must become disinterested. One must lose his concern about others, recognizing that (1) there is no real difference between good and evil and (2) all things are as they must be. Hence, whether one helps the suffering or ignores them, he should do so with complete disinterest—as though doing one was the same as doing the other. Whichever road you take, it will be guided by fate. It doesn't matter what you do, as long as you don't care which is right or wrong.

Reincarnation does not guarantee spiritual progress

Sometimes reincarnationists use evolution as a proof that we are constantly becoming better, higher, and more spiritually oriented life forms. The problem is that there is no evidence that such evolution has occurred in the biological or the spiritual realms. After more than a hundred years of experimentation and scientific observation since Darwin, no one has ever proven from the fossil record or produced in the lab any change from one major life form to another. One evolutionist admitted that:

With the failure of these many efforts science was left in the somewhat embarrassing position of having to postulate theories of living origins which it could not demonstrate. After having chided the theologian for his reliance on myth and miracle, science found itself in the unenviable position of having to create a mythology of its own: namely, the assumption that what, after long effort, could not be proved to take place today had, in truth, taken place in the primeval past.[15]

If major evolutionary changes did not take place in the biological sense, is there any reason to assume that it has happened in the spiritual sense? Are we progressing toward a new kind of being with higher God-consciousness? A glance at the morning news is sufficient to give an emphatically negative answer.

Furthermore, there is no reason to think that moral progress must be gradual. Why can't there be an immediate, radical change in a person? Even reincarnationists believe that quantum leaps in moral development are possible and that some dramatic changes occur between death and the next incarnation. No matter how many finite lifetimes it takes, we can never progress to the same level and the infinite goodness of God. There will always be an infinite difference between us. The only way to bridge that gap would be a sudden and miraculous transformation, which would eliminate the need for a long process of moral enrichment. One life would be enough if it ended with a dramatic change after death. But this is what the Bible teaches (2 Cor. 5:1-5), not reincarnation.

There is also reason to think that a hundred or a thousand lives would not be enough. There are no guarantees that anyone will ever reach *moksha*. No matter how many bodies they take, each one might fail to pay off its own karmic debt, or even increase it. How can we be sure that we would ever make it? If we messed up so bad this time, what makes us think we will do better next time? As for the Christianized versions that say it gives men a second chance to accept Christ, it does not make sense to say that it takes more than one lifetime to make a lifetime decision. If one life is not enough, there is no guarantee that any number of reincarnations over any amount of time will ever be enough.

With these kinds of fundamental problems in the logic of reincarnation, it just might not be worth the trouble. But what about the Bible—what does it teach about the afterlife? What does it have to say about reincarnation? Let's look at both the doctrine of resurrection and that doctrine's significance to reincarnation.

WHAT IS RESURRECTION?

We said before that reincarnation is the belief that after death the soul passes on to another body. By contrast, resurrection is the belief that after death the same physical body is made incorruptible. Rather than a series of bodies that die, resurrection makes alive forever the same body that died. Rather than seeing man as a soul in a body, resurrection sees man as a soul-body unity. While

REINCARNATION	RESURRECTION
Pantheistic	Theistic
Soul/Body dualism	Soul/Body unity
Mortal body	Immortal body
Many-times event	One-time event
Intermediate states	Ultimate state
In process	Perfected
Based on Karma	Based on Grace

reincarnation is a process toward perfection, resurrection is a perfected state. Reincarnation is an intermediate state, while the soul longs to be disembodied and absorbed in God; but resurrection is an ultimate state in which the whole person, body and soul, enjoys the goodness of God. Quite a difference, huh?

It surprises a lot of Christians to learn that we will have a real physical body in the afterlife, but why shouldn't we? Jesus did! After His resurrection, He said, "See My hands and My feet, that it is I Myself; touch Me and see, for a spirit does not have flesh and bones as you see that I have" (Luke 24:39). Not only did He have flesh and bones, but His friends could recognize it as the same body, not just some body. He even ate some fish with them! (vv. 41-43) If you try to do that in a subtle body like the reincarnationists talk about, it would fall right through. His resurrected body was made of human flesh like the body He had in His earthly life (John 20:11-29; 21:1-23; Acts 1:4-9).

But it had some differences too. He could appear and disappear at will (Luke 24:31; John 20:19, 26). And He ascended into the clouds without a jet pack (Acts 1:9-11). These differences show that the raisings of Lazarus (John 11:1-44) and of the widow's son (Luke 7:11-17) were not resurrections, but only revivification of their mortal bodies (since they both died again). So the resurrected body was material, but immortal. It was physical, but imperishable (1 Cor. 15:50-54).

Paul does not speak in terms of a spiritual existence in heaven either. He says that we will be changed. Calling Christ "the first-fruits of those who are asleep" (v. 20), he sees Jesus' resurrection as the pattern for those who are to follow. The contrasts that Paul makes do not suggest a disembodied state, but a perfected body. He says, "We shall all be changed, in a moment, in the twinkling of an eye" (vv. 51-52). This change is from perishable to imperishable, mortal to immortal, dishonor to glory, weakness to strength. The body is perfected, not by doing away with it, but by removing its imperfections. When Paul says that to be absent from the body is to be present with the Lord (see 2 Cor. 5:6), we can easily see that he means absent from this earthly body. At the resurrection, we will be reunited with it as it is made an immortal body.

When will the resurrection happen? The Bible speaks of two resurrections: one to life and the other to judgment (Dan. 12:2; John 5:29; Heb. 11:35). The clearest text is Revelation 20:4-6, which indicates that the first resurrection occurs when Jesus returns at the Second Coming and involves only those who will be resurrected to eternal life; but the second resurrection occurs later and involves those who will be judged (vv. 11-15 expands on this). What happens to the dead between now and then? Paul assures us that death means to be with Christ (2 Cor. 5:6). It is "very much better" (Phil. 1:23) than this life. It is a conscious bliss in God's very presence (Rev. 6:9).

HOW DOES RESURRECTION WORK?

You already know that reincarnation says that when we die, we lose our body but our soul lives on, acquires its karmic debt, and is given new bodies to live as many lives as necessary until all its karma is gone, when it is united with God (either personally or impersonally). Resurrection works in a very different manner. The differences begin with the nature of man and follow from there to the natures of death, judgment, and the final state.

The nature of man

Reincarnation is based on a pantheistic worldview that denies the reality of matter. Even in the systems that are panentheistic, like John Hick and the personal form of Hinduism, matter is regarded as evil and a corruption of reality. From this starting point, it is no wonder that reincarnationists see perfection as the elimination of matter. Theism, the worldview of the Bible, says that matter was created by God and is good (Gen. 1:31; 1 Tim. 4:4). Man was created by mixing dust plus breath—body and spirit (Gen. 2:7) and is to be perfected in spirit, soul, and body (1 Thes. 5:23). Even the name Adam comes from the Hebrew word for dust. Without his body, man is just not complete, according to the biblical view.

The nature of death

The famous Hindu teacher Swami Radhakrishnan acknowledged:

> There is a fundamental difference between Christianity and Hinduism; it is said that it consists in this: that while the Hindu to whatever school he belongs believes in a succession of lives, the Christian believes that "it is appointed to men once to die, but after this the judgment."[16]

This verse (Heb. 9:27) is indeed central to the Bible's view of death. Not only does it clearly assert that man has but one life, but it associates death with judgment. This association clarifies the difference between the two views even further. Rather than being put into a body because of sins, God judged Adam's sin by introducing death—the separation of body from the soul. Perfection of the body comes when this curse is removed, when sin and all of its effects are done away with. Reincarnation teaches that life in this world is a curse and death is an escape, but resurrection asserts the opposite. Life is a blessing and rich gift of God, and death is the punishment for sin (Rom. 6:23).

The nature of judgment

On what basis is man to be judged? The reincarnationists say that each man will work off his own karma. But this flies in the face of the grace of God given as the basis of judgment in the Bible. The Scriptures speak of salvation as a "gift" (John 4:10; Rom. 3:24; 5:15-17; 6:23; 2 Cor. 9:15; Eph. 2:8; Heb. 6:4) which is received by faith. Rather than working to merit God's favor, the believer is given grace, or unmerited favor, by which he is pronounced righteous. As Christ said very plainly:

> For God so loved the world, that He gave His only begotten Son, that whoever believes in Him should not perish, but have eternal life. . . . He who believes in Him is not judged; he who does not believe has been judged already, because he has not believed in the name of the only begotten Son of God (John 3:16, 18).

The basis of judgment is whether or not an individual has believed that Jesus is God's Son, sent into the world to save him.

But what about the justice of God? It can't be just of God to let sin go unpunished! This is where the doctrine of atonement enters. The New Testament teaches that Jesus was punished for the sins of the whole world in His death. Our sins were not simply ignored or swept under the rug. Jesus "satisfied" (Rom. 3:25; Heb. 2:17; 1 John 2:2; 4:10) God's demand for justice by bearing our guilt as our substitute. This penalty paid by Christ is also

---

Is Substitutionary Atonement Just?
How can it be just to punish the innocent instead of the guilty? Surely "the wickedness of the wicked will be upon himself" (Ezek. 18:20). The Bible is clearly against the suffering of the innocent, but there is another principle involved here: "Greater love has no one than this, that one lay down his life for his friends" (John 15:13). Which of these precepts was Christ to follow? If He obeyed only the first, how could mankind be saved? But if He died for sin, then the former principle of justice is denied. The solution rests in seeing that some moral principles are more important than others, just as saving lives was more important to the Hebrew midwives in Egypt than obeying the God-established government (Ex. 1:15-21). Here, demonstrating the love of God by providing salvation for all men is a command that outweighs the justice of Ezekiel's saying. It is more important to save the lives of all men, and still punish their sin, than to insist that they bear their own guilt. After all, which shows the greater love?

ATONEMENT

Personal	Vicarious
Made by the offending party	Made by the party offended
Given by the criminal	Received by the criminal
Incompatible with mercy	Highest form of mercy

spoken of as a "ransom" (Mark 10:45), "reconciliation" (Rom. 5:10; 2 Cor. 5:18-20; Col. 1:22), "redemption" (Rom. 3:24; 8:23; Eph. 1:7, 14; Col. 1:14; Heb. 9:12-15), and "justification" (Rom. 4:25; 5:1, 9, 16-18; Gal. 2:16-17; Titus 3:7). Jesus is called the "Sin-bearer" (2 Cor. 5:21; Heb. 7:26-27; 1 Peter 2:24), the Suffering Servant (Acts 3:13; 8:32ff), the "curse-bearer" (Gal. 3:13), and the Lamb of sacrifice (John 1:29, 36; Acts 8:32; 1 Peter 1:19).

There is an important difference between personal atonement (paying for your own sins) and vicarious atonement (having the penalty paid by another). The former is the law of karma, and the latter, the rule of grace.

Since Christ was sinless (Heb. 4:15), His death was not necessary to pay for His own sin. Rather, His life was voluntarily (John 10:17-18) given to pay the penalty for the sins of others. "He made him who knew no sin to be sin on our behalf, that we might become the righteousness of God in Him" (2 Cor. 5:21). As Robert Morey has phrased this in the language of reincarnation:

Christianity eventually replaced Karmic transmigration with its doctrine of Christ's substitutionary atonement in which He paid all of our "Karmic debt" through His own suffering. He had no Karma of His own, but He suffered and died for our sins.[17]

The nature of the final state

While reincarnationists are almost exclusively universalists (everyone will be saved), the Bible teaches that some will be forever punished. Though some complain that this is not compatible with God's love, the objection rests on a misunderstanding. Pantheism sees all things as necessary outworkings of God's being, but theism recognizes the freedom of God's will to do as He chooses. With this in mind, it is clearly an error "to base man's salvation solely on God's attributes, such as His love or goodness." His love is not mandated by His nature; it is a choice. It is the actions by which God *shows* His love that are really at issue here.

Thus God's love, in and of itself, cannot save anyone, much less all of humanity. None of God's attributes, in and of themselves, can save anyone. It is the manifestation of God's love in Christ that saves sinners, not "love" as mere sentiment.[18]

How has God chosen to demonstrate His love? "While we were yet sinners, Christ died for us" (Rom. 5:8). He might have let us work off our own karma, but He didn't.

We may not like the idea of hell, but the Bible leaves no good way around it. The Scriptures teach clearly that believers will be resurrected to life with God on the basis of their faith in Jesus Christ. Unbelievers will be resurrected also, and judged, as many

---

Is Hell a Hypothesis?
John Hick says that Jesus used the concept of hell merely as a threat, though He had no intention of sending anyone there. Philosopher Paul Helm noted that, if hell is only a hypothetical threat, not a real one, then this must mean that either:
1. the threats could be carried out but will not be, or
2. God structures human nature so that all will be saved and the threats do not need to be carried out.

If the second view is true, then we must question the integrity of Jesus, who certainly gave the impression that the threats were real. Besides, why threaten people who are going to believe anyway? Moreover, the first view is no different than if the threats were real. God's moral character remains the same whether He allows the possibility for man to choose evil, or if they actually do choose evil. Men are responsible for choosing heaven or hell; God just wants to make those options clear to them.

of them want to be, according to their deeds (Rev. 20:11-15). However, no one who does not believe in Christ ("whose name is not written in the Book of Life") escapes the punishment of the lake of fire on the basis of the records of their deeds ("the books" in v. 12). Everyone is going to get a new, immortal body. The only question is where that body will spend eternity—with God, enjoying His goodness and love, or separated from Him forever in hell.

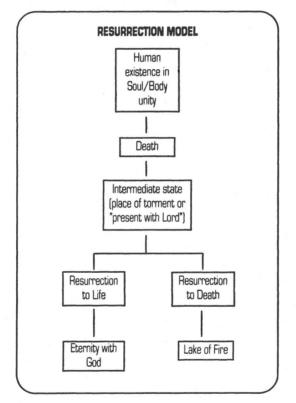

NOTES

1. William A. Henry III, "The Best Year of Her Lives," *Time*, May 14, 1984, p. 62.

2. Plato, *Republic*, Book X, 614d.

3. _____, "Meno" [81b], in *The Dialogues of Plato*, trans. by B.

Jowett (New York: Random House, 1937), vol. 1, p. 360.

4. _____, *Republic,* Book X, 620.

5. Ian Stevenson, "The Explanatory Value of the Idea of Reincarnation," *The Journal of Nervous and Mental Disease,* September 1977, p. 305.

6. Jennifer Boeth, "In Search of Past Lives: Looking at Yesterday to Find Answers for Today," *Dallas Times Herald,* April 3, 1983, H1.

7. Quincy Howe, Jr., *Reincarnation for the Christian* (Philadelphia: Westminster Press: 1974), p. 51.

8. Ibid., p. 107.

9. Geddes MacGregor, *Reincarnation in Christianity* (Wheaton, Ill.: Theosophical Publishing House, 1975), p. 168.

10. _____, "The Christening of Karma," in *Karma: The Universal Law of Harmony* (Wheaton, Ill.: Theosophical Publishing House, 1975), p. 4.

11. Howe, *op. cit.,* p. 107.

12. John H. Hick, untitled review, *Religion,* Autumn 1975, p. 175.

13. Allan Watts, *The Way of Zen* (New York: Vintage Books, 1957), p. 52.

14. C.S. Lewis, *Mere Christianity* (New York: Macmillan Co., 1943), p. 25.

15. Loren Eisley, *The Immense Journey* (New York: Random House, 1957), p. 199.

16. S. Radhakrishnan, *The Principal Upanishads* (London: George Allen & Unwin, 1958), p. 114.

17. Robert A. Morey, *Death and the Afterlife* (Minneapolis: Bethany House, 1984), p. 12.

18. Ibid., p. 233.

12

QUESTIONS ABOUT TRUTH

"What is truth?" Pilate's words ring with the cynicism of a man who has searched for it but never found it. His implication is that there is no such thing. Pilate is not alone. Many have followed the same road, so that what is taught in the schools is the same cynical conclusion: There is no truth.

For the Christian, that view is not an option. Jesus said, "Thy word is truth" (John 17:17), and He said again, "I am . . . the truth" (14:6). There is truth; but what is the nature of truth? More important, how can we know truth?

Have you heard this one yet? "Whatever is true for you may not be true for me." Or how about, "I'm really glad you found something that works for you." What good does it do to tell someone about Jesus if he doesn't realize that you are saying, "This is true for everyone, everywhere, at all times, and it is not compatible with any opposing system of beliefs"? If we are going to tell the world that we have the truth, then we better have some idea of what truth is. How else can we make them understand?

IS TRUTH RELATIVE OR ABSOLUTE?
The claim that truth is relative might be understood as relative in two ways. Either truth is relative to time and space (it was true then, but not now), or it is relative to persons (true for me, but not for you). On the other hand, absolute truth implies at least two things: (1) that whatever is true at one time and in one place

is true at all times and in all places, and (2) that whatever is true for one person is true for all persons. Absolute truth doesn't change; relative truth changes from time to time and person to person.

The relativist would say that the statement, "The pencil is to the left of the pad," is relative since it depends on which side of the desk you are standing. Place is always relative to perspective, they say. But truth can be time-bound as well. At one time, it was perfectly true to say, "Reagan is President," but one can hardly say that now. It was true at one time, but not now. The truth of such statements is irrevocably contingent on the time at which they are said.

Likewise, the relativist claims that truth is dependent on the person making the statement. If a Christian says, "Ye are gods" (John 10:34), it means that we have the image of God and are His representatives. If a Mormon says it, he is speaking of his hope to be the deity of his own planet. If a pantheist says it, she means that humans are God. The truth depends on the views of the one who makes the statement and his intended meaning. Also, "I feel sick" may be true for me but not for everyone else in the world. All these statements are true only in relation to the person who makes them.

But there seems to be a misunderstanding here. The interpretation of the relativist appears to be misguided. As regards time and place, the perspective of the speaker, temporal and spatial, is understood in the statement. For example, "Reagan is President," when said in 1986 is true and it always will be true. At no time will it cease to be true that Reagan was President in 1986. If someone uses the same words in 1990, then he is making a new and different truth claim, because the present tense is now four years removed from the context of the other statement. The spatial and temporal context of statements is an inherent part of the context which determines the meaning of that assertion. However, if "Reagan is President" (said in 1986) is always true for everyone everywhere, then it is an absolute truth. The same can be said about the pencil on the desk. The perspective of the speaker is understood as part of the context. It is an absolute truth.

But what about the second version of relativism, that truth is

"All Truth Is Perspectival"

Many people will tell you that all truth is really true from a certain way of seeing things or perspective. The old story of six blind men and the elephant is often used to illustrate and support this position. One blind man, feeling only the trunk, thought that it was a snake. Another discovered only the ears and concluded that it was a fan. The one who came across the body said that it was a wall and, after finding a leg, another said it was a tree. Another holding the tail declared it was a rope. Finally, the last blind man felt a pointed tusk and informed them that it was a spear. To some, this proves that what you think is true is only a matter of your perspective of things. It should be pointed out, though, that all of the blind men were wrong. None of their conclusions were true, so this illustration says nothing about truths. There really was an objective truth that all of them failed to discover. Also, the statement, "All truth is perspectival," is either an absolute statement or a perspectival one. If it is absolute, then not all truths are perspectival. If it is perspectival, then there is no reason to think that it is absolutely true—it is only one perspective. It does not succeed either way.

relative to persons? If we take the case of the Christian, the Mormon, and the pantheist, we see that the same problem of excluding perspective is involved. Using the same words does not guarantee the same meaning. We must consider what the actual claim is in its context before we can tell if it is true. What about, "I feel sick"? Guess what: personal pronouns don't even transfer as well as verb tenses. It doesn't matter that the same words are used; when said by different people, they take on a different meaning. Are these statements true for everyone? Yes, it is true that the person called "I" in the sentence did feel sick at that time and that must be acknowledged as true by everyone (though we have to take "I's" word about how he felt). In the same way, the meanings attached to the words "ye are gods" truly reflect the views of the people who said them, and it will never be not true for anyone, anytime, that those were their views when they stated them (even if they change their views later).

Now about this time a relativist might say, "You are agreeing with me. You are saying that truth is relative to the context." That's close. We are saying that meaning is relative to the context.

As for truth, we are saying that once the context is brought into the picture, the meaning is understood and it becomes obvious that these are absolute truths. We are not agreeing at all.

But relativism runs into other problems. If relativism were true, then the world would be full of contradictory conditions. That pencil that we mentioned would be on all four sides of the pad at the same time. "I" would have to be sick, well, angry, delighted, hungry, stuffed, excited, and ambivalent all at once. How confusing! Such contradictory conditions are impossible.

Also, no relativist can say, "It is absolutely true that this is true for me." If truth can only be relative, then it must only be relatively true for him. But wait a minute! THAT can't be claimed in any absolute sense either—it can only be relatively true that it is relatively true for him. Should we keep going? Either the claim that truth is relative is an absolute claim, which would falsify the relativist's position, or it is an assertion that can never be made, because every time you make it you have to add another "relatively." It is just the beginning of an infinite regress that will never pay off in a real statement.

"Life Is but a Dream"
Some might tell you that we each create our own reality. What is real to you is not real to me because your dream is not my dream. In fact, you only perceive me in your dream and don't know whether I am real or not. Not only is truth subjective, there is no absolute reality to be known. All reality is nothing but imagination run wild. Something intuitively tells us that this view can't be true. First, "nothing but" statements assume "more than" knowledge. But how can anyone have knowledge that is beyond their own dream? For that matter, how can you have knowledge that is "more than" all of reality? One would have to be omniscient to say this. Furthermore, is this a statement about absolute reality or only about one person's dream? If it is really a statement about "all reality" in an absolute sense, then it cannot be true—for at least this statement is true whether someone imagines it or not. But if it is only a subjective statement about one person's dream, then it makes no claim to be true and can be dismissed. It might not hurt to remind such a person that he should not talk in his sleep.

Of course, there are some benefits to relativism. It means that you can never be wrong. As long as it is right for me, I'm right even when I'm wrong! Isn't that convenient? The drawback is that I could never learn anything either, because learning is moving from a false belief to a true one—that is, from an absolutely false belief to an absolutely true one. Maybe we'd better give absolutism another look.

Some people see problems in absolutism. "Don't you have to have absolute evidence to believe in absolute truth?" No. The truth can be absolute no matter what our grounds for believing it are. We might not even know a truth, but it is still absolute in itself. The truth doesn't change just because we learn something about it.

"What about in-between things—like what warm means, or when not shaving becomes a beard—how can those things be absolute?" The fact that it is in-between to me is an absolute fact for all men, even if it is not in-between to them. Also, the condition itself, the real temperature and the exact length of the beard, are objective and real conditions. That truth doesn't change either.

"You Christians Are So Closed-Minded"
Open-mindedness has become a self-evident virtue in our society and a closed mind, a sign of ignorance and depravity. However, this thinking is based on half-truths. Surely, it is good to admit the possibility that one might be wrong and never good to maintain a position no matter what the evidence is against it. Also, one should never make a firm decision without examining all the evidence without prejudice. That is the half-truth that ropes us into this view, but a half-truth is a whole lie. Are we still to remain open-minded when all reason says that there can be only one conclusion? That is the same as the error of the closed mind. In fact, openness is the most closed-minded position of all because it eliminates any absolute view from consideration. What if the absolute view is true? Isn't openness taken to be absolute? In the long run, openness cannot really be true unless it is open to some real absolutes that cannot be denied. Open-mindedness should not be confused with empty-mindedness. One should never remain open to a second alternative when only one can be true.

"If truth never changes, then there can't be any new truth." New truth can be understood in two ways. It might mean "new to us," like a new discovery in science. But that is only a matter of us discovering an old truth. The truth has always been there, but we are just finding out about it. The other way we might understand new truth is that something new has come into existence. Absolutism has no trouble handling this either. When January 1, 2022 arrives, a new truth will be born because then it will be true to say, "This is January 1, 2022." That can never be true before then. "Old" truths don't change but "new" truths can come to be.

IS TRUTH CORRESPONDENT OR COHERENT?

There are two basic views of what truth is. One says that truth is what corresponds to reality. The other says that a view is true if it coheres or holds together as an internally consistent set of statements. The former says that truth is what corresponds to reality. Truth is "telling it like it is." The latter compares truth to a web hanging in space so that its own network of connections upholds it. Like a chain, each link is dependent on the others to hold it together.

The implications of the coherence theory are that some truths are truer than others because they cohere better. There are degrees of truth and any statement is true only to the extent that it fits into the system.

Saying that there are degrees of truth, as the coherentist does, and that all truths are dependent is just another way of saying that all truth is relative. If all statements are dependent (contingent) on the system, then no truth can be absolute. Even the system as a whole is not absolute, because it depends on the coherence of all of its contingent parts. If one statement can be more or less true than another statement, isn't that the same as saying that its truth is relative to the truth of the other? But we have already shown that truth is, and must be, absolute. If the coherence theory says that truth is relative, then the theory must be wrong.

HOW TO JUSTIFY TRUTH

Another objection to the coherentist view is that it makes truth dependent on an infinite regress that will never arrive at any truth. If every truth claim presupposes some other claim, and so on to infinity, then we have an infinite regress that will never assure us that we have arrived at truth. For every explanation we give of why our belief is true, we would have to explain its presuppositions, and then explain that explanation, and so on forever. We could never finish explaining anything. If we did find an explanation that needed no further explanation, then we will have arrived at a foundation (a self-evident truth or undeniable first principle), and the coherence view was wrong to begin with. C.S. Lewis put it this way:

> But you cannot go on "explaining away" forever: you will find that you have explained explanation itself away. You cannot go on "seeing through" things forever. The whole point of seeing through something is to see something through it. It is good that the window should be transparent, because the street or garden beyond it is opaque. How if you saw through the garden too? It is no use trying to "see through" first principles. If you see through everything then everything is transparent. But a wholly transparent world is an invisible world. To "see through" all things is the same as not to see.[1]

If we have to look behind or "see through" every explanation, then we will never find anything. But don't we search for truth because we expect to find something?

This infinite regress makes coherentism impossible. It is really a chain of unsupported claims. After all, a chain can't just hang in the air by itself; there has got to be a peg somewhere that holds the whole chain up. And spiders don't build webs in empty space. They attach them to the walls. No system can stand without some absolute truth to support it. Also, the best that a coherentist can do in evaluating other systems of belief is to say that his system coheres better. He can never say that any other coherent system is false. In that case, we could never refute pantheism, because once you throw out logic, everything coheres.

Truth must be based on a firm foundation of self-evident truths or first principles that correspond to reality. We will discuss self-evident truths a little later, but let's focus on the correspondence part of the definition for right now. There are several reasons for accepting it, both from the Bible and from philosophy.

The Scriptures use the correspondence view of truth quite a bit. The ninth commandment certainly presupposes it. "You shall not bear false witness against your neighbor" (Ex. 20:16) implies that the truth or falsity of a statement can be tested by whether it checks out with the facts. When Satan said, "You shall not surely die," it is called a lie because it does not correspond to what God actually said.

Joseph also used the correspondence theory when he said to his brothers, "Send one of you that he may get your brother . . . that your words may be tested, whether there is truth in you" (Gen. 42:16). Moses said that a prophet should be tested by seeing if his prophecies correspond to actual events (Deut. 18:22). When Solomon built the temple he said, "Let Your word that You promised Your servant David my father come true" (1 Kings 8:26, NIV). Anything that does not correspond to God's Law is considered

---

Jack Rogers' View of Truth
Jack Rogers, a professor at Fuller Theological Seminary, has given the definition of truth that is currently being used to say that the Bible is infallible in its intentions (purpose), but not inerrant in its affirmations. He says, "to confuse 'error' in the sense of technical accuracy with the biblical notion of error as willful deception diverts us from the serious intent of Scripture." He rejects the idea that truth must correspond to reality with "technical accuracy." Rather, he asserts that the "biblical notion of error" involves knowingly telling a lie. Truth resides in the intention of the author rather than what he actually said. This is confirmed when he says that inerrancy distracts us, not from the message of Scripture, but from its "intent." As long as the prophets and disciples did not know any better than to make unscientific statements, they cannot be considered errors because there was no intentional deception. Though Jesus may have known better, He chose to accommodate to the popular views so that people would not be distracted from His intended message, the Gospel. Those who hold this view are sincere, but they are sincerely wrong.

false (Ps. 119:163). And in the New Testament, Jesus says that His claims can be verified by John the Baptist, saying, "You have sent to John and he has borne witness to the truth." The Jews also told the governor that he could "learn the truth" (Acts 24:8, 11) about the charges they brought against Paul by examining the facts.

Philosophically, lying is impossible without a correspondence to reality. If our words do not need to correspond to the facts, then they can never be factually incorrect. Without a correspondence view of truth, there can be no true or false. There would be no real difference in the accuracy of how a system describes a given fact because we could not appeal to the fact as evidence. Statements could not be judged as true or false, but only more or less cohesive. There has got to be a real difference between our thoughts about things and the things themselves for us to say whether something is true or false. Furthermore, all factual communication would break down. Statements that inform you of something must correspond to the facts about which they claim to be giving information. But if those facts are not to be used in evaluating the statement, then I really haven't told you anything. I have merely babbled something that you ought to consider and weigh its relevance to your own system of thought. Now this could be quite dangerous if you were crossing the street and my statement was to inform you that a Mack truck was coming. How long should you take to see if that fits into your overall network of beliefs? (And does not the Gospel carry the same kind of urgency?) Correspondence to reality is a philosophical prerequisite for truth and truthful communication.

IS TRUTH INTENTIONS OR PERSONS?

Another theory is that truth is not a quality of propositions, but of intentions. Adherents of this theory say that the meaning of any statement lies not in what it says about reality, but in what the person intended to affirm when he said it. A statement is considered true if it achieves its intended purpose and false only if it is intended to mislead someone. Hence, a person can make statements which do not correspond to the facts but are not lies or errors because the person meant to tell the truth—he did not

TWO VIEWS OF TRUTH

	Correspondence	Non-correspondence
Basis:	Factual	Practical
Nature:	Propositional	Personal
Referent:	Reality	Results
Medium:	Language	Life
Location:	Affirmation	Intention
Nature of error:	Falsehood Mistake	Lie Deceit
Implication:	All mistakes are errors	Not all mistakes are errors

intend to deceive. This view has special relevance to the debate about whether there are errors in the Bible in that some claim there can be factual inconsistencies in the Bible and still call the Scriptures infallible. It is claimed that they infallibly accomplish their purpose of leading men to Christ and the authors never intentionally deceived anyone.

The correspondence view says that truth resides in propositions. Meaning is a disclosure of the author's intentions, but it can only be discovered by looking at what he actually said. Since we cannot read the author's mind when we want to know the meaning of a statement, we look at the statement itself. Only when we see the proper relation of all the words in the sentence, and the sentence to the paragraph, etc., do we understand the big meaning of the affirmation. Then we check it against reality to see if it is true or false.

Is truth ever in a person rather than a proposition? Out of the hundred or so times that "truth" is used in the New Testament, only one passage indisputably uses truth of a Person (John 14:6). Other texts refer to truth being in a person (1:14, 17; 8:44; 1 John 2:4) or walking in truth (2 John 4). However, the context of these clarifies that the truth is tested by the correspondence between the person's behavior and God's commands, which are propositions. So even here truth is correspondence. Persons, their character, and conduct can correspond to reality as well as propositions can. The emphasis of the biblical text is certainly on propositional truth. And passages where truth is used of a person can be understood as relating to the truthfulness of that person's words or works, as to whether or not they correspond to God's reality.

Even if some passages do use truth as a quality of persons, only the correspondence view can accommodate both interpretations. The personal view says that truth does not reside in propositions, but a correspondence view can say that the persons or actions in question must correspond to God's expectations. And the passages where truth is clearly seen as propositional and correspondent cannot all be explained in a noncorrespondence way.

Just to top it off, any attempt to deny that truth is expressible in propositions is self-defeating because it is a truth claim expressed in a proposition. Hence, the correspondence view of truth must be accepted for truth to reside in both persons and propositions.

IS TRUTH KNOWABLE?

Even among Christians there is a wide range of beliefs about how and how much we can know about truth, especially truth about God. If what we have said so far is true though, then only one of these positions is really reasonable.

AGNOSTICISM/SKEPTICISM

There is a real difference between agnosticism and skepticism but the answers to both of them are almost identical. Agnosticism says that nothing can be known, but skepticism only says that we should doubt whether anything can be known. Skepticism came along first, but as Immanuel Kant read David Hume's doubts about absolute knowledge, he decided to take it one step farther and disclaimed all knowledge of reality. Really both of these views are self-defeating. If you know that you don't know anything, then at least you know that much. But that means you have positive knowledge of something and you no longer have to be agnostic. Likewise, you may say that you should doubt everything, but you don't doubt *that*. That is, you don't doubt that you should

---

Dealing with Skeptics

One great philosopher had an effective way to deal with skepticism. When encountered by people who claimed to doubt everything, he would ask, "Do you doubt your own existence?" If they answered yes, then he would point out that they must exist in order to doubt and *that* certainty should remove their doubts. If they answered no, then he could show them that there are at least some things which are beyond doubt. To counter this assault on their doctrines, the skeptics decided to simply remain silent. Then they would not be caught in his trap. The philosopher was not shaken though. At that point, he simply said, "I guess there is nobody here after all. I may as well go talk to somebody who exists." And he walked away.

---

doubt. Now if there is one thing that you can be certain of (to the skeptic), or one thing that you can know (to the agnostic), then there might be other things, and your position has proven itself to be false.

RATIONALISM

Rationalism is not merely a view that says we use reason to *test* truth. Rationalism says that we can *determine* all truth by logic. It says that we can rationally prove the existence and nature of God. For a rationalist, no appeal to evidence can overturn a logical demonstration. That is why Spinoza, having proven to his own satisfaction that all reality was unified in absolute being, denied that anything in the world had existence distinct from God, or that there was any free will. That is why Leibniz maintained that this is the best of all possible worlds, no matter how bad things get. He was convinced by rationalism that only the greatest good can exist. All truth is logically necessary to a rationalist.

The big problem with rationalism is that it is a castle built in the air that has no link with reality. It assumes—but does not prove—that the rationally inescapable is the real. In fact, in all of its logical rationalizing, it never proves that *anything* real even exists. The only way that rationalism can overcome these weaknesses is to quit being rationalism and begin accepting some empirical evidence. Also, my own existence is *actually undeniable*, but it is not *logically necessary*. There is nothing in my existence that even suggests that I, or anything else, must exist, yet rationalism says, again without

Irrational Rationalism

Oddly enough, the most stubborn rationalists in the world are pantheists, who don't believe in reason. Even from pantheism's earliest statements in Western culture, pantheists have begun with one principle and derived all others from it: All is one. Now if that is true, they say, then whatever seems to be more than one must be illusion. Hence, there is no matter, no evil, no right and wrong, etc. All of these things follow from the one principle and are determined by a rationalistic method that allows no evidence to contradict it. Most extraordinarily, rationalism leads them to the rejection of reason. For once the distinction between true and false is removed, then rationalism demands that logic be revoked. Reason, having gotten them this far, must now be jettisoned because of the determinative nature of their original principle. Rationalism becomes the foe of reason.

solid proof, that this is logically necessary. Finally, when rationalism tries to prove its own principles to offer a justification for itself, it fails doubly. The attempt itself is futile because everyone from Aristotle to the present has agreed that first principles cannot be proven; they must be self-evidently true and in need of no further explanation. Otherwise you have to go on explaining forever. But rationalists fail again in that they don't agree on what the first principles are. Some end up in pantheism, some in theism, some with finite gods, but none with the rationally necessary basis that they claim will justify their beliefs.

FIDEISM

Fideism holds that the only way we can know anything about God is by faith. Truth is subjective and personal, so we can believe it but not prove it. There are no rational proofs or empirical evidence that can lead us to knowledge of God. We must simply believe that what He has said in His Word and done in our lives is true. Ultimately, as the old hymn says, "You ask me how I know He lives; He lives within my heart." Søren Kierkegaard is a spokesman of this view.

Now we certainly don't want to demean the importance of faith. In fact, we often cite the phrase of Augustine, "I believe in order that I may understand." Also, logical arguments are certainly

---

"Truth Is Subjectivity"

Søren Kierkegaard, the father of existentialism, wrote an essay with this title. He was concerned that, if Christianity was accepted only as a set of propositions, then it would never lead one to a relationship with God. Hence, rather than focusing on the objective truth of the faith, he stressed that it must be true to the individual or it is not true at all. Faith "that" something was true was surpassed by faith "in" something.

"But the above definition for truth is an equivalent expression for faith. Without risk there is no faith. Faith is precisely the contradiction between the infinite passion of the individual's inwardness and the objective uncertainty. If I am capable of grasping God objectively, I do not believe, but precisely because I cannot do this I must believe. If I wish to preserve myself in faith I must constantly be intent upon holding fast the objective uncertainty, so as to remain out upon the deep, over seventy fathoms of water, still preserving my faith." [*Kierkegaard's Concluding Unscientific Postscript,* trans. by David F. Swenson (Princeton: Princeton University Press, 1963), p. 182.]

---

not the basis of religious commitment. However, fideism has the right answers for the wrong reasons. We can't begin by assuming that God exists and has revealed Himself in the Bible and works in the lives of His people. Those are the very things that the unbeliever questions.

The main problem is that fideism doesn't recognize the difference between belief *in* and belief *that*. Evidence and logical proofs can assist us toward belief *that* God exists, the Bible is His Word, etc., but they cannot make us commit our lives to those truths. Commitment is belief and trusting *in* the Lord. Fideists only see the latter and overlook the need for the former. Hence, they make no distinction between the *basis* of belief in God (the truth of His Word) and the support or *warrant* for that belief. They require men to believe *in* God without allowing them to first understand *that* there is a God to be believed (see Heb. 11:6).

Besides, if faith alone is the only way to know truth, why not have faith in the Koran or the Book of Mormon? Fideism doesn't really attempt to justify any beliefs, so we could simply believe anything that we wanted. The net result is that fideism really makes no truth claims. It has to offer some way to test truth before it can make a truth claim. Since it doesn't have any test for truth, it can't really make any claim to be true. It isn't even in the marketplace pushing its claims as true. Now if someone does begin to offer some explanation or defense of why he is a fideist, then he has ceased to be one. The minute he offers anything other than, "Believe it," as support for his position, he has stopped being a fideist and begun using justifiable beliefs. Either fideism is making no truth claims or it is self-defeating. In either case, it cannot answer the question of how we know about God.

REALISM

The final view says that we can know some things about God. The other views are either inconsistent or self-defeating. This one stands. We can't know everything (rationalism), for there is no way that a finite mind can comprehend all of an infinite being. But we do know something because agnosticism is self-defeating. This is a reasonable and realistic view. But the question remains, How do we know what we know about God? And that is the last question we have to consider.

CAN WE KNOW TRUTH?

Agnosticism:	Self-defeating—how do they know we can't know?
Skepticism:	Self-defeating—do they even doubt skepticism?
Rationalism:	Inconsistent—can't rationally prove that something is rationally inescapable
Fideism:	Self-defeating—either unjustified belief or not fideism
Realism:	We can know something

IS TRUTH LOGICAL?

We can know what we know about God because thought applies to reality. In that context, knowledge is possible. If thought does not apply to reality, then we can know nothing. Logic is a necessary presupposition of all thought. Without logic (the laws of thought), we can't even think. But is it only a presupposition? How do we know that logic applies to reality? We know it because it is undeniable.

Now this gets us back to those self-evident first principles that we mentioned earlier. Don't let that scare you. You can understand Winnie-the-Pooh, can't you? Well, Pooh had an adventure that illustrates how self-evident principles work. He was walking through the forest when he came to Rabbit's house.

> So he bent down, put his head into the hole, and called out: "Is anybody at home?"
>
> There was a sudden scuffling noise from inside the hole, and then silence.
>
> "What I said was, 'Is anybody home?' " called out Pooh very loudly.
>
> "No!" said a voice; and then added, "You needn't shout so loud. I heard you quite well the first time."
>
> "Bother!" said Pooh. "Isn't there anybody here at all?"
>
> "Nobody."
>
> Winnie-the-Pooh took his head out of the hole, and thought for a little, and he thought to himself, "There must be somebody there, because somebody must have *said* 'Nobody.' "[2]

See, it's that simple. We've been doing it together all through the book. A self-evident principle is one that cannot be denied without assuming that it is true in the process of the denial. Rabbit's statement is really the reverse of this. It's self-defeating, and you have seen that word several times in this chapter. If you have to assume that a statement is true in order to deny it, it is actually undeniable. First principles, which are the starting point of all truth and the foundation of all thought, are these kind of statements.

Logic applied to reality is a key example. Now all logic can be reduced to one single axiom—the law of noncontradiction. This law says that no two opposite statements can both be true at the same time in the same sense. Logicians usually simplify that to A is not non-A. If we try to deny that, we get, "Two contradictory statements can be true," or "A is not [not non-A]." Both of these statements have a problem. They assume what they are trying to deny. In the first, it still assumes that there can be truth without the law of noncontradiction. But if opposites can be true then there is no difference between true and false, so this statement cannot be true, as it claims to be. The symbolic form does the same thing by clinging to the idea that A is still identifiable from anything else. The law of noncontradiction cannot be denied because any denial assumes that opposites cannot be true, and that is exactly what is being denied. So we find that the basis of logic is an undeniable first principle.

But the statement, "Logic applies to reality," is also undeniable. To say that logic does not apply to reality, you have to make a logical statement about it. But if it takes a logical statement to deny logic, then your actions defeat the purpose of your words. Either way, logic must apply to reality. And if logic applies to reality, then we can use it to test truth claims about reality.

But let's back up. Why do there have to be some self-evident, undeniable first principles? As we said before, agnosticism is self-defeating. We do know something. And we know that it is impossible for every truth claim to be dependent on another truth so that an infinite regress develops. Therefore, there must be some truths that stand all by themselves and don't need any further justification. We can't get behind them or "see through" them to find out why they are like that. That is why they are called *first* principles—they have no other principles before them. It's not that they are without justification; rather, they justify themselves by being undeniable.

Really, we can recognize that these ideas are self-evident by intuition, without having to test them by attempting to deny them. But sometimes we don't understand what they really mean, and the denial test brings this out. In other words, sometimes they are self-evident in themselves, but not to us because we don't understand them well enough. That explains why these truths are not universally accepted and why we sometimes have to examine them to see that they are undeniable.

What are some self-evident truths? We can find examples in every area of thought. Without attempting an explanation, here are a few. All of these have been used at least once in this book. See if you can recognize them as you use the book.

I. Self-evident propositions about logic
   A. Law of noncontradiction (A is not non-A).
   B. Law of identity (A is A).
   C. Law of excluded middle (either A or non-A).
   D. Laws of valid inference.
II. Self-evident propositions about knowledge
   A. Something can be known.
   B. Opposites cannot both be true.
   C. Everything cannot be false.
III. Self-evident propositions about existence
   A. Something exists (e.g., I do).
   B. Nothing cannot produce something.
   C. Everything that comes to be is caused.

These principles become the foundation for all knowledge. From this point, logic and evidence can confirm that God exists and that Christ is His Son. Truth has an absolute foundation in undeniable first principles and it can be tested through logical means because it ultimately corresponds to reality. Christianity claims to be true and it bids all to come in and dine at the table of truth.

NOTES

1. C.S. Lewis, *The Abolition of Man* (New York: Macmillan Co., 1947), p. 91.

2. A.A. Milne, *Winnie-the-Pooh* (New York: Dutton, 1961), p. 24.

13

QUESTIONS ABOUT MORALS

Abortion ... gay rights ... sex education ... drug abuse ... pornography ... all of these are issues where Christians are taking a clear stand and which are, at the heart, moral issues. As we have become more vocal, the outside world has become harsher in its criticism of our views. They can't quite conceive of why we think that we are right. Where did these values come from? Some ancient book that can be interpreted in hundreds of ways and was written by men who could never have imagined what the modern world would be like? And how can we seriously believe that such precepts are always and absolutely right? Christian morality seems so black and white. Aren't there any gray areas?

In the words of *Cool Hand Luke*'s warden, "What we have here is a failure to communicate." While our vision of virtue seems to be growing sharper, the rest of the world seems to be rapidly slipping into blindness and running from the light. As Allan Bloom says:

The danger they have been taught to fear from absolutism is not error, but intolerance. Relativism is necessary to openness; and this is the virtue, the only virtue, which all primary education for more than fifty years has dedicated itself to inculcating. Openness—and the relativism that makes it the only plausible stance in the face of various claims to truth and various ways of life and kinds of human beings—is the great insight of our times. The true believer is the real danger.[1]

In light of such a mind-set, the believer must be prepared to defend his ethical principals at their foundations. Is there a good reason to believe that morals are absolute? Is there a rationalization for why we are not "open-minded" about matters of values? How can we explain these things to unbelievers?

We don't need to defend every command of God, and there is not room here to deal with specific issues. What is needed is simply to show that the belief in absolute moral values is reasonable. We can do this by showing that values are absolute and that they have an absolute basis. We might need to go beyond this by answering the common objection that absolute values sometimes conflict, so that a person cannot obey both of them.

ARE THERE ANY ABSOLUTE VALUES?

Relativism is nothing new. The ancient Greek philosopher Heraclitus said, "No one ever steps into the same river twice, for fresh waters are ever upon him." This indicates the constant change that permeates our existence. But if everything is in flux (changing), then nothing stays the same. All is relative to the way things are at the moment. How can any value be absolute?

Since Heraclitus' day, several other moral theories have challenged the absolute nature of moral imperatives. Some have said that there are no rigid laws. Kierkegaard said that all ethical commands are transcended by religious duties, just as Abraham had to go beyond all morality to sacrifice Isaac because of a "leap of faith." A.J. Ayer said that all value statements were literally nonsense because they could not be verified by experience. Some have said that ethics are really only general principles that serve the purpose of structuring society. Jeremy Bentham and John Stuart Mill agreed that the general rules of society should be observed so that man can be happy, but they are not ultimately binding. Some, like Joseph Fletcher, think that all norms have to be evaluated by the individual in each situation.

Joseph Fletcher's situation ethics are built on the idea that "our obligation is relative to the situation."[2] He says that love is the only absolute; all other moral commands are relative to this. The only way to judge right and wrong is to look at the results. What

Situation Ethics

Joseph Fletcher's book, *Situation Ethics,* contained no new ideas when it first appeared in 1966, but it clarified the position and popularized it. He stated plainly that his presuppositions are pragmatism (the end justifies the means), relativism (only love is absolute; all other values are relative), positivism (moral principles are believed, not proven), and personalism (people are more important than things). Regarding the Bible, he says, "Either cheap melancholy or utter frustration will follow if we turn the Bible into a rules book, forgetting that an editorial collection of scattered sayings, such as the Sermon on the Mount, offers us at the most some paradigms or suggestions" (p. 77). In defense of pragmatism he asks, "If the end does not justify the means, what does?" (p. 120) He is at least consistent in that he goes on to recognize that ends also need to be justified. Love is the only end that justifies itself (p. 129). This raises the question, If love can justify itself, why can't other goods be good in themselves? If they were, then they wouldn't be means any longer, but ends in themselves.

"works" or "satisfies" is right. Values, then, are made neither by God nor society, but by the individual, who must decide what is right for him in a given situation. When asked, "Is adultery wrong?" Fletcher says, "One can only respond, 'I don't know. Maybe. Give me a case. Describe a real situation.'"[3] This, he believes, eliminates the cruelty of legalism by focusing on persons rather than precepts.

THE IMPOSSIBILITY OF DENYING ABSOLUTES

As reasonable as these proposals sound, there is a fundamental inconsistency to a denial of absolutes: in order to deny absolutes, one must imply that there are absolutes in the process of the denial. To deny absolutes, you have to make an absolute denial. It's just like saying, "Never say never." You just did. Or, "It's always wrong to say always." You have to say it to say it. How can you be absolutely sure that there are no absolutes?

Besides, if relativity were true, then there must be something to which all things are relative, but which is not relative itself. In other words, something has to be absolute before we can see that everything else is relative to it. That is the nature of relations: they exist between two or more things. Nothing can be relative by itself, and if everything else is relative, then no other relations are real. There has to be something which does not change by which we can measure the change in everything else. Even Einstein recognized this and posited absolute Spirit as something to which all else is related. John Dewey in his progressivism made progress an absolute and Heraclitus had an absolute Logos that measured his "river" of flux.

AFFIRMING ABSOLUTE VALUES

Just showing that relativism is wrong does not prove that Christian values are right. The relativist says, "So there are some absolute values? Name one." C.S. Lewis named several in his writings. He showed that many things are universally recognized as wrong, such as cruelty to children, rape, murder without cause, etc. He also noted (in the appendix to *Abolition of Man*) that values do not change greatly from one culture to another, but are very similar. But our challenge is to name just one.

Some thinkers have tried to reduce all moral principles to one central absolute. Immanuel Kant came up with a "categorical imperative," which ought to be followed in all circumstances. It can be discovered by asking, for each decision, "Would I want this action to be a universal practice for all men?" If you answer no, then don't do it. Would you want all men to lie to you? Then don't lie. Would you want all men to murder? Then don't mur-

---

The Heart of the Matter

If you want to get to the heart of the matter and find out what someone really believes about values, find out what his expectations are. A person can easily say that people are of no greater value than things, but he will balk if you treat him like a cigarette butt and step on him. He still expects to be treated as a person with value, even if he denies that worth with his words. Even someone who claims that there are no values still values the right to his opinion and expects you to do the same. This fact helps us greatly in affirming absolute values because it makes values actually undeniable. Whenever someone denies absolute values, they expect to be treated as a person of absolute value.

der. Do only those things that you would want all men to be able to do.

Martin Buber said that the most important moral principal is to treat people as persons, not things. He said that we can go through life seeing everything else as an "It" or we can recognize that some things have a similarity to ourselves and should be called "Thou." To Buber, it is the "I-Thou" relationships that bring meaning to life and are the basis for all values. People should be treated as ends in themselves, not as means to an end. People should be loved, not used.

It is not hard to see that both Buber and Kant agree in principle with Jesus about the single most important value. Jesus said, "However you want people to treat you, so treat them." When asked what the most important Law of the Old Testament was, Jesus replied, "'You shall love the Lord your God with all your heart, and with all your soul, and with all your mind.' This is the greatest and foremost commandment. The second is like it, 'You shall love your neighbor as yourself.' On these two commandments depend the whole Law and the Prophets." What is Kant's categorical imperative but a restatement of Christ's Golden Rule? And what is the greatest commandment if not an imperative to maintain "I-Thou" relationships with all persons, especially the Ultimate Thou? On this one principal, all other ethical norms are

---

I and Thou
Martin Buber (1878–1965), the famed Jewish existentialist, explored the realm of relationships in a book entitled *I and Thou*. He uses the familiar term for "you," which expresses intimacy. Noting that we experience life on three levels, he says, "Extended, the lines of relationships intersect in the eternal you" (p. 123). Defining love, he writes, "Love is responsibility of an I for a You: in this consists what cannot consist in any feeling—the equality of all lovers, from the smallest to the greatest and from the blissfully secure whose life is circumscribed by the life of one beloved human being to him that is nailed his life long to the cross of the world, capable of what is immense and bold enough to risk it: to love man" [Martin Buber, *I and Thou* (New York: Charles Scribner's Sons, 1970), pp. 66–67].

established: the Christian ethic of love.

Love is an absolute value that is universally recognized. Even Bertrand Russell, famous for his essay *Why I Am Not a Christian,* said, "What the world needs is Christian love or compassion." Humanistic psychologist Erich Fromm said that all psychological problems come from a lack of love. Confucius had the same idea, but he stated it negatively: Do not do unto others what you do not want the to do to you. Who would argue against love?

At the heart of Kant's test question is the issue, "How do I want people to treat me?" Surely we all desire to be loved. If we want to be loved, then we ought to love others. Not to love others is to deny their personhood, for we love persons as such. In fact, isn't that why we expect to be loved—because we are persons and persons should be loved? If we ought to be loved, then all persons ought to be loved. To conclude anything else would be inconsistent and arbitrary. Love is an absolute moral value that is universally accepted and expected by all people.

WHERE DO VALUES COME FROM?

THE SOURCE OF LOVE

People express love and expect love, but they are not love by nature. The love of people changes and is limited. Love is something that people have, but not something that they are. If love is an absolute, though, then there must be some unchanging, unlimited love somewhere that is the source of all other love. All moral absolutes must have an absolute prescriber, and humans are not absolute. So where does love come from? The Christian answer is that all love comes from God. In fact, the Bible says, "God is love" (1 John 4:16). Since God is by nature love, He can give love to His creatures. We *have* love; He *is* love. The nature of God is the source of all love and it is reflected in the men that He has made in His image. No meaningful love ethic can avoid dealing with the God of love.

But if we are to love, then we must know what love means. And if God is love, then the command to love is a command to know God first, so that we can know the nature of love. "Ignorance of

God Is Love

That phrase sounds great! It has so much emotional appeal and makes us feel so good, but does it have any real meaning? Is God a great big ball of good feelings for—everyone? The key to the Christian doctrine of love is found in the Trinity. God has one nature, but that nature explodes into three Persons (rather than one nature/one person like us). The Father is the Lover. The Son is the Loved (or Beloved), and the Holy Spirit is the Spirit of Love flowing from Them. Love itself is a trinity. Each has perfect intimacy with the other two Persons. They love each other. Hence, the nature of God is love. If God were only one Person, this could not be true. Creation is, then, the Godhead proclaiming, "Open the fellowship, so that more may enjoy Our love." When man sinned, the gates of fellowship closed; but in Christ's death, the veil that separated man from God was torn (Luke 23:45; Heb. 10:19-20) and the proclamation went out again, "Open the fellowship, so that all may enjoy Our love."

the nature of God will mean ignorance of the nature of absolute love. In brief, the Christian love ethic is no more secure than its source and no more applicable to life than our knowledge of that source."[4] So how can we know about love? The same way we know about God.

There are two ways that we can learn about God: through general revelation (in nature; Ps. 19:1-6) and through His special revelation (in the Bible; v. 7ff). The latter is certainly more explicit, but experience is more accessible. Anyone can and should know that God is love just from thinking about general revelation.

Paul told the heathen at Lystra that God "did not leave Himself without witness, in that He did good and gave you rains from heaven and fruitful seasons, satisfying your hearts with food and gladness" (Acts 14:17). Don't these simple blessings show us that there is a God who cares about us? "Thou dost open Thy hand, and dost satisfy the desire of every living thing" (Ps. 145:16). Just the fact that we have pleasure should tell us that God is good and loving. But Paul also told the philosophers on Mars Hill that God provides more fundamental gifts of "life and breath and all things" (Acts 17:25). So God has left a witness to His concern for us in the world that we live in and this helps us to know His love.

But we also can know God's love through the people He has made. "Love is from God; and everyone who loves is born of God and knows God" (1 John 4:7). Anytime that we love, we display the love that comes from God. This love in itself shows that we know something about God and demonstrates God's love to others. As we said before, the finite and changing love that men have must have an absolute source if it is to be valued absolutely. Men, made in God's image, love in the image of His love.

The most explicit knowledge of God's love comes from the Scriptures. In the Old Testament, God's love was acknowledged even in the giving of the Law for "showing loving-kindness to thousands" (Ex. 20:6). Jonah complained about God being too loving when He saved Nineveh from destruction, saying, "I knew that Thou art a gracious and compassionate God, slow to anger and abundant in loving-kindness" (Jonah 4:2). The repeated chant of Psalm 136 is "For His loving-kindness is everlasting." In the New Testament, God's love is further revealed in Jesus Christ. "For God so loved the world, that He gave His only begotten Son" (John 3:16). "Greater love has no one than this, that one lay down his life for his friends" (15:13). "God demonstrates His own love toward us, in that while we were yet sinners, Christ died for us" (Rom. 5:8). Here we have a disclosure of God's love.

THE CHARACTERISTICS OF LOVE

Defining love is never easy. In 1 Corinthians 13:4-7, Paul gives a description of love, but not a definition. He does give us one of the key characteristics of love: *Love is desiring (and doing) the good of the other.* Just as God desires to do good to all creatures by giving them existence and providing for their needs, those who would love must emulate Him by "seeking not our own," but seeking to do good for another. Jesus could have stayed with God forever and never suffered death, but He was interested in doing good for us.

Another characteristic of love is that *love gives with no demand for return.* Human love comes in three types: (1) love that gets but doesn't give (egoistic), (2) love that gives but expects a return (mutualistic), and (3) love that gives without expecting anything (altruistic). The Greeks had different words for each of these: *eros, philia,* and *agape.* Eros love is self-seeking by definition. It is only concerned with its own desires. Philia is brotherly love, such as friendship, in which there is a give-and-take kind of relationship. The returns make the sacrifice worthwhile. But agape is completely unconditional. It gives, and gives, and gives, but never demands that it receive anything. Jesus gave all His time and energy to helping people who could not pay Him back; then He gave His life without any demand that anyone ever believe in Him. That is the kind of love that God has. That is the kind we should imitate.

There is one more characteristic of love that the Bible won't let us ignore. *Love is tough.* Of His people, He says, "For those whom the Lord loves He disciplines, and He scourges every son whom He receives" (Heb. 12:6). The only loving thing to do for someone who needs correction is to correct him. God's love is tough enough to confront our stubborn wills without violating our freedom. Love can take a stand too. Jesus was no namby-pamby: He made His own whip to cast all the merchants out of the temple (John 2:12-16). He didn't mince words with the religious leaders. He called them hypocrites, fools, blind guides, whitewashed tombs, and a brood of vipers (Matt. 23). Love is not mere sentiment, but a commitment to do what is good for another, even when love has to be tough. Going to the cross was no easy decision made because Jesus had the warm fuzzies. Nor is it an easy decision God made to honor the wishes of those who refuse to respond to His love.

> If God would allow any unbelievers to enter heaven it would be worse than hell for them. How can those who detest prayer and praise to God bear to remain eternally in a place which does this continually? If they felt uncomfortable for only an hour in church doing this, think of the eternal discomfort if they had to do it forever. Or, to put it more strongly, since heaven is a place where men will bow in worship to God, how could it be loving for God to force men to go there when they do not will to worship God, but hate Him? It seems more congruent with the nature of divine love not to compel men to love Him against their wills.[5]

Surely no one *wishes* to go to hell, but some certainly do *will* it. God refuses to coerce anyone into loving Him because forced love is rape. But He demonstrates a tough love by allowing people to go their own way. If God's perfect and steadfast love has failed to win them, what could possibly change their minds? Hell is simply the place where the unbeliever is no longer bothered by God pestering him with His love.

WHAT HAPPENS WHEN ABSOLUTES CONFLICT?

Saying that we have absolute values can cause trouble. There is perfect harmony in heaven between the Lover, the Beloved Son, and the Spirit of Love. But when love comes to earth some of these duties conflict. Responsibilities overlap and we are torn between two absolute commands. Sometimes neither one seems like the loving thing to do.

Abraham had to make such a choice. Should he offer Isaac as a sacrifice, or disobey God? (Gen. 22) The Hebrew midwives had to decide if they would obey Pharaoh's orders or save the lives of the Israelite babies (Ex. 1). The Bible commands that we obey parents, but what if our parents object to us serving God? (Matt. 10:37) Or if a man fears for the safety of his wife, should he lie to protect her? (Gen. 20:12)

Christians have given three different answers to this problem. Each has some good reasons to commend it, but there are problems with some of them. We will examine all three and evaluate each.

NO CONFLICTS

The first view says that there are really no conflicts. Absolutes may seem to overlap, but in reality, they don't. Conflicts are only apparent. Really there is only one absolute duty and that is to love. All other commands are only general principles of love. They usually are right, but sometimes we just have to let love lead the way. Surely in cases where lying or adultery is the loving thing to do, the general principle can be broken. This view maintains the absolute nature of love, it is simple, and it does not hold anyone guilty for doing the best that they can in a tough situation.

Loving on Two Levels

Jesus offered two great commands: Love God and love man. This puts love on two different levels. Vertically, we are to love God with our whole selves; horizontally, we love men as ourselves. Moses also divided the Law into two tablets. The first related to our duties toward God and the second explained our duties toward men. Note the priority here: the "first and greatest command" and the "second." We are to love God first, and men second. We should love God supremely, with all our being; but man should be loved only according to our own humanity. Loving on two levels implies a third level of things. Things are not persons and do not have value in themselves. They are to be used, not loved. But what happens when our duties to different levels conflict? Sometimes loving God means that we should love men (Matt. 25:40; 1 John 4:20). But in other cases we must love God more than man (Luke 14:26).

This view has its problems though. First, there is not just one duty of love. There are at least two levels: love God and love your neighbor. Sometimes these do come into real conflict. Look at Isaac and Abraham. Wouldn't love have led you to spare Isaac? Both of these levels of love come from God's nature and cannot be overlooked. Also, the Proverbs appear to be general rules, but are the Ten Commandments really just the Ten Suggestions? Jesus did not seem to think that love was a love that could be separated from the specific commandment, for He said, "If you love Me, you will keep My commandments" (John 14:15). Third, how is love defined? How does one know what the loving thing to do is? To just say, "love" is like telling a man to do "X," or to "zirkle." What does that mean? Unless love is defined by a specific set of laws, one cannot know what is truly loving.

A variation of this view says that there are no real conflicts and that the faithful and obedient person never needs to worry about them because there is always a third alternative. This points to 1 Corinthians 10:13, which says that God always, "with the temptation will provide the way of escape." They look at Abraham ready to offer Isaac and see that God provided a third alternative. There are no real conflicts; there is always going to be a way out. If one did not take advantage of the way out (say he didn't wait long enough for God to deliver him), then he is responsible for the law that he broke, for the laws are absolute. If any law is ever broken, God must punish that as sin. This view holds that moral commands are absolute and more realistic about the conflicts of moral duties. It also really promotes checking out all possibilities before taking any action.

The problem with this answer is that it doesn't really face the conflicts. It tips its hat to them, then it ignores them. For there is not always a third alternative. True, Abraham did not have to kill Isaac, but he certainly had to *intend* to do it. Hebrews 11:19 tells us that he was not looking for a way out, but expected to have to kill Isaac and let God raise him from the dead. Jesus pointed out the real conflict between obeying parents and obeying God, but His solution was hardly a third alternative. He said in that case his disciple must "hate his own father and mother and wife and children and brothers and sisters" (Luke 14:26). Rather than going between the horns of the dilemma, this takes the dilemma by the horns.

Also, some people who hold this view find their own way out by redefining the commandments. One man wrote that it is a "fallacious assumption that to be truthful we must *under all circumstances* speak and act in terms of the data which comes in the purview of others who may be concerned with or affected by our speaking or acting."[6] But doesn't this make the absolute commands less than absolute? Should the circumstances really define what the command means? If so, this view makes ethics situational.

A third objection might be that it relies heavily on God's intervention. Not that God can't intervene to help us, but it seems presumptuous to think that He must. What if just one time He didn't do anything and we were forced to choose one of the two commands. Are *we* responsible for not obeying both commandments, or is *God* responsible, since He let us down?

A final criticism is that all too often this view maintains the law and forgets about love. It tends to be legalistic, rather than compassionate for the person caught in the conflict. Kant said that he would not lie to save a life because he would never want lying to be a universal norm. But wouldn't he want lifesaving to be prac-

Are All Absolutes Equal?

Christians often say that the "little sins" and the "big sins" are all alike in the eyes of God. It is true that all sin is sin, but Jesus taught a very different doctrine. He said that justice and mercy were "weightier matters" than tithing, even though the Law required both (Matt. 23:23). He taught that profaning the Sabbath was of less importance than helping a human being in need (12:5; Mark 2:27). On these grounds He not only healed on the Sabbath, but also allowed His disciples to grab a snack by "plucking ears of grain." He said that these things were "lawful," "guiltless," and doing "good" (Matt. 12:7, 12), not lesser evils. Christ even spoke of the "least" commandment (5:19). Punishment for sin is seen to be lesser and greater (11:24; John 19:11; Rev. 20:12) and reward for doing good is too (3:11; 1 Cor. 3:12-13). Combining this with the facts that we are to love God more than man (Matt. 22:38-39), and that absolutes sometimes do conflict, we must admit that some absolutes are more important than others.

ticed by all? Sometimes this view stresses the absoluteness of less important law without giving due consideration to the higher laws of mercy. It also makes a person guilty for doing the best that she can when God does not come through with a way of escape. Can a woman really be held liable for leaving the house to prevent her alcoholic husband from beating her and her children?

This raises a whole new question: Are all absolutes equal? Or are some more important than others? This view would treat all absolutes alike. But don't some relationships have priority over others? We know that there are at least two levels of love; is one level higher than the other in precedence? The next two views say that there are such levels and some laws are more important than others.

LESSER OF TWO EVILS

This view says that there are real conflicts and sometimes there is no way out. When that happens, our duty is to do the lesser evil. That is, we must perform the less nonloving act. If it is impossible to keep both commandments, then we should break the one that will cause the lesser amount of harm. This is often called doing the lesser of two evils. Of course, if one breaks a commandment, he is still held accountable for it. Even if sin is unavoidable, he is still guilty. At least by choosing the lesser evil, he is less guilty than otherwise. This preserves absolutes, admits real conflicts, and there is no special pleading to God for deliverance or subtle redefining of terms. It also introduces a new idea in recognizing that some commands are of greater weight and that these should be obeyed over the lesser commands.

But how can a man be held accountable for what is unavoidable? If a man cannot avoid sinning, is it fair to find him guilty? Moral guilt implies that there was a choice to do wrong. If there is no choice, how can he be responsible? This causes even greater problems when we come to Christ, "One who has been tempted in all things as we are, yet without sin" (Heb. 4:15). Either we have to say that Christ never faced a conflict between absolutes, in which case He was not tempted in the same way we are, or else Christ faced conflicts and sinned. If sin is unavoidable, there is no way to avoid this conclusion. Yet we must reject both of these answers. There must be a way for Christ to have confronted real moral conflict and yet avoid sinning. Beyond this, it is illogical to say that one is morally obligated to do a lesser evil. No one can be obligated to do evil. Goodness is the only basis for moral duties. No one can have a moral responsibility to do evil.

GREATEST POSSIBLE GOOD
Many people have confused this view with the former one, thinking that there is only a semantic difference between them. But they are actually very different. In the last view, one should do the lesser evil, for which he is guilty. But here the focus is on doing the greatest good, and you can't be guilty for doing good. In the former, man is condemned for doing what was unavoidable; but here man is praised for doing his best.

Sometimes called graded absolutism or hierarchicalism, this view says that when a conflict arises, the person is only obligated to obey the higher command. His duty is to follow the higher command given by God, which is the greatest good. But what about the lower command? It is temporarily suspended as long as one obeys the higher. Each command in the Bible is absolute and there are no exceptions; but when a conflict occurs, the greater duty is to fulfill the higher law. By doing the greater good, one is exempted from doing the lesser good. The lower is trumped by the higher.

But how do we know which is the greater good? There are clues throughout the Bible which help us to establish an absolute hierarchy of which relations are more important. *First, love for God is always above love for man.* Abraham's love for God took precedence over his love for his son (Gen. 22). Jesus called His followers to break off family ties if necessary to obey God (Matt. 10:37). God is always seen as the first priority. *Second, persons are more important than things.* Jesus taught that we should not "lay up for yourselves treasures upon earth. . . . You cannot serve God and mammon" (Matt. 6:19-24). But things are not as important as finite persons either, "For what does it profit a man to gain the whole world, and forfeit his soul?" (Mark 8:36) Paul even said, "The love of money is the root of all sorts of evil" (1 Tim. 6:10). People are to be loved and things are to be used. Though incomplete, this list shows that the higher and lower laws are not a matter of subjective feelings. God has established a real and absolute hierarchy of values.

Whenever there is an unavoidable conflict between two of these levels, the higher takes precedence over the lower. Of course, it is sometimes more complex, as when there is a conflict between persons. Should we return our neighbor's gun if he wants to kill his wife with it? No! Our duty to save the life of an innocent

---

God vs. Government

There is no doubt that God intends that we should obey government. Romans 13:1ff, Titus 3:1, and 1 Peter 2:13-14 make this quite clear. But what if the commands of the government conflict with the laws of God? We have several such instances in the Bible. Daniel was told to eat unclean meats (Dan. 1:8) and stop praying (6:7ff), but in each case he chose obedience to the higher authority. Likewise, Peter and John were told not to preach the Gospel any longer, but they responded, "We must obey God rather than men" (Acts 5:29). To them there was no question as to which absolute command they should obey. Love for God always outweighs our duty to the government.

person is greater than our obligation to return property to a would-be murderer.

There is a pyramid of values that can be diagrammed as follows:

This view is different from all the other views that we have described. It is different from the "no conflict" view in that it recognizes real conflicts between absolute commands. It says that sometimes there is no third alternative and the conflict must be faced head-on. While the "lesser of two evils" position is similar by recognizing a gradation of absolutes, this view does not hold a person morally guilty for doing the greatest good possible.

"But isn't graded absolutism really relativism in disguise?" No, it is absolutism in three ways. First, it believes that all values are based on the absolute nature of God. Morality can't change any more than God can change. Second, each command is absolute as such and should be obeyed absolutely. Normally, there is no question that we are obligated to do what the moral law requires. Only when there is a conflict between absolutes is the hierarchy used to decide which relationship takes precedence. Third, the gradation of values itself is absolute. The way that conflicts are resolved is not subjective, but by an absolute structure of what values are more important. Again, this gradation has its roots in the nature of God who made the world so that persons are of greater value than things, and God is over all.

So the absolute values of a Christian worldview can be affirmed, defended, and explained. We must affirm them because they are undeniable. Those who deny all values affirm the value of their denial. We can defend values because they come from the very nature of God, who is love. We can explain them because this God has revealed Himself in nature and in Scripture.

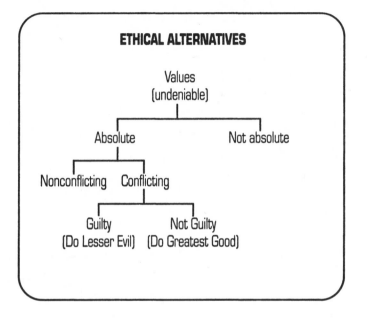

NOTES

1. Allan Bloom, *The Closing of the American Mind* (New York: Simon and Schuster, Inc., 1987), pp. 25–26.

2. Joseph Fletcher, *Situation Ethics: The New Morality* (Philadelphia: Westminster Press, 1966), p. 27.

3. Ibid., pp. 142–43.

4. Norman L. Geisler, *The Christian Ethic of Love* (Grand Rapids: Zondervan, 1973), p. 16.

5. Ibid., p. 22.

6. John Murray, *Principles of Conduct* (Grand Rapids: Wm. B. Eerdman's Publishing Co., 1957, 1971) p. 145.

Appendix

Reasoning to Christianity from Ground Zero

1. There are self-evident truths (e.g., "I exist," "Logic applies to reality").
2. Truth corresponds to reality.
3. Truth is knowable (all other views are self-defeating [chap. 12]).
4. One can proceed from self-evident truths to the existence of God.
   a. The argument from Creation (proceeds from "I exist")
   b. The argument from morals (proceeds from "Values are undeniable")
   c. The argument from design (proceeds from "Design implies a designer")
5. God is a necessary Being (argument from being [chap. 2]).
6. My existence is not necessary (evident from the definition of a necessary Being).
7. Therefore, theism is true (there is a necessary Being beyond the world who has created the contingent things in the world and intervenes in the world [chap. 3]).
   a. The objection from the problem of evil can be solved (chap. 4).
   b. The objection to miracles can be solved (chap. 5).
8. The Bible is a historically reliable document.
   a. History is an objective study of the past.
   b. There is great historical, archeological, and scientific evidence to confirm the reliablity of the Bible (chaps. 9–10).

(corollary) The Bible gives a reliable record of the teaching of Jesus Christ.

9. Jesus claimed to be both fully human and fully God.
10. He gave evidence to support this claim.
    a. The fulfillment of prophecy
    b. His miraculous and sinless life
    c. His resurrection (chap. 6)
11. Therefore, Jesus is both fully human and fully God.
12. Whatever God teaches is true.
13. Jesus (God) taught that the Old Testament was the inspired Word of God and He promised the New Testament.
14. Therefore, both the Old and New Testaments are the inspired Word of God (chap. 7).

GLOSSARY OF TERMS

a posteriori From experience, as opposed to a priori.

a priori Prior to or independent of experience.

abstract That which exists in the mind rather than the external world; the conceptual as opposed to the objective; the general as opposed to the particular.

absurd In logic, a contradiction, as in "round square." In existentialism, the impossibility of objective or ultimate meaning.

accidental In metaphysics, an attribute of something which is not necessary to that thing.

agnosticism The belief that one cannot, or at least does not, know reality, or especially, God.

analogy A correspondence in some respect between things otherwise different.

apologetics Literally, "defense"; in philosophy, the discipline of rationally justifying one's beliefs.

atheism The worldview which claims that no God exists; the universe is all there is.

being That which is or exists; the real.

bipolar In panentheism, the two poles of God's being.

Brahman In Hinduism, it denotes the principal and ultimate reality which is identical with all that is (see pantheism).

cause The necessary and sufficient condition for an effect.

causality, law of A basic principle in logic and science that states, "Every event has a cause."

Christian Science A modern pantheistic cult founded by Mary Baker Eddy; denies the reality of sin, sickness, and death and denies the unique deity of Jesus Christ.

Church of Jesus Christ of Latter-day Saints (Mormons) The name of the religious cult founded in 1830 by Joseph Smith, Jr.; denies biblical authority and doctrine, espousing polytheism.

clairvoyance An occultic practice or ability of seeing objects or persons psychically.

coherence theory of justification In epistemology, the theory that there are no immediately justified beliefs; justification is a relationship among beliefs, none of which is epistemologically prior.

coherence theory of truth A definition for truth as that which is systematically consistent.

contingent Dependent on another for its existence or function.

correspondence theory of truth Definition of truth as that which corresponds to reality.

cosmological argument The argument from the contingent, changing world (cosmos) to the existence of God.

deduction Arguing from the general to the particular; also a logical argument whose conclusion follows necessarily from one or more premises.

deism The belief that God created the world and is transcendent; denies that God is immanent in the world, especially in any supernatural way.

demiurge Plato's concept of a finite creator or god who formed the world out of the chaos (prime matter).

determinism The belief that all events in the universe (including man's actions) are controlled by previous conditions.

Docetism An ancient heresy that said Jesus Christ only appeared to be a man, but was really a spirit being.

dualism The worldview which teaches the existence of two ultimate realities (such as God and evil, or spirit and matter).

efficient cause The agent by which an effect is produced.

emanation In pantheism (Plotinus), the flowing of the universe necessarily from God, as rays flow from the sun or radii flow from the center of a circle.

empiricism The theory of knowledge which holds that all knowledge begins in sense experience.

epistemology The study of knowledge or how we know.

equivocation Use of the same term with two different meanings.

essence Qualities or attributes of a thing which are necessary; its nature.

essentialism, ethical The ethical view that God wills moral rules because they are right, and flow from His essence or character (see voluntarism).

ethics The study of right and wrong, of what one ought to do.

eternal That which exists without beginning, end, or change; not simply of endless duration, but the absence of time.

ex nihilo The Christian belief that God created the world "out of nothing."

exemplar cause The pattern or blueprint after which something is made.

existentialism A philosophical movement which stresses that existence is prior to essence; the concrete and individual is over the abstract and universal.

fallacy A logical error of inference, relationship, or conclusion.

fideism The view that there are no rational ways to justify one's beliefs; faith alone is necessary.

final cause The end or goal for which an agent acts; the ultimate.

finite Having specific boundaries or limits.

finite godism The worldview that affirms there is a God but that He is limited in power and/or love (see theism).

first principle Basic axiom or proposition; self-evident assumption.

formal cause The structure or form of which something consists.

foundationalism In epistemology, the belief that knowledge is based on first principles or immediately justified beliefs.

gnosticism Early religious cult which held God is good, matter is evil, and man is saved by knowledge (gnosis) of special hidden truths.

hedonism The ethical view which claims that pleasure is the greatest good.

humanism The belief that man is the highest value in the universe.

Hyksos A group of foreign invaders who dominated ancient Egypt for some time. Velikovsky identifies them with the Amalekites.

hypnotherapy A psychological therapy which involves the use of hypnosis.

hypnotic regression The process by which one is said to recall past-life memories through hypnosis.

idealism The philosophy which holds that reality consists of minds and ideas rather than matter.

identity, principle of The law of logic which says a thing is identical to itself; that is, A is A.

immanent Indwelling. God's immanence is His presence within the universe (see transcendent).

immortality The doctrine that man will live forever.

indeterminism The belief that at least some events, especially human behavior, are uncaused.

induction Arguing from the particular to the general.

inerrancy The term used to describe the Bible as being wholly without error in all that it affirms in the original manuscripts.

infallible The term used to describe the Bible as being a reliable guide only in matters of faith and practice (not in science, history, etc.).

infinite Without limits or boundaries.

infinite regress The belief that causes are infinitely dependent on dependent causes; it is impossible to arrive at a first principle or cause.

instrumental cause The means or tools through which an agent acts.

intuitionism In ethics, the view that in every situation, the right action is self-evident.

jiva, jivatman Commonly translated and understood as referring to what Westerners call the "soul"; that individual which endures throughout one's reincarnations.

karma The law of cause and effect which says that for every action (in this life) there is a reaction (in the next life). What we sow in this life we will reap in the next life.

liberation theology A panentheistic view of God used to justify Marxist rebellion.

logic The study of valid thinking and argument.

logical positivism The philosophy which holds that all metaphysical and theological propositions are meaningless unless they are empirically verifiable.

material cause The stuff or matter out of which something is made.

materialism The belief that all of reality is material, that no spiritual entities, such as the soul or God, exist.

metaphysics The study of being or reality.

metempsychosis Ancient Greek word which essentially means the same thing as reincarnation.

moksha The final state of "deliverance" from the burdensome cycle of reincarnation.

monism The metaphysical view that all reality is one.

mysticism The belief that there are states of mind or reality beyond sensation or reason.

natural law In ethics, the view that there are innate or natural moral laws known by all men. In physical science, the principles which describe the normal operation of the universe.

naturalism The belief that the universe is all there is; everything operates by natural law (without miracles).

necessary being A being who cannot not exist, whose very essence is existence.

necessity That which must be or cannot be other than it is.

nirvana Literally, "cessation" or "extinction"; this term is interpreted in a variety of ways in Buddhism. But it minimally means the cessation from being trapped in the wheel of rebirth and selfish craving.

noncontradiction, law of A proposition cannot be both true and false at the same time in the same sense.

noumena According to Kant, the "thing in itself" or real world, as opposed to the world of appearance (see phenomena).

objectivism The belief that there are external objects outside mere states of consciousness.

ontological argument The argument devised by Anselm for God's existence which claims that from our idea of God's essence we can conclude God must exist.

ontology The study of being.

panentheism The worldview which holds that "all is in God"; God is to the world as a soul is to a body.

pantheism The worldview which denies God's transcendence and identifies God with His immanence in the universe.

parapsychology The field of scientific study which purports to examine phenomena which cannot be explained by conventional theories of psychology.

phenomena According to Kant, the world of appearance, as opposed to reality (see noumena).

phenomenology A philosophical movement which attempts to avoid all presuppositions and begin with the pure data of human consciousness.

pluralism The metaphysical view that reality is many (see monism).

polytheism The belief in many gods.

positivism The philosophy which repudiates metaphysics and attempts only a scientific understanding of the world.

pragmatism The philosophy which makes practical consequences the criterion for truth.

privation The lack of some good quality which ought to exist in an object (e.g., sight in a man).

proposition The meaning conveyed by a sentence. Some philosophers claim that a proposition is identical with a sentence.

rationalism The epistemological view that stresses reason or rational explanations. Uses reason as a determinative principle, sometimes in opposition to empirical data.

reincarnation The belief that the soul after death passes on to another body.

relativism The belief that there are no absolutes; that the truth and/or value of a proposition are relative to that of other propositions.

samsara The continual cycle of rebirth.

self-defeating or self-stultifying Any statement which presumes, either in its content or in the act of affirmation, the opposite of what it attempts to affirm.

skepticism The belief that one should doubt or suspend judgment on philosophical questions.

solipsism Metaphysically, the doctrine that "I alone exist." Epistemologically, the view that one knows only himself, nothing more.

specified complexity Any pattern which is diverse and ordered so that it carries information (e.g., human language, DNA).

subjectivism In ethics, the belief that there are no objective, universal principles of conduct. In epistemology, the view that a statement is only true when considered to be true by the individual.

substance According to Aristotle, the underlying essence; that in which all qualities of a thing inhere.

sufficient reason The principle (from Leibniz) that everything must have a rational explanation or cause.

syllogism A concise deductive argument, consisting of two premises and a conclusion.

syncretism The reconciliation or union of conflicting beliefs.

tautology In logic, a statement that is true by definition, such as, "All triangles have three sides." Hence, an empty statement which affirms nothing about the real world.

teleological argument The argument from design or purposiveness of the world to the existence of a Designer (God).

teleology In ethics, the view which stresses the end, result, or consequences of our actions.

theism The worldview that affirms the existence of a personal, infinite Creator of the world, who is immanent in the world, unlimited in power and in love.

transcendent That which is more than our experience or goes beyond the world. Theists say God is transcendent because He is outside of or beyond nature (see immanent).

transmigration The movement of the soul from one body to another. Often used to refer to reincarnations in other life forms, such as animal, vegetable, and mineral as well as human.

uniformity The scientific principle which says that those causes which produced a given effect in the present would have produced the same effects in the past.

universal That which is true at all times and all places. The general concept or idea of a thing, as opposed to a particular instance or example.

undeniability The principle by which some statements cannot be denied because their truth must be assumed in the process of the denial.

utilitarianism In ethics, the view that one should act to bring about the greatest good for the greatest number of people.

vinnana In Buddhism, it is the "unconscious disposition" of the deceased which is reborn; as opposed to the conscious self, soul, or mind.

voluntarism, ethical The ethical view that traces all moral principles to God's will; something is right because God wills it (see essentialism).

yin/yang Buddhist concept of the ultimate unity of all things, especially opposites, such as light and dark, good and evil.

SUGGESTED READINGS

Chapter One
Edward J. Carnell. *An Introduction to Christian Apologetics* (Grand Rapids: Eerdmans, 1950).

William Lane Craig. *Apologetics: An Introduction* (Chicago: Moody Press, 1984).

Fredrick Howe. *Challenge and Response: A Handbook of Christian Apologetics* (Grand Rapids: Zondervan Publishing House, 1982).

Chapter Two
Reginald Garrigou-Lagrange. *God: His Existence and His Nature* (St. Louis: B. Herder Book Co., 1934).

Norman L. Geisler. *Philosophy of Religion* (Grand Rapids: Zondervan Publishing House, 1974), Part 2.

Stuart Hackett. *The Resurrection of Theism* (Chicago: Moody Press, 1957).

C.S. Lewis. *Mere Christianity* (New York: Macmillan, 1957).

_____. *God in the Dock* (Grand Rapids: Eerdmans, 1970).

Eric Mascal. *He Who Is* (New York: Longmans, Green, 1943).

J.P. Moreland. *Scaling the Secular City* (Grand Rapids: Baker Book House, 1987), Chapters 1–4.

R.C. Sproul. *Classical Apologetics* (Grand Rapids: Zondervan Publishing House, 1984).

Chapter Three
Norman L. Geisler and William D. Watkins. *Worlds Apart: A Handbook on World Views* (Grand Rapids: Baker Book House, 1989).

James W. Sire. *The Universe Next Door: A Basic World View Catalog* (Downers Grove, Ill.: InterVarsity Press, 1976).

Chapter Four
Norman L. Geisler. *The Roots of Evil* (Grand Rapids: Zondervan Publishing House, 1978).
C.S. Lewis. *The Problem of Pain* (London: G. Bles, 1942).
_____. *A Grief Observed* (London: Faber and Faber, 1964).
Phillip Yancey. *Where is God When it Hurts?* (Grand Rapids: Zondervan Publishing House, 1977).

Chapter Five
Augustine. *City of God* (New York: Random House, 1950), Book X.
Norman L. Geisler. *Miracles and Modern Thought* (Grand Rapids: Zondervan Publishing House, 1982).
C.S. Lewis. *Miracles* (New York: Macmillan, 1966).
Danny Korem. *The Fakers* (Grand Rapids: Baker Book House, 1980).
_____. *Powers: Testing the Psychic and Supernatural* (Downers Grove, Ill.: InterVarsity Press, 1988).

Chapter Six
William Lane Craig. *The Son Rises* (Chicago: Moody Press, 1981).
Norman L. Geisler. *Christian Apologetics* (Grand Rapids: Baker Book House, 1976), Chapter 17.
Peter Kreeft. *Socrates Meets Jesus* (Downers Grove, Ill.: InterVarsity Press, 1987).
Josh McDowell. *Evidence that Demands a Verdict* (San Bernardino: Here's Life Publishers, Inc., 1972), Section 2.
_____. *More Than a Carpenter* (Wheaton, Ill.: Tyndale, 1977).
Frank Morrison. *Who Moved the Stone?* (London: Faber and Faber, 1958).
J.P. Moreland. *Scaling the Secular City* (Grand Rapids: Baker Book House, 1987), Chapters 5 and 6.
John Warwick Montgomery. *Christianity and History* (Downers Grove, Ill.: InterVarsity Press, 1964).

Chapter Seven
Gleason Archer. *A Survey of Old Testament Introduction* (Chicago: Moody Press, 1964).

Norman L. Geisler and William E. Nix. *A General Introduction to the Bible* (Chicago: Moody Press, 1968).

Norman L. Geisler, ed. *Inerrancy* (Grand Rapids: Zondervan Publishing House, 1979).

Josh McDowell. *Evidence that Demands a Verdict* (San Bernardino: Here's Life Publishers, Inc., 1972), Section 1.

John D. Woodbridge. *Biblical Authority: A Response to the Rogers/McKim Proposal* (Grand Rapids: Zondervan Publishing House, 1982).

Chapter Eight

Gleason L. Archer. *Encyclopedia of Bible Difficulties* (Grand Rapids: Zondervan Publishing House, 1982).

J.W. Haley. *Alleged Discrepancies of the Bible* (Nashville: Goodpasture, 1951).

Chapter Nine

Gleason L. Archer. *A Survey of Old Testament Introduction* (Chicago: Moody Press, 1964).

F.F. Bruce. *The New Testament Documents: Are They Reliable?* (Grand Rapids: Eerdmans, 1960).

Gary Habermas. *The Verdict of History* (Nashville: Thomas Nelson, 1988).

Clifford A. Wilson. *Rocks, Relics and Biblical Reliability* (Grand Rapids: Zondervan Publishing House, 1977).

Merrill Unger. *Archaeology and the Old Testament* (Grand Rapids: Zondervan Publishing House, 1954).

Chapter Ten

Norman L. Geisler and J. Kerby Anderson. *Origin Science: A Proposal for the Creation—Evolution Controversy* (Grand Rapids: Baker Book House, 1987).

Duane T. Gish. *Evolution? The Fossils Say No!* (San Diego: Creation Life Publishers, 1973).

Robert Jastrow. *God and the Astronomers* (New York: Norton, 1978).

J.P. Moreland. *Christianity and the Nature of Science* (Grand Rapids: Baker Books House, 1989).

Charles B. Thaxton, Walter L. Bradley, and Roger L. Olsen. *The Mystery of Life's Origin* (New York: Philosophical Library, 1984).

Chapter Eleven

J. Kerby Anderson. *Life, Death and Beyond* (Grand Rapids: Zondervan Publishing House, 1980).

Norman L. Geisler and J. Yutaka Amano. *The Reincarnation Sensation* (Wheaton, Ill.: Tyndale House Publishers, 1986).

Stuart Hackett. *Oriental Philosophy: A Westerner's Guide to Eastern Thought* (Madison: University of Wisconsin Press, 1979).

Robert A. Morey. *Death and the Afterlife* (Minneapolis: Bethany House, 1984).

Stephen H. Travis. *Christian Hope and the Afterlife* (Downers Grove, Ill.: InterVarsity Press, 1980).

Chapter Twelve

Norman L. Geisler. *Christian Apologetics* (Grand Rapids: Baker Book House, 1976), Part 1.

Chapter Thirteen

Norman L. Geisler. *Ethics: Alternatives and Issues* (Grand Rapids: Zondervan Publishing House, 1971).

Erwin Lutzer. *Necessity of Ethical Absolutes* (Grand Rapids: Zondervan Publishing House, 1981).

J.P. Moreland. *Scaling the Secular City* (Grand Rapids: Baker Book House, 1987), Chapter 4.

Topical Index

All indexes compiled by THOMAS A. HOWE

TOPICAL INDEX

PERSONS INDEX

SCRIPTURE INDEX